the
fearless
home
seller

the fearless home seller

Elizabeth Razzi

STC Paperbacks

Stewart, Tabori & Chang

New York

Published in 2007 by Stewart, Tabori & Chang
An imprint of Harry N. Abrams, Inc.

Text copyright © 2007 by Elizabeth Razzi

Library of Congress Cataloging-in-Publication Data

Razzi, Elizabeth.
  The fearless home seller : Razzi's rules for staying in control of the
deal / Elizabeth Razzi.
      p. cm.
  Includes index.
  ISBN-13: 978-1-58479-532-2
  ISBN-10: 1-58479-532-8
  1. House selling—United States. I. Title.

HD259.R394 2007

643'.120973—dc22   2006030841

Editor: Marisa Bulzone
Designer: Jay Anning, Thumb Print NY
Production Manager: Anet Sirna-Bruder

The text of this book was composed in Electra
Printed and bound in the United States of America

10 9 8 7 6 5 4 3 2 1

harry n. abrams, inc.
a subsidiary of La Martinière Groupe

115 West 18th Street
New York, NY 10011
www.hnabooks.com

To Guy, Lisa, and Stephen.
My home is wherever you are.

Acknowledgments

I have never held a real estate license. I've never shown a property to buyers or tried to sell a home by myself. Instead, through my work as a consumer journalist, I have had the privilege of interviewing hundreds of top-notch agents and brokers from across the country, as well as the people who train them in their craft, plus mortgage lenders, economists, and all types of advocates and experts in the housing field. I also have been particularly privileged to have spoken with scores of people who have bought and sold homes, some happily, and some who only got through their deal with more than a little unwelcome drama. Thanks to all of them, I have learned a lot, and I hope to pass that knowledge along to you through this book.

The *Fearless* approach to selling your home is based on a simple idea: The better you understand the process, the more in control of it you will be. Armed with the right information, you will be able to hire the brightest real estate agent to help you sell. Or, if you're so inclined, you'll have the confidence to attempt a sale on your own, fully understanding the size of the task you're about to take on. This book is not an exhaustive explanation of all the technicalities of real estate — though there are plenty of them. Instead it's a simple conversation, full of the practical advice I've offered to friends and acquaintances over the years as they went about trying to sell their homes. It's advice offered by a friend who is *not* in the business, and who doesn't have a dollar at stake in your decisions but who nevertheless understands how the whole thing is supposed to work, and how you might keep it from going wrong.

I would like to thank the many real estate agents and brokers who have shared their insights with me over the years. In particular, I'd like to send a thank you to Merelyn Kaye and Rosemary Hayes Jones, two Realtors in Northern Virginia who, in the course of shepherding me through many properties over the years, have as a by-product shown me some notable examples of how for-sale homes *really* look to buyers. Also, Ben Anderson, a Realtor and auctioneer in Destin, Florida, who is chairman of the National Association of Realtors' Auction Forum, provided a great deal of useful information about how that sales method works. My editor, Marisa Bulzone, and her team at Stewart, Tabori & Chang are responsible for the wonderful flow of the pages that follow.

Finally, I would like to thank my husband, Guy Razzi, and our children, Lisa and Stephen, for their patience and support through all the months I worked on this guide. They are proof that the best kind of home is full and messy and anything but a showplace—at least until you try to sell it.

—ELIZABETH RAZZI

Contents

PART THREE
Closing the Deal

When It's Time to Sell Your Home

I F ONLY IT WERE ALL ABOUT MONEY. IN TRUTH, SELLING YOUR home feels quite a bit like volunteering for a referendum on your lifestyle. First, you have to come up with a dollar value — your asking price — for the place that has sheltered you for years, possibly decades. Maybe you grew up there or raised your children there. Maybe it's the family homestead or the vacation place that you enjoyed summer after summer. Maybe it's a tiny in-town condo where you spent a few, fun years early in your career. Whatever the case, your needs have changed and it's time to move on.

Next, you have to invite strangers in to size up your lifestyle and your taste, and every one of those strangers who walks through and doesn't immediately decide to buy your home seems to deliver an implicit criticism: your home is not good enough for me. On the other hand, if buyers rush forward with full-price offers as soon as your home hits the market, you'll almost certainly fear that you've sold off your precious home for too little. How could you cheat yourself this way? For these reasons, not to mention the sheer hassle of prepping and showing a place, a home sale tends to be less than fun.

Parade of Agents

You don't have to go through the process alone. You'll deal with a number of real estate agents throughout, including the one you choose as your representative in the deal, plus untold others representing an untold number of buyers. Each will pick apart your home as if it were a used car (even if they're too polite to let you hear the criticism, you can be sure they'll do it in private). Nosy neighbors will tramp through during open houses; prospective buyers will look into your closets and through the back reaches of your basement. Before you're done, home inspectors will crawl all over the place looking for flaws. Pest inspectors will hunt for signs of termites or other damaging insects. Appraisers will take a look and come up with a dollar value of their own for the place—which could be different from the value you and the buyer agreed upon. Through it all, you will be expected to keep your home so pristine that it doesn't even look as if real people live there.

The stakes are high, and the process tends to be inconvenient, at best. But you can take away much of the worry and discomfort if you know the path ahead of you, and if you have all the information you need to keep the decision-making power right where it belongs—with you. The fearless approach is straightforward: if you understand the selling process, including the motives of all the professionals you pay so dearly to help you, you can stay in control of the transaction and keep stress to a minimum.

Rolling Up Your Sleeves

Whether you're in a rush to sell or you have the luxury of time, your first job is to prepare your home for sale. Before you even think of picking up a phone to call a real estate broker, you need to pick up a mop . . . and a caulk gun . . . and a paintbrush. If you need to pay for professional help with the cleanup and fix-up, consider it a low-risk, short-term investment; there's an excellent chance that you'll recover more than the cost through a higher selling price. Even a home that has been lavished with TLC over the years needs a couple of weeks for presale prep. If you've been too busy to pay much attention to housekeeping and repairs, well, now it's payback time. Roll up your sleeves (or open up your wallet) and get the place in shape. The work could take weeks—even months, if you have to get on a painter's or a carpenter's schedule.

Once your house is painfully clean, you have a big decision to make: will you go the usual route and hire a real estate agent to help you sell, or will you attempt to sell on your own without an agent? If you decide to try to sell on your own, at least for a while, you'll find lots of details about the process in chapters 9 and 10.

If, like most sellers, you decide to use the services of a real estate brokerage, allow yourself a week or two to fully investigate your options. Take the time to interview at least three of the strongest local agents, and give yourself a couple of days to check their references (call their three most recent clients). The very best credential any agent can offer is a history of satisfied clients.

Once you sign a contract with one of the agents to represent you in the sale, it's showtime! It can sometimes be tough to predict what kind of response you're going to get once you place your home on the market. You might find yourself flooded with potential buyers, all dying to get a peek. Or you might get a steady trickle of lookers, week after week, but no offers. It all depends on the strength of your local market and the attractiveness of your home—including the attractiveness of its price. The seasons and the weather come into play, too. Cold, sloppy weather in a stagnant market can translate into a very lonely time for a home seller.

Eventually, practically every seller gets a nibble. And then the process speeds up dramatically. Negotiations over a purchase contract might only take a day or two of back-and-forth offers and counteroffers, and the purchase contract you ultimately hammer out will specify how much time will elapse before closing day. Typically, the time between contract and closing is two or three months, but you can get that down to as little as a few weeks if you and the buyer are in a hurry—and if you're well prepared.

Basic Tools of Selling

As you read through this book, you will become acquainted with the basic tools of selling. Although the Internet and e-mail are tremendously important tools for real estate sales, some of the old, low-tech tools still help sell homes, too. If you sell without an agent, you'll need to employ as many of these tools as you can; if you hire an agent, you'll need to make sure that agent includes them in the marketing plan. Here's a brief rundown of today's top tools, which are examined in greater detail later in the book:

- **The Multiple Listing Service (MLS):** The MLS is a massive database of homes listed for sale by brokers. It was designed as a way for brokers to post notices of homes they were selling, along

16

with an offer to split the sales commission with any other broker or agent who brought forth a buyer.

- **The Internet:** The vast majority of home buyers start their search online. In fact, in 2005, nearly a quarter of home buyers first learned about the very home they eventually bought on the Internet, according to the National Association of Realtors (NAR). You'll want to be sure buyers find your home well represented there. The general public can search MLS-listed homes on the NAR-sponsored Web site www.Realtor.com.

- **Yard signs:** It's the lowest of low-tech, but the humble old sign in the yard still sells homes. That's how you might snag a passerby who didn't even intend to hunt for a new home—until she saw that your place, the one she's always admired, is finally on the market!

- **Lockbox:** With your permission, the real estate agent will lock a box containing a key to your home on your doorknob or porch rail. Other local real estate agents can use their pass card or combination to open the box and get the key so they can show the home without making an appointment with you or your agent.

- **Open houses:** Shortly after your home goes on the market, an agent may host a weekend open house lasting several hours. Agents usually hold a separate agents-only open house as well.

- **Advertising:** Even though buyers are increasingly reliant on the Internet to find homes, newspaper classifieds still draw attention. Often agents will run a photo of your home in their own larger "display ad," especially in less-expensive community newspapers.

If you are trying to sell without an agent, you'll be particularly reliant on classified and display ads.

The Path Ahead

There are many tasks that need to be accomplished before you hand the keys over to new owners. Generally they can be broken into the following steps, roughly in this order: declutter, scrub, and repair your home in preparation for sale; find the best real estate agent to help you (or decide to try to sell on your own); estimate how much money you will net from the sale; live like a fugitive— ready to tidy up and leave for showings at fifteen minutes' notice— while your home is being marketed; manage the negotiations; and, finally, stay on top of all the inspections and paperwork that will bring this deal to a happy ending. This book carries you through these tasks in the sequence that you will most likely face them, but you may find it useful to flip back to material in the appendices for extra resources, such as a list of helpful Web sites and examples of commonly used contracts.

Along with a steady stream of strangers tramping through your home (if you're lucky), there also will be a sizable number of professionals involved in the deal, including real estate agents, mortgage lenders, appraisers, home inspectors, insurance agents, lawyers, and pest exterminators. That's one of the reasons the home-buying process is so complicated and expensive; each of these service providers stands to earn a commission or a fee from the sale of your home. Many of those fees will be borne by the buyers, of course, but others will be yours to bear. Regardless, they all chip away at your bottom line, because money the buyers have to spend on transaction fees is ultimately money they can't afford to pay you for the home! (One of the goals of this book is to alert you to any subtle pressures these service providers might place on the transaction. Truly understanding the home-selling process will equip you with the confidence you need to deal with any such pressure.) Below, you'll find a cast of characters who commonly appear in real estate deals (please turn to the glossary at the back of the book for further definitions and a list of useful Web sites).

Cast of Characters

Real estate agent: Usually, the person with whom you work most closely is your real estate agent. An agent is someone who acts on behalf of someone else. A licensed real estate agent works on behalf of a broker, who, in turn, is an agent of the buyer or seller who hired him. If your buyer has chosen to be represented by her own buyer's agent, that agent is supposed to negotiate with your (seller's) agent in hopes of striking a deal at the lowest price and best terms for the buyer. Your agent, of course, is pushing for the highest price and best terms for you.

Real estate broker: Typically, a real estate agent works under the supervision of a licensed broker; it is the broker with whom you have a contract for representation.

Buyer's broker or buyer's agent: A real estate salesperson who has agreed to represent the buyer is a buyer's broker/buyer's agent. Some make a living out of working only with buyers and call themselves *exclusive* buyer's brokers/buyer's agents. But many agents today will work with buyers or sellers, depending on the deal. An agent should not try to represent both parties in the same transaction, although some will try to act as neutral go-betweens if state law allows it and if both buyer and seller are informed of the arrangement.

Appraiser: Before making a loan, lenders will insist on having an appraisal performed by one of their approved appraisers. Appraisers are licensed by the state to estimate the market value of homes, based on recent completed sales of comparable properties and taking into account a home's special assets and flaws.

Mortgage bank: A business that originates, sells, and services mortgage loans is a mortgage bank.

Mortgage broker: A person who deals with a number of different loan originators and can shop a borrower's loan application around for the best combination of interest rate and terms is a mortgage broker. Brokers earn a fee for each mortgage they originate. Although good mortgage brokers will shop hard on behalf of borrowers, they are not required to represent the interests of the borrower. Therefore, reputation is critical in choosing a mortgage broker.

Loan officer: The person who takes a borrower's application and ushers it through the loan-approval process is a loan officer.

Escrow officer/closing officer: In California and some other western states, when a buyer and seller agree on terms of a sale, they enter into escrow, a time when all the demands of the buyer, seller, lender, and government need to be satisfied so the deal can be made final. They hire a neutral third party—either a state-licensed escrow company, a title insurance company, a bank or trust company, or an attorney—to act as their escrow officer, a neutral third party who manages the flow of money, inspections, and paperwork necessary to complete the deal. In other states a title company or an attorney acts as the closing officer, performing many of these same functions.

Title company: A title company will perform a title search, an examination of the land-ownership records on file with the local government to verify that the seller is the rightful owner of the property and that there are no outstanding claims against it, such as tax liens or undisclosed mortgages. The title company then will offer a title-insurance policy that will pay legal fees (or damages) if someone comes forward after closing with a claim against the title. Lenders require that buyers purchase a title-insurance policy that would pay the lenders if a dispute were to come up; borrowers can (and should) pay extra to extend that coverage to themselves as well.

At the end of each chapter in this book, you'll find "Razzi's Rules to Live By," a summary of that chapter's key points. They're little reminders of the strategies and principles that will help you maintain sure footing as you maneuver through the twists and turns of the typical home-buying process. You'll also find a complete list of the rules in appendix one.

I invite you to visit http://www.fearlesshome.com for updates on material in this book and its companion volume, *The Fearless Home Buyer*. You are welcome to send e-mail through that site, as well. I would love to hear from you.

PART ONE
getting ready

CHAPTER ONE

When to Sell

"Hence! Home, you idle creatures,
  get you home: Is this a holiday?"

WILLIAM SHAKESPEARE, *Julius Caesar*

WOULDN'T IT BE WONDERFUL IF WE COULD SELL OUR HOMES the way we sell a stock. Imagine calling up your broker and placing a "sell" order at the prevailing market price. Before the end of the day, you'd have a sale—maybe not at exactly the price you'd hoped for, but close to it—and you could continue about your life. Home sales, instead, normally take weeks or months to pull off. The strength of the local housing market, the strength of the local job market, the seasons, and even the weather all affect how quickly you can make a deal, and at what price.

We don't always have control over when we'll be selling, either. During the first half of the decade, when buyers were elbowing each other aside for the honor of paying full price on anything with a roof and walls, it was a fabulous time to sell (especially if you planned to relocate to a tent in the woods without reentering that crazy market as a disadvantaged buyer). But despite high prices and heavy demand, most homeowners did not choose to sell their homes just to take advantage of the booming market. They had no need or desire to move at that time. The timing of a home sale is usually driven by something other than market conditions: Maybe you finally feel you have enough income to handle a bigger home payment. Maybe you can't stand that closet-size kitchen any longer. Outside events often force us into the housing market, even when that market is not looking terribly friendly to sellers. Marriage, a job transfer, divorce, retirement, incapacity, or a death in the family can send us searching for a real estate broker to help us unload a home. Under happy circumstances we may even volunteer for the hassles of a home sale because we've found a nicer, more appropriate place to live.

Financial Triggers

Important financial considerations may also prompt us to sell a home. Maybe you've finally tired of the tight budget you're left with after making the too-big mortgage payment on a too-expensive home. Or, maybe, now that retirement is approaching, you'd like to sell the big home in the high-cost-of-living suburbs and take up full-time residence in a town with a lower cost of living.

Tax planning also can make it wise to start thinking about a home sale. Thanks to the huge run-up of home values during the first half of the decade, many homeowners are likely to find themselves bumping against the ceiling on the home-sale profit they can exclude from federal income taxes when they eventually sell their home. Under the federal-income-tax laws, a married couple can keep up to $500,000 in profit from the sale of their principal residence, tax free (you must have owned and lived in the home for at least two of the five years preceding the sale). Singles can keep up to $250,000 in profit, tax free. Any profit beyond that means you face paying capital-gains tax.

You may be especially vulnerable to bumping into that ceiling if, under the tax rules in effect before 1997, you rolled over the profit from home sales into the home you're living in today. Let's look at an example: Say you owned a couple of homes before the tax laws changed. The modest price of those first homes seems quaint, when you look back on it, but over the years property values rose steadily, and you ended up accumulating $250,000 in capital gains (or profit) from your combined previous sales. Back in 1996, or earlier, when you bought your current home, the tax laws dictated that you roll that old profit over into the accounting for your new home, through a process called "adjusting your basis."

Say you paid $500,000 for your lovely home in 1996 (for simplicity's sake, we'll imagine you didn't make any down payment). For tax purposes, you had to roll over your $250,000 profit from the sale of all those previous homes into the accounting for your new home. On paper, that reduced the investment in your new home by $250,000. Essentially, you shrunk the cost of your new home ($500,000 minus $250,000), giving you an "adjusted basis" of $250,000. Because, on paper, you reduced the investment in your new home, you'll eventually reap a bigger profit (on paper) when you sell.

Let's also assume prices in your neighborhood have soared since 1996, and that your lovely home is now worth $750,000. If you were to sell now, your capital gain would be $500,000 ($750,000 minus your adjusted basis of $250,000). You and your spouse could shelter every penny of that half-million-dollar profit from taxes (for simplicity's sake, we'll assume you don't have to give up some of

your profit to a real estate agent's commission). But what would
happen if you chose not to sell now . . . but to wait and sell five
years from now, at a price that's $10,000 higher? You could then
expect to pay capital-gains tax on that full $10,000. Why?
Remember, under today's federal-income-tax laws, a married couple
can keep up to $500,000 in profit from the sale of their principal
residence, tax free—but any more than that is subject to capital-
gains tax. If you're in a situation like this, it might be in your best
financial interest to sell now and reset the meter on your capital
gains so future profits will be tax free as well.

Best Seasons for Selling

The time of year can dramatically affect how long it will take to sell
your home. In most parts of the country, springtime is peak selling
time. The weather is good, and families are eager to find a new
home and get their move finished in time for the kids to have a
fresh start in a new school come September. Also, most homes look
much more attractive once the lawn has greened up, the flowers are
blooming, and the trees have blossoms or leaves. The "springtime"
selling season can start as early as Super Bowl Sunday, as buyers
start thinking ahead toward springtime. That should be your cue to
start your cleanup and fix-up work.

Markets usually slow down, sometimes drastically, during the
hot summer months. Many families have already made their move,
and other buyers are away on vacation or are otherwise too busy
having fun to focus on such practicalities as a house hunt. There's a
flurry of sales again after Labor Day, which slows to a trickle come
November. Markets all but die off during the November/December
holiday period; cold, icy weather certainly doesn't help bring the

buyers out. The buyers you do find are serious, though, and are often buying because they absolutely must be in the market when the pickings are slimmest, perhaps due to a job transfer. They may be a bit desperate—but they'll figure you're somewhat desperate, too, and will push for a bargain.

The Homeowner's Dilemma: Buy First or Sell First?

It's the classic dilemma for homeowners looking to move into a better home: which should you do first, buy the new home or sell the old one? Your overall finances and the condition of your local housing market will help you determine the answer.

Far and away the safest course, financially, is to sell the old house before making an offer to buy a new one. That way you find out exactly how much cash you will net from the sale and, therefore, how much you can afford to pay for your new home. If the home doesn't sell for quite as much as you thought it would, you might have to spend a little bit less on the new place.

In an ideal world, you would then quickly find a new home, and you could arrange things so the sale and purchase deals got finalized at about the same time, allowing you to move directly from the old home to the new one. Sometimes, it really unfolds in just that way. But reality is often not so cooperative. After your lovely current home gets snapped up in a flash, you could have trouble finding a replacement that's nice enough to make all the hassle and expense of moving worthwhile. You could be pressured to settle for a less-than-ideal home, or you could be forced to move into a rental temporarily while you continue your hunt. This is the risk of selling first.

Delaying your sale until after you've found the perfect new home eliminates that risk. You simply don't move unless and until you find something better. But this strategy carries its own set of risks, of course, most of them financial. It's very easy to get stuck paying two mortgages. And if interested buyers learn that you're soon to be (or already are) on the hook for two mortgage payments, you can be sure they'll try to win your home with a low offer.

Buying Before You Sell

So there's risk either way: you risk not getting the right move-up home, or you risk the expense and worry of carrying mortgages on two homes at the same time. Only you can say which risk is easier for you to stomach. Let's suppose, just for curiosity's sake, that you decided to go the buy-first route. It's a trickier path to follow because you have to find a new source of down payment money. How would you pull it off?

Take out a bridge loan: A bridge loan allows you to dip into the equity you've built up on your current home to make the down payment on your new one. One of the easiest ways to do this is to set up a home-equity line of credit at your bank or credit union. Typically, the interest rate on such a loan is the prime rate plus a 0 to 1 percentage-point markup, and you can make interest-only payments during the early years of the loan. Banks compete heavily on these loans and may offer to pick up all your closing costs, which typically amount to a couple of hundred dollars. But if you pay off the line of credit within one to three years (as you almost certainly will, if you're using it as a bridge loan), banks will demand that you reimburse them for those closing costs.

Establish a finding-a-suitable-home contingency: You probably won't get away with this in a market with a lot of competing homes, in which buyers have the upper hand. Requesting it might even cause buyers to dismiss you as a less-than-serious seller; they might not even want to make a bid. But if there's not much available on the market, and multiple buyers are clamoring for your home, you can make your home sale contingent on your ability to find a suitable replacement home within thirty to sixty days (or so). That's not such a great deal for the buyers; they know their deal could collapse if nothing suits your fancy. But some may be willing to live with that uncertainty if it's the only way to get their hands on your very special home.

Commit to a delayed, but firm, closing date: Buyers may find your playing for time more palatable if, while you shop, you at least remain obligated to sell. You can do this by selling your home without establishing any special finding-a-home contingencies, but by delaying closing for several months—during which you conduct your home search. The delayed closing might suit the buyers' timetable better, too, depending on their circumstances. Be sure to include this request in your counteroffers (you'll find more on the negotiating give-and-take in chapter 15). But remember that if closing day comes and you still haven't found the home of your dreams, you'll have to honor your contract, even if that means putting your furniture into storage and moving into an apartment for the time being.

Buyer's Markets versus Seller's Markets

Aside from the seasonal ebb and flow of home buyers, market conditions will affect the ease with which you're able to sell your home for a good price. Are you in a "buyer's market," a "seller's market," or a "balanced market"? First, a few definitions: If there are many buyers on the market chasing few available homes, you're in a "seller's market." Buyers have to pay top dollar and may have to wage battle in a bidding war. They settle for homes that aren't everything they were looking for. They find they have to agree to more of the seller's demands during negotiations. If the seller wants to rent back the home for a few weeks after closing, for example, buyers may have to swallow this condition, even if it causes them terrible inconvenience. It's that or lose the home to another bidder. You'll sell fastest and at the highest price during a seller's market.

If there are relatively few buyers on the market, choosing among lots of homes, you're in a "buyer's market." Buyers can afford to be choosy and will drive a hard bargain on price. They'll throw you a low-priced offer, just to see if you'll bite. If you don't, they figure that they can either come back with a higher offer or simply move on to one of the other lovely homes on the market. To sell in such a market, you may have to sweeten the deal with extra enticements such as a decorating allowance or a prepaid home warranty to set your home apart from the pack. It will take longer to sell during a buyer's market, and you may have to compromise on price.

In between those extremes is the "balanced market." If you're in a balanced market, there's a healthy balance of buyers and sellers, and neither party can dictate all the terms of the deal. Neither party is particularly desperate. Homes that are in good condition and that are fairly priced tend to sell within the period that's typical for that community and that price range, generally within a couple of months.

Six months' inventory is key. That's the dividing line separating a balanced market from a buyer's or seller's market. If it would take about six months to sell everything on the market, it's a balanced market. If it would take less time, conditions favor sellers. If it would take more time, conditions favor buyers.

Even in a balanced market, very expensive or unusual homes generally take longer to sell than other homes because there is a limited pool of buyers interested in them. If you're selling an architectural masterpiece for a couple of million dollars, you need to be patient. There are relatively few people who'll appreciate the home—and few who can afford it. You simply have to wait longer for the market to work. Real estate agents who specialize in luxury homes can help you gauge a reasonable selling period; it could stretch to a year or more.

Ask your agent what kind of market you're in, and be aware that markets can change quickly. What was a seller's market last month might have cooled off a bit this month. Be alert for signs that the balance of power is starting to shift in your market. Ask all the agents you talk to (as you interview them before choosing one to list your home) how many homes are listed in the MLS compared to last month and the month before. Ask about the average length of time homes remain on your market. If the number of available listings and the time on the market is starting to inch up, your market is cooling—becoming more of a buyer's market. If the number of available listings and the time on the market is shrinking, your market is heating up—becoming more of a seller's market.

Surfing a Changing Market

Sellers are usually a little bit slower to detect a changing market than buyers are, especially when the tide is starting to turn against them. If the neighbors down the street got $300,000 for their home two months ago, then certainly you can get $325,000 for your (you think) much nicer home, right? It's only human to think that way, but it will pay off if you can force yourself to be more objective. If prices are slipping, it means dollars in your pocket if you sell quickly, before prices slide further. In other words, you might want to consider listing your $300,000 home for only $290,000—just to get it sold quickly, before the market drags your price even lower.

A top-notch real estate agent will help you face the reality of a changing market, but some agents are prone to self-delusion, too. And some fear you will list with someone else if they give you too much dour news at a listing presentation. They'll list your home at the higher price, but recommend price reductions if a few weeks go by without any nibbles. If you're jumping into a cooling market as a seller, you'll probably walk away with the best price if you anticipate the market and offer sellers a good deal—and unload your home *before* the market cools further. Of course, if the market is starting to turn up again, this strategy will cost you precious dollars. That's why it pays to know the true temperature of your local market when you decide to sell.

Razzi's Rules to Live By

🏠 We can't always time our home sale.

Life events such as marriage, job transfers, divorce, illness, and death dictate when we must sell a home, regardless of whether it's a buyer's or seller's market.

🏠 Selling now may preserve future gains.

If your profit on a home sale would hit $500,000 as a married couple or $250,000 as a single person, selling now would reset the meter, and allow future profits to go untaxed as well.

🏠 Buyers bloom in the springtime.

It's the peak season for selling because buyers like to get the deal settled in time for a summer move. Homes also tend to look their best in spring. There's another brief spurt of interest between Labor Day and Halloween.

🏠 Snowbirds are serious.

The few buyers who are out looking at homes during winter tend to be serious buyers who *need* to complete a deal. But they'll drive a hard bargain, too.

🏠 Selling first is safest, financially.

Selling your old home before buying a new one is the safest course for your money. But you may have to compromise on the selection of your new home.

🏠 A bridge will take you there.

If you're truly determined not to give up your current home unless you find the perfect replacement, you may have to buy first. A bridge loan (often simply a home-equity line of credit) can help you make the jump.

🏠 Six months' inventory is key.

That's the dividing line separating a balanced market from a market favoring buyers or sellers. If selling everything on the market would take about six months, it's a balanced market. If it would take less time, it's a seller's market. If it would take more time, it's a buyer's market. Ask your agent for a market reading.

🏠 Watch for signs of a shifting market.

You'll make the most money if you react quickly to a market that's shifting from one that favors buyers to one that favors sellers, or vice versa. Hold out for a better price if the sellers are getting the upper hand; cut your price fast for a quick sale in a market where buyers are gaining an edge.

CHAPTER TWO

Estimating Your Bottom Line

"A house is a machine for living in."

Le Corbusier

JUST HOW MUCH MONEY CAN YOU EXPECT TO CLEAR FROM THE sale of your home? You need to come up with some kind of estimate before you make any decisions concerning how much you can spend on a new home or whether you'll really come out ahead from a job transfer.

Real estate agents can give you their opinion of how much your home is likely to fetch on the market. Unfortunately, even good agents with a keen sense of the current market can't do much more than offer an informed guess about price. The market itself will dictate your price; the most agents can do is to try to read the market. Even the best agents often find themselves proposing a price reduction after a month or two (or even a week or two) on the market. Or they may find themselves juggling multiple offers if the initial price was too low.

Keep in mind that real estate agents are an optimistic species. After all, what self-employed salesperson could survive without being an optimist? Imagine how odd it would be if agent after agent came to your home for a listing interview and said, "Oh, this house is just run-of-the-mill. You probably won't sell for nearly as much as you think." Even if it were the truth, you'd probably be a little bit offended, and that agent wouldn't get hired too often (and if you *do* find agents being so openly pessimistic about your home, that means you need to invest in some serious sprucing up before you dare try to sell that dog). Bottom line: Remember that an agent's estimates may err on the high side, especially before that agent has officially committed to the task of selling your home.

Before listing your home for sale with any particular agent you should interview at least three agents who are well acquainted with your neighborhood (you'll learn more about finding agents in chapters 5 and 6). Ask for price estimates from each of them, backed up by the actual sales price of homes that have sold recently. You'll find lots more on the nuances of setting your price in chapter 8 , but for now, you're simply trying to get a ballpark of how much you might clear from a sale. Talking with a few real estate agents will yield that starting number; it wouldn't hurt to visit a couple of open houses too—at homes you consider comparable to yours—just to get a better feel for the market.

With that very rough target price in mind, you can go on to look at the rules and tax breaks that will have a big effect on your bottom line. Let's take a look at IRS rules to see if any of your home-sale profit will be siphoned off for taxes.

Profit, of course, is not determined solely by the sales price. Profit is the difference between the sales price and the price you originally paid for the asset. For tax purposes, though, it gets more complicated. Your "adjusted basis" is the important number; it takes into consideration the actual price you paid, adjusted for things like selling expenses, remodeling investments, and (possibly) the untaxed profits from long-ago home sales.

Tax Breaks on Home Profits

As discussed in the previous chapter, under the tax laws in place since 1997, homeowners are able to sell their main residence and keep a huge piece of the profit tax free. Married couples can claim as much as $500,000 in profit tax free; singles get up to $250,000. It doesn't matter if you sell the house and move into a more expensive mansion or a less expensive cottage—or even a rental apartment. You could pitch a tent in the woods and call that home. The profit is yours, tax free. And you can take advantage of this great tax break as often as once every two years. Bear in mind, however, that it applies only to your main home; vacation homes and investment properties don't qualify.

The old tax rules were in effect for many, many years, and they still linger in the back of some people's minds—particularly retirees thinking about downsizing. It used to be that the only way to shield your capital gain from a home sale was to buy a more expensive home and roll your profit over into that. Once—and only once—in a lifetime could you downsize to a smaller home and shield some of the profit from taxes. The old law put an awful lot of pressure on people nearing or in the early years of retirement. You had one chance to downsize, and you didn't want to do it prematurely and then face a big tax bill if you needed to move on to an even less expensive home (or a rental) sometime later. Rest assured: the old law is dead, dead, dead. The taxman has very little say now in how much you should spend on a new home.

Resetting the Meter to Protect Future Profit

With the way housing values have rocketed in recent years, a quarter or even a half a million dollars in home-sale profit ain't the huge sum it used to be. As discussed earlier, if you've been a homeowner for many years, and, under the old tax rules, you rolled your profit over from previous home sales into your current home, you might want to consider selling, just to preserve future home appreciation from taxes.

Timing Counts

To qualify for the $500,000/$250,000 tax break, you must meet two important conditions. First, *either* you or your spouse must have *owned* the home for two out of the five years before the sale. Second, you must have *lived* there for at least two of the five years. They don't have to be the two years immediately before the sale, and they don't even have to be two years in a row. Your time in the home simply has to add up to at least 730 days over the course of five years.

There are some important exceptions to the two-out-of-five-years rule that could mean you qualify for at least part of the tax break:

* Members of the military or the foreign service (along with the commissioned corps of other uniformed services such as the National Oceanic and Atmospheric Administration and the Public Health Service) who are on extended duty at least fifty miles away from home or who are under orders and live in

government quarters may be able to apply an earlier stretch of time spent living in the home to qualify for the two-out-of-five-years rule and for the entire tax break.

- Relocating at least fifty miles from your current home so you can take a new job may entitle you to claim part of the tax break.

- Home sales that become necessary because of big, unforeseen life changes may qualify you for a partial tax break. These changes include job loss that qualifies for unemployment compensation; divorce or legal separation; the birth of twins, triplets, or other multiples; health problems (yours or those of close relatives) that force you to sell in order to seek treatment; and death.

The bottom line is that if duty or hardship (or a happy surprise like the birth of twins) truly forces you to sell your home before the two-out-of-five-years rule is satisfied, it's worth checking with the IRS to see if you qualify to shield at least part of your home-sale profit from taxes. At www.IRS.gov, you can download Publication 523, "Selling Your Home," for specific rules.

Special Rules for Inheritances and the Recently Widowed

If you inherit a home, your basis (the figure representing your original investment in the home) is the value of that home as stated on the estate's tax return. Even if you're inheriting the family homestead, which has appreciated by hundreds of thousands of dollars over the decades, that appreciation is water under the bridge as far as you are concerned. The meter on your taxable appreciation starts anew when you take ownership at today's value.

However, if you're a recent widow or widower and you owned the home jointly with your spouse, your basis adjusts only partially. Your late spouse's half of ownership transfers to you and gets valued at half of the property's current market value. However, since you already owned half of the home, your half of ownership is valued just as it was before your spouse passed away. The IRS gives this example: Your jointly owned home had an adjusted basis of $50,000 on the day your spouse died. The current market value of the home was $100,000 on that day. As the survivor, your new basis will be $75,000, reflecting the $25,000 for one-half of the old basis, plus $50,000 for half of the market value.

Accounting for Remodeling Investments

If you bought your home for $200,000 and then turned around and built a $100,000 addition or rehab, you really spent $300,000 to buy that home, didn't you? That's how the IRS sees it, too. Investments you make in remodeling are added to your basis (and reduce your profit when you sell). Keep a file with copies of all the contracts and receipts associated with any remodeling jobs done over the years—on all your homes. You never know when you might need to document those investments for the IRS.

Adjusting for Home-sale Expenses

The expenses involved in selling your home not only affect that important on-paper figure, your adjusted basis, but they take cash out of your pocket in a very real way. Trying to cut corners on these expenses can backfire, however, by yielding a smaller sales price. To calculate your net proceeds from the sale, you will deduct these expenses from your sales price (if you list your home with a real estate agent, that agent will break these numbers out for you at the listing presentation). That agent's commission, as much as 5 or 6 percent of the sales price, is usually the biggest of those expenses by far. The following costs are deducted from your sales price to determine your net proceeds:

- Cost of professional window washing or other cleaning services before listing for sale.

- Cost of repair expenses before listing for sale.

- Cost of painting before listing for sale.

- Cost of new carpeting installed before listing for sale.

- Advertising fees (if you sell without an agent).

- Transfer taxes (a special sales tax on real estate levied by some communities. It's usually a matter of negotiation whether these will be paid by the buyer or seller).

- Condo, co-op, or homeowners-association document packages (buyers may pay this expense, depending on local custom).

- Inspections you pay for (sellers may pay for items such as a termite inspection or a property survey, depending on local custom).

- Loan points (prepaid interest) you pay on behalf of buyers.

- Legal fees.

- Brokerage commission.

Deducting Refinanced Mortgage Points

After your home sale is complete, don't forget to claim an income-tax deduction for unclaimed points left over from an old, refinanced mortgage. Although points paid on a mortgage used to buy your primary home are deductible the same year you took out the loan, that's not the case with points paid on a refinance. You must spread deductions for refinance points over the life of the loan. If, for example, you paid $2,000 in points when you refinanced into a new thirty-year mortgage, you can only deduct $67 ($2,000 divided by 30) each year. But you play catch-up when you pay off that loan, and the remaining undeducted points can be claimed against your taxable income that year.

Deducting Moving Costs

The IRS also allows you to deduct the costs associated with packing and moving your belongings if you are relocating a significant distance for your job. You're eligible for the deduction if your new job is at least fifty miles farther from your old home than your old job was. Say, for example, your old home was a quick five-mile commute away from your office. If you transfer to a new job that's at least fifty-five miles away from your old home, you can deduct the costs of that move. In that case, your packing, moving, storage, and travel expenses (excluding food) are deductible. You can find complete rules and a worksheet in IRS Form 3903, "Moving Expenses," available at www.IRS.gov.

Razzi's Rules to Live By

🏠 It's just an opinion.

Even experienced real estate agents can only give you an educated opinion on an appropriate asking price. The best they can do is to try to read the market, and sometimes they don't get it quite right.

🏠 Real estate agents are optimists.

They have to be, or they wouldn't choose to make a living as self-employed entrepreneurs in a sales-oriented field. Just remember that while they're gushing about the prospects of selling your home at top dollar.

🏠 You need price estimates from at least three agents.

Requesting them is a regular part of the listing interview.

🏠 Sales price doesn't determine profit.

At least not alone. The price you paid for your home matters just as much as the price you sell it for.

🏠 Roll-over, you're dead.

Tax rules no longer force you to trade up to a more expensive home in order to avoid paying tax on part of your home-sale profit.

🏠 Half a million ain't what it used to be.

Even though tax laws allow a married couple to keep up to $500,000 and singles to keep up to $250,000 in home-sale profit tax free, you could find yourself exceeding that thanks to today's home prices. That's especially true if you have old, untaxed home profits from homes sold before 1997.

🏠 Timing counts with the IRS.

That $500,000/$250,000 tax break on home-sale profit is available to you only if you've owned and lived in the home for two of the five years leading up to the sale.

⌂ The IRS sometimes makes exceptions.

You may still qualify for part of the $500,000/$250,000 tax break even if you lived in the home less than two years, under the following conditions: your home sale was forced by major events or circumstances such as military service, job relocation, the birth of twins or other multiples, job loss, divorce, illness, or death.

⌂ The IRS gives you a break on death and taxes.

If you inherit a home, you don't face a tax bill for capital gain that built up over the years before ownership shifted to you.

⌂ Remodeling investments count, too.

Hang on to records, contracts, and receipts for all your remodeling jobs over the years. They count toward your basis in the home—the total amount you've invested—and can lower the amount of home-sale profit that you might owe tax on years from now.

⌂ Save by tracking expenses.

Home-sale expenses such as real estate commissions and lawyers' fees are subtracted from the sales price to arrive at your net proceeds—the number that really counts.

⌂ Don't forget your refinance points.

Now's the time to deduct any points from a mortgage refinance that you haven't already deducted on your income tax returns.

⌂ Moving costs might be tax-deductible.

If you take a new job that's at least fifty miles farther from your old home than your old job was, you can claim an income-tax deduction for moving expenses.

CHAPTER THREE

Remodel or Repair Before Selling?

"In a little house keep I pictures suspended,
 it is not a fix'd house,
It is round, it is only a few inches from
 one side to the other;
Yet behold, it has room for all the shows
 of the world, all memories!"

WALT WHITMAN, *My Picture-Gallery*

T HE MINUTE YOU DECIDE TO SELL YOUR HOME, IT STOPS BEING your home. Sure, you may still live there and collect the mail each day, but you need to break off the love affair right away. You have to stop thinking of it as home if you hope to sell it quickly and at the highest possible price. It's now merely an object waiting to be sold, an item to be dressed up like a department-store window. Your comfort, your personal sense of style, your convenience — all those things that used to be important about your life in that home cease to be important. You need to fade out of the picture, and allow this home to become the object of someone else's desire.

Flip through some home-decorating magazines or walk through an open house in a development of brand-new homes. The one thing you'll always notice about these ideal presentations is that there are no people present and little of the useful stuff—not to mention debris—that people use all the time. Look through the photos, and note the little necessities that are missing from each view: There are no dish racks or cookie jars on the kitchen counter; there's an elegant flower arrangement instead. There's no stack of incoming junk mail, no dog dish, no muddy baseball cleats. A clothes hamper in the bathroom? Ha! That would imply that there's dirty laundry somewhere. Children's rooms have few, if any toys. Maybe there's a strategically placed teddy bear or fire truck as a prop. And you certainly won't find any insights into the would-be owners' interests. There are no diplomas on the wall, no religious icons, no family portraits, no sports-team banners.

Magazine editors and new-home marketing departments pay a lot of money to stylists who come up with these pared-down tableaux of domestic bliss or urbane style. Your task as a seller is to transform your house, townhouse, or condo into a similar state of picture-perfect blandness. It's very, very difficult to scrub yourself out of the picture, but you must do it if you want to compete effectively.

Let's go through the steps.

Fixing the Flaws You've Lived With

One of the first things you need to do is to tackle fix-it jobs that require a lead time for hiring contractors—or the dedication of several weekends of your own time. But while it's important to fix all the nagging little things that you've learned to live with, it's unwise to pour thousands into a big remodeling job. Let's go over which jobs to tackle and which to leave for future owners to address according to their own liking.

Nagging, inexpensive fixes should be at the top of your to-do list. Even though they've probably grown practically invisible to you, these little flaws send a message to potential buyers that the home hasn't been maintained well. In the rush of touring houses, buyers may very well forget about your home's sun-filled windows, but remember that the doorknobs were wobbly and the doorbell didn't work. Fix 'em all! That includes broken appliance knobs, loose grout in the tub, sluggish drains, cracked windowpanes, torn screens, sagging rain gutters, and those shaky steps leading to the backyard. The buyers will almost certainly ask you to fix these things after their professional home inspection anyway, so you might as well get them done now, before you invite the world in for a look.

Big Fixes and Remodeling

Whether you should undertake big-ticket jobs is not always so clear-cut. Your goal should be to keep your home in line with what buyers expect, given your neighborhood and price range. If, for example, a typical $500,000 home in your community contains at least three full bathrooms, but yours only has two (or—gasp—one), it might be wise for you to invest the $24,000 or so it would cost to put another in (an estimate from *Remodeling* magazine) before putting the home on the market. Many buyers won't even consider a home without multiple bathrooms these days, and without them, you can expect your home to linger on the market and fetch a low price. Fixing a big deficiency like this could actually reap a price that's more than high enough to cover your investment.

But you should think long and hard before committing to a major kitchen remodeling, which, depending on local construction costs and the level of luxury you hope to achieve, can cost anywhere from about $40,000 to $80,000 and up, according to *Remodeling*. (Each year *Remodeling* conducts a survey with *Realtor* magazine estimating the average costs for common projects, along with how much that work is likely to recoup in sales. You can find more information at www.Remodeling.hw.net.) There are exceptions, but you generally won't recover the full expense when you sell. Anyway, do you really want to go through months and months of disruption for such a major remodeling job when you won't even be living there to enjoy your new kitchen?

That's not to say you don't want to spiff the place up a bit, especially if there are only a few worn areas in a home that's in good shape overall. Kitchens and bathrooms are the keys to buyers' hearts, and they're the rooms that take the biggest beating in our day-to-day lives. If the dishwasher or range is shabby or in disrepair, consider replacing it. If the silver backing on the bathroom mirror has worn away, put in a new one. If the kitchen light fixture is out-of-date, look for a brighter, more fashionable model—many cost less than a hundred dollars. These inexpensive fixes can really brighten the place up and help you sell.

Certainly you should freshen up any shabby areas with a new coat of paint. Dingy wall-to-wall carpet should be torn up and replaced (if you have nice hardwood hiding beneath that carpet, this is the time to let it shine). Any carpet, paint, or wallpaper in a dated color—even if you still love it—has got to go. Mauve carpeting? Get rid of it now. Any real estate agent honest enough to level with you about out-of-fashion colors and trends should score bonus points in your book; they'll help you get the most from your house. You can get diplomacy from your friends, but when you're paying good money for a real estate agent's expertise, you want the hard truth.

Nuts-and-bolts Repairs

Should you put thousands of dollars into repairs that don't show? Things like the roof, water heater, furnace, or air conditioner? What about basement waterproofing? There's not always an obvious answer, and the question is intimately tied up with a seller's obligation to disclose defects that could affect a buyer's decision (you'll find more on disclosure obligations in chapter 16). Basically, the many rules concerning sellers' disclosure obligations boil down to the Golden Rule: Do unto others as you'd have them do unto you. In real estate you might think of it like this: Disclose anything that you'd want to know if you were the buyer.

So if the roof, water heater, furnace, or air conditioner is in need of replacement, you should disclose that to buyers. Unless you're enjoying a roaring seller's market that has buyers grabbing any property they can get, they will lower their price in reaction to this information, reflecting the fact that they have to budget a few thousand dollars right away for a replacement. Or you could pay for the upgrade before putting the house on the market, and crow in your advertising that the home has a new roof, water heater, furnace, or air conditioner. Just don't expect buyers to get too excited about your new roof or utility—it's just not that big a turn-on. After all, they *expect* the house to come with reliable heat. But you at least will have removed a negative from the situation.

Basement waterproofing is a bit more problematic. Leaky basements worry buyers—and their homeowners' insurance companies. The biggest worry is that flooding or seepage could give rise to mold growth, a problem that can be tough and expensive to conquer if it gains too much headway. And it can take a while to find out if a basement leakage problem has been successfully corrected. Water can travel a big distance between the point it enters and the point it shows up as a stain on your wall, and you might have to wait until the next downpour to find out if the spot you waterproofed was actually the correct spot. So, if you have a wet basement problem, you certainly must disclose that fact. If you make any repairs to correct the situation, you need to make copies of the repair contract, payment receipt, and warranty information and present them to prospective buyers. Some buyers may still hesitate (at least if competing homes don't have similar problems), but others won't. And you shouldn't have to worry about a buyer coming to you with a lawsuit a year after the sale, complaining of having been deceived.

Inspections and Warranties

Some home-inspection companies try to sell the idea that home-owners should pay to have their own professional inspection done before they list their home for sale, just so they can get an early look at problems that could become an issue later on. The idea is that sellers then have the opportunity to fix problems and take them off the bargaining table. Savvy buyers will still pay to have their own in-spection performed before their contract becomes binding and they are committed to the deal. And it is true that buyers often use the home-inspection report as an excuse to reopen negotiations over price, or even to back out of the deal. But I think you can safely save the few hundred dollars that a presale home inspection costs.

After all, you've been living in this house — most likely for years. You already know how much (or how little) time and money you have devoted to maintenance over those years. Certainly the home inspector hired by the buyers may reveal some flaws that you hadn't expected (maybe some water damage in the attic, which you rarely visit, for example), but then again, that inspector might find little fault. And, even if you do pay for your own presale inspection, the buyers' later inspection could produce a different laundry list of fixes that you're expected to make.

Your real estate agent also may recommend that you buy a home warranty that will cover the buyers if major systems or appliances (such as the furnace or air conditioner) break during their first year. These policies typically cost less than five hundred dollars and usually cover heating, cooling, plumbing, and electrical systems, plus major built-in appliances such as the range, dishwasher, and refrigerator. If something breaks as a result of normal wear and tear during the first year, the new owners can simply call the warranty company's toll-free number to arrange for service; they'll pay a nominal fee for the visit.

For home buyers, I think warranties are a mediocre deal; they certainly shouldn't deter them from inspecting the home for flaws and negotiating hard on the price. In practice, warranties can sometimes be frustrating for homeowners because most of the warranties have significant exceptions that limit how useful they will be should things break; leaks from a shower enclosure or broken handles on a microwave or refrigerator may not be covered, for example. But for people trying to sell an older home, a warranty might be worthwhile simply as a marketing tool. If the other sellers in your market are offering warranties on their homes, you probably should, too, just to stay competitive. And if you're competing against a lot of newer homes, a warranty could help level the playing field, at least a little bit.

Razzi's Rules to Live By

🏠 The minute you decide to sell your home, it stops being your home.

It becomes nothing more than a dolled-up object in a department-store display. Scour yourself out of the picture.

🏠 Fix it, finally.

All those little jobs that you've been meaning to do need to be done now, and all the little flaws that have grown practically invisible to you need to be repaired before fresh eyes examine your home. You don't want those minor flaws sending a major message to potential buyers.

🏠 Keep up with the Joneses.

If buyers shopping in your neighborhood and price range expect to find at least three full bathrooms, but yours has only one or two, spending the money to bring your home up to par could result in a big payoff.

🏠 Don't overdo it.

Don't commit to a major remodeling just in preparation for sale. Usually you won't recover the full investment—but you *will* undergo the full hassle.

⌂ Let kitchens and baths shine.

They're the key to buyers' hearts, and they take the heaviest day-to-day wear. Focus your presale improvements on these areas.

⌂ You can get diplomacy from your friends.

But when you're paying good money to a real estate agent, you deserve the cold truth about flaws in the home you're trying to sell.

⌂ Follow real estate's golden rule:

Disclose unto others as you'd have them disclose unto you. If your home has a flaw that would affect a buyer's decision to buy and/or the price they'd pay, then you must disclose that to the buyer—or risk a legal tussle.

⌂ A new furnace is *not* a hot button.

Don't expect buyers to get too excited about your new furnace, roof, or other utility. They expect these things to be in working order. But putting money into a repair or replacement can remove a flaw.

⌂ Let the buyers do the inspection.

Don't spend a few hundred dollars on an inspection before putting a home up for sale. Savvy buyers will want their own inspection anyway, and you can use that money for any needed repairs.

⌂ A warranty is a sales tool.

Home-repair warranties typically have frustrating exclusions and exceptions, making them a mediocre deal for homeowners. They're better thought of as a sales tool, a little extra that might reassure a buyer.

CHAPTER FOUR

Dressed to Kill

"In the middle of the room there is a big ottoman;
and this, with the carpet, the Morris wall-papers,
and the Morris chintz window curtains and brocade
covers of the ottoman and its cushions, supply all
the ornament, and are much too handsome to be
hidden by odds and ends of useless things."

BERNARD SHAW, *Pygmalion*

I REMEMBER SOME OF THE HOMES I DIDN'T BUY. THERE WAS THE
ONE with the pink carpet practically everywhere. There was the
one with the shoebox-size dining room containing four fully
mirrored walls (that one also had an odd little room filled with
shelves of miniature liquor bottles, the kind sold on airplanes).
There was a lovely home full of baseball memorabilia (the owners
seemed to favor the St. Louis Cardinals). And there was a house
brimming with Republican mementos, including that Washington
classic, a room full of grip-and-grin photos with politicians. In one
house, an ill family member had apparently been living in the great
room, as evidenced by the abandoned bed set aside in the corner,
piled high with medical supplies. (That hardly told a cheery tale.)

Another place had a big fan going in the basement in an attempt to air out a moisture problem.

That's not really how you want your home to be remembered by buyers, is it? But I also recall another house or two that were decorated so perfectly I might have moved in on the spot. I think of one as the Ralph Lauren house. In fact, I was so smitten I had to force myself to focus on some big, permanent flaws, such as a very badly laid-out kitchen. That kind of seductive tableau is the effect you need to strive for before you invite the first buyer through the door.

The View from the Curb

Many buyers take a quick drive past a home to see if it's a candidate for consideration before ever asking a real estate agent for a showing. I know I do. You need to snare buyers on those unannounced drive-bys, which often occur in the evening. That's one reason you should keep the lights on in your front windows and turn on all the exterior lights the entire time your home is on the market. You never know when a buyer might pass by, ready to fall in love.

Real estate agents call these efforts "boosting your curb appeal." And a home lacking curb appeal will suffer on the market. Hire someone to do the work, or roll up your sleeves and do it yourself. You absolutely must do the following outdoor jobs:

- Trim low-hanging trees and shrubs. Remove them altogether if they're wild or if they obstruct the view of the home.

- Remove dead brush and leaves.

- Mow the lawn as frequently as necessary.

- Spread fast-acting fertilizer on the lawn to green it up—even if it's more weeds than grass. You at least want lush, green weeds.

- Spread fresh mulch on all plant beds.

- Edge the lawn abutting sidewalks and driveways.

- Plant bright, new annuals, if weather permits.

- Paint the front door, and, if they need freshening, the window shutters.

- Clean or replace outdoor light fixtures and address numbers.

- Paint or seal the porch floor if it looks at all shabby.

- Place a pair of nice rocking chairs, a swing, or wicker chairs on the porch.

- Power wash any mildew or dirt from the home's exterior, and repaint if necessary.

- Clean the rain gutters and nail up any sagging areas.

- Repair any loose steps or pavers leading to the door.

- Put a few abundant pots of full-grown flowers near the entry.

- Place a new welcome mat in front of the door.

- Add an attractive wreath or flag to the front, if it suits your home's style.

- Train a couple of inexpensive garden spotlights on the front of your home. (Position them close, to highlight the texture of brickwork, stone, or siding, but don't make the wattage too high.

Aim for a subtle wash of light. Another small spot illuminating your For Sale sign wouldn't hurt.)

The View Inside

Your ruthless cleaning must also extend beyond the exterior, to thoroughly encompass the interior. That even includes the insides of closets and the dark recesses of the basement and garage, because serious buyers will nose around everywhere. Your first step is to drastically declutter and get rid of any belongings that you don't really want to keep. Remember, this house isn't your home now. It's just a thing you're trying to sell.

Be merciless as you decide what to throw out or donate to charity. If you keep something, you'll only have to pay someone to carry it to your new home—and then you'll have to find a place to put it once you're there; make sure you only keep what you really need and want. A yard sale is a time-honored way to lighten your load—and it gives neighbors an inkling that your lovely home will be coming on the market soon (maybe they've had an eye on it all these years, or they know of a friend who might like to buy it).

Once you've pared down your belongings to those that really deserve a place in your new life, it's time to cut back further. You need to edit the belongings that will be on view to buyers. This is one reason you have to be ruthless about throwing things away; you're going to put a lot of your belongings into boxes and pack them away in the closet. You may even want to rent an off-site storage shed to accommodate them until after your home has sold.

Your goal is to achieve that uncluttered home-decor-magazine look. The first to go should be pieces of furniture that, while useful, may not complement that decorator look. Are there any odd chairs, ottomans, bookcases, magazine racks, or antiques that could be stored for a while to make rooms feel more spacious? After you've made that round of culling, brace yourself for the next step: depersonalizing your home. You want to put away your treasures and mementos and make your home more of a blank canvas, ready to accept the buyer's style. Museums employ this technique all the time, taking some items off exhibit in order to emphasize new ones, so think like a curator.

Get some good, strong boxes and pack up the following items, which you won't need until it's time to settle into your new home:

- Family photographs. *Maybe* two or three beautifully framed photos will enhance the look of a room, but beyond that, stow them away.

- Collectibles. Pack up your prized collection of figurines, first-edition books, antique cameras, and so on. Put away your awards, diplomas, religious icons, and other personal items. They'll only distract buyers and probably won't add to that clean, magazine-inspired look. Besides, then you won't have to worry about strangers breaking or stealing any of your favorite things. You never know what will ring an emotional bell (positively or negatively) with the strangers who tour your home. For all you know, that Ivy-league diploma you so treasure could just remind a buyer of a despised ex. It's better to pack it away!

- Items that won't be included in the home sale. If you don't intend to part with your one-of-a-kind chandelier, or the fireplace doors, or a pair of wall sconces, you need to protect them *now*. Don't even let buyers see them, and there won't be any squabbles later with a buyer who's angry that those beautiful pieces aren't being included in the sale. (You wouldn't show a toddler a dish full of candy and then say he can't have any, would you? Keep the same idea in mind with buyers. You don't need tantrums.) Buy replacements and install them so that's all the buyer ever sees.

- Utilitarian books and manuals. If you don't need them every day and they don't look attractive on the bookshelf, pack 'em away.

- Small appliances and tools. Are you really going to be baking cakes while your home is being marketed? Probably not, so put your heavy stand mixer into storage. Ditto for the bread machine, the food processor, and oversize pots and pans. You won't need them, and getting rid of them makes your kitchen look spacious and easy to clean. Small appliances that you do use every day, such as the toaster and the coffeemaker, can live in the cupboard when you're not actually using them. Remember, those magazine photos rarely show these workaday items—beyond the heroically upscale espresso machine.

- Children's toys. Certainly you wouldn't ship all their favorites off to a storage shed (speaking of tantrums). But, if your home is at all typical, there's an abundance of toys filling the family room and the kids' bedrooms. Let the kids earn some money for themselves by adding some of their outgrown toys to your yard sale (they can spend the money on a treat for their new home— maybe some new lawn toys or a video-game console). And some of their favorites could be decommissioned for a while, at least until the home is no longer on display. They'll love their toys all the more when they're reunited with them, and your preshowing cleanups will be much easier to pull off.

- Extra blankets, towels, and linens. If you keep on hand only those sets that best complement your decor, say two sets per person or per bed (one to use and one for the laundry basket), then you can tidy up your linen closet and make it look beautifully roomy.

- Old cans of paint, insect sprays, weed killers, and other toxics. OK, you've been meaning to haul them off to your town's hazardous-waste-recycling center forever—now's the time. You'll have to get rid of them before you move anyway, and such items will only raise questions in the minds of prospective buyers, as in "Do they have a roach problem?"

- Long-term storage and seasonal items. Move out that baby furniture that you're holding on to in hopes of using it for your grandchildren someday. The bulky holiday decorations that won't be needed for half a year or more? They can safely be sent to off-site storage. Buyers like to see that there's lots of storage space in your basement, attic, or garage, and clearing out your stuff makes it look that much roomier.

- Houseplants. It's time to finally put your struggling houseplants out of their misery—or at least in the care of a friend. You may want to buy two or three brand new, vigorous plants in shiny new pots to take their place. A well-chosen silk plant or two may fit the bill. Indoor plants can give the perfect touch to a space, but only if they're healthy and beautiful and don't add to the clutter. If your little indoor jungle takes up a big corner of the room or obscures the window, it's time for a transplant.

Living in the Washington DC area, I've learned an important lesson from some of the many military- and diplomatic-corps families who constantly move into and out of our neighborhoods. Because another move is only a year or two away, all their belongings have to carry their weight. Their homes are rarely filled with a lot of excess stuff; it simply doesn't travel well. So follow their lead and pare down to essentials.

Protecting Your Valuables

Remember that you're about to invite strangers into every room of your home. Your real estate agent may even post 360-degree panoramas of each room on the Internet. You certainly don't want to show off any items that might appeal to a thief. Remember, strangers will have the run of the place while you aren't at home, and they'll open cabinet doors and peek inside closets. You don't want them going into your jewelry box—or coming back later for a thorough burglary. Put your jewelry, guns, and other valuables in a bank's safe-deposit box for the time being.

Cleaning—Like a Demon

Once you've decluttered your home top to bottom, it will be easier to pull off the cleaning job of a lifetime. Clean homes look good—and they *smell* good. And buyers like nice, fresh homes, even if they're a hundred years old. If these tasks are too much for you to handle yourself, it will pay to hire someone to do them for you. Your must-dos include the following:

• Wash all windows, inside and out.

• Shampoo (or replace) wall-to-wall carpet.

- Wash and polish wood and tile floors.

- Wash and polish all light fixtures; put in the maximum wattage bulb that's safe for that fixture (buy attractive, clear bulbs while you're at it).

- Wipe finger marks off woodwork and light switches.

- Wash and polish wood cabinet doors.

- Clean the insides of all appliances, including the refrigerator and oven.

- Degrease the range hood and run the filter through the dishwasher.

- Scrub or replace trash bins, especially in the kitchen.

- Bleach or replace tile grout in showers and bathrooms.

- Recaulk tubs, if at all necessary.

- Remove any calcium or lime deposits from shower doors and fixtures.

- Send draperies to be dry-cleaned.

- Vacuum and shampoo sofas and wash or dry-clean slipcovers if necessary.

- Clean or replace furnace and air conditioning filters.

- Touch up the paint as necessary.

That's a whole lot of work, isn't it? But no real estate investment in the world yields better dividends than these low-cost, high-elbow-grease efforts do. By the time you're finished, if you've done your job right, you'll be seriously reconsidering moving out of this lovely, well-repaired home.

Managing Your Dear Pets

They're members of the family, but even the best-behaved dog or cat is a nuisance when it's time to show a home. Some real estate agents go so far as to recommend that you send Spot and Fluffy off to live with a friend or a relative while you market the home, but that's a bit extreme, if not impossible, for many pet lovers. However, you absolutely must make any lingering pet aromas disappear. And when you evacuate the home for showings, you're better off taking the dog (and even the cat, if at all possible) with you. You'll find more about that in chapter 12.

For now, though, assume your home has a pet aroma. We grow accustomed to the scents we live with in a home, and they disappear for us. But buyers bring fresh noses on the scene, and you don't want them to remember your home as the one that smelled like dog. Or cat. Shampooing (or replacing) the carpet and sofa are a must, especially if that's where your pet spends a lot of time (or had some accidents back in puppyhood). Book extra appointments with the groomer to keep Spot smelling more like shampoo and less like Spot (if Spot has a particularly strong odor, a visit to the veterinarian may be in order, to check for skin or ear infections or to get a teeth cleaning). Wash pet bedding frequently, and use a scent-eliminating spray liberally in between washings. Replace raggedy, smelly pet toys with fresh new ones; tidy up the lawn daily; and clean the cat's litter box once a day (at least), replacing the litter frequently.

Apply the same odor-control vengeance in dealing with other

pets such as birds, reptiles, guinea pigs, hamsters, and the like. That damp, cedar smell coming from the guinea pig's home isn't fooling anybody! Freshen pets' habitats daily. And if your home shelters any creatures that could be hazardous if handled without your permission, say exotic snakes or tarantulas, do yourself a favor and have them vacation at the home of a knowledgeable friend. Who needs to worry about the possibilities?

Minding Your Nose

Pets, unfortunately, aren't the only critters that can leave a house smelling bad. We do our share, as well. While your home is on the market, do not allow anyone to smoke indoors. Don't allow a tobacco smell to build up in the garage or carport, either. And nobody wants to see ashtrays full of butts out on the patio. Nonsmokers are incredibly sensitive to these smells, and their presence can sour them on your home.

Even your dinner menu may have to be modified for the time being. Don't even think about cooking onions, garlic, fish, curry, fried foods, or anything else that leaves a lingering aroma. Leave those foods for restaurant meals.

And while you're at it, put an extra hamper in the garage or mudroom to quarantine smelly sneakers, cleats, and athletic jerseys. Douse it with air freshener regularly—and get the household athletes to commit to a few extra workouts with the washing machine, at least while your home is on display.

Setting the Stage

There's one more step you should consider in preparing your home for sale. Good real estate agents often recommend ways to "stage" a home for sale, or they may refer you to someone who specializes in home staging. For a fee of several hundred dollars (perhaps more for a large home), such specialists will help you rearrange your furniture and belongings to greatest effect. They'll often loan you some props, such as throw rugs, potted plants, or small pieces of furniture to help pull off a more put-together effect.

In fact, staging is essential if you've already moved out of the home. Most buyers have surprising difficulty imagining themselves and their belongings in an empty house. It can actually yield more money (and a faster sale) if you bring in props and enough furniture to set up appealing, homey tableaus.

Again, remember that this place isn't your home anymore; it's something being dressed up for sale. Create those little scenes, even if it means taking that old TV with the rabbit ears out of the den and replacing it with the armchair and ottoman from your bedroom—you can do without TV in the den for a while. Create a still life from books and a lamp on a nearby table, to give it that "Father Knows Best" den feeling. Put a bowl of fruit on the kitchen counter, a bowl of natural sponges on the bathroom counter. Arrange a tableau of chic bottled water, glasses, lemons, and breadsticks on the patio table. Toss a straw hat on the bedpost. Buy an inexpensive new bedspread if the old one looks out-of-date or you need to brighten up the room with some color. Buy fresh new bath mats and shower curtains for the bathrooms. Borrow an area rug (or buy a cheap imitation Oriental one) to pull together a grouping in the living room. Take down dated window coverings and either replace them with inexpensive, up-to-date coverings or allow windows to go naked, especially if the woodwork is beautiful. Remember, that's often how it's done in magazines.

It doesn't matter that you don't really live this way; you're simply setting a stage. Sure, it goes against the grain to spend money decorating a house that you don't plan to live in, but these little touches can easily pay for themselves in a higher home price and a faster sale.

Razzi's Fearless Rules to Live By

🏠 Be ready for evening drive-bys.

Buyers often drive past in the evening just to see if your home is a candidate. Leave lights on in the front rooms and outdoors so they can see it at its best. Homes without curb appeal don't stand a chance.

🏠 Green thumbs bring greenbacks.

Put some time and money into making the front lawn look as good as possible, even if all that beautifully manicured green stuff is nothing but weeds.

🏠 Be merciless about clutter.

You need to get rid of junk that isn't worth its keep; store unneeded belongings off-site, and put unsightly necessities out of view.

🏠 Clean with a vengeance.

Clean homes look good and smell good. And they sell faster and for more money.

🏠 Spruce up until you no longer want to leave.

That's the sign that you're ready to invite buyers in so they can fall in love with it, too.

⌂ Notice what's *not* there in magazine pictures.

Homes look best without necessities like dish racks, toothbrushes, and toasters. Put them away.

⌂ Assume that Fido and Fluffy smell.

Visitors will pick up scents that you've naturally grown accustomed to, so be diligent in eradicating pet scents.

⌂ Set the stage.

Remove items that don't add to that glossy-home-magazine setting, and rearrange belongings so they tell a lovely domestic tale. Buy (or borrow) items, if necessary; the investment will pay off.

CHAPTER FIVE

The World of Brokers—and How They're Paid

"True, it was a good advertisement at Boosters' Club lunches, and all the varieties of Annual Banquets to which Good Fellows were invited, to speak sonorously of Unselfish Public Service, the Broker's Obligation to Keep Inviolate the Trust of His Clients, and a thing called Ethics, whose nature was confusing but if you had it you were a High-class Realtor and if you hadn't you were a shyster, a piker and a fly-by-night."

SINCLAIR LEWIS, *Babbitt*

MOST HOMEOWNERS BY FAR USE A REAL ESTATE brokerage company to sell their home—a full 87 percent of sellers, according to statistics published by the National Association of Realtors (NAR). There's plenty of information in chapter 9 that can help you decide if you're cut out for trying to sell on your own, but first, let's take a look at how the world of real estate brokers and agents works.

The hiring of a real estate brokerage company is a big-ticket purchase in itself. Real estate commissions these days run about 5 or 6 percent of the sales price. And the median price of a home is roughly $210,000. (The median is a statistical midpoint. Half of all homes sell for higher prices than the median; half sell for lower prices.) A 5 percent commission on a $210,000 home is $10,500. Ten grand is a pretty big expenditure, of course, but many, many people pay quite a bit more. Remember, half of the homes in the country are selling for more than $210,000. On a $500,000 home, a not-uncommon price in many metro areas, 5 percent amounts to a $25,000 commission; 6 percent amounts to a $30,000 commission. In other words, the commission for selling a nice three- or four-bedroom home in the suburbs of a big city can easily be about the same as the sticker price on a Cadillac sedan. For that kind of money, you should do some serious tire kicking before you buy any real estate broker's services.

As soon as the talk turns to commissions, real estate brokers and agents will point out that they do not pocket that whole commission. And it's true that the commission is divided and divided again, often leaving the individual agent who sits across the kitchen table from you with maybe 1.5 percent out of that whole 6 percent commission. That money gets sliced up quite a bit. First the commission is divided (typically fifty-fifty, but not always) between the seller's agent and the buyer's agent. Then your agent splits her share with the broker under whose auspices she works. The ratio of that split depends on how much of a hotshot your agent is. Newly licensed rookies typically hand over 50 percent to the broker, whereas top-selling agents sometimes keep as much as 90 percent themselves. Even getting only 10 percent, their broker makes money because those agents handle many transactions, and likely at high prices, too. There are some exceptions to this business model, however; the RE/MAX franchise allows agents to keep a higher-than usual share of the commission, and instead charges them a fee for office overhead, the right to use RE/MAX logos, and other costs of business that are typically picked up by the broker. And the number of brokerage companies that pay real estate agents a salary instead of a commission is increasing; they're often companies that charge discounted fees to consumers or offer various real estate brokerage services à la carte.

For sellers, the appeal of the traditional system of agents and brokers working for a commission is obvious: you don't owe a penny unless the home sells. And you won't ever have to write out a big check to your broker. The fee for brokerage services comes straight out of the sales price at the closing table. The agent and broker assume all the up-front expenses for advertising, which include renting an attractive For Sale sign, creating and printing flyers or brochures, taking digital photographs, hosting open houses, and posting the listing on the MLS. They don't get paid anything for all the hours they spend researching sales prices on comparable properties, escorting buyers through your home, or managing paperwork. Plus, because their earnings are directly tied to the selling price of your home, brokers have an incentive to push for the highest possible price. On the other hand, when you start looking at the 1.5 percent or so that actually makes it into your agent's pocket, you discover that an extra $10,000 in selling price only earns your agent an extra $150; you definitely stand to benefit more from a higher selling price than your agent does. Keep that in mind when an agent urges you to pounce on an offer that's lower than you expected.

Buyers' Agents: Who Pays Them?

The agent who brings a buyer to your home and tries to negotiate your price down is actually paid by *you*, out of the commission split discussed above. You see, before things began to change in the 1980s and '90s, real estate agents always represented the sellers. Homeowners hired a brokerage company and a specific real estate agent to represent them in selling their home; that brokerage would then list the home in the local Multiple Listing Service (MLS). More than simply an advertising database, the MLS is a broker-to-broker offer of cooperation and commission splitting. When brokers or agents list a home in the MLS, they are announcing, "Hey, all you licensed agents who belong to the MLS! Find a buyer for this home and I'll split my commission with you." What *buyers* didn't realize (and many agents driving them around didn't necessarily understand, either) was that this system made the agents—legally— representatives of the *seller*. So, if an agent learned that a buyer was willing to come back with a full-price offer if the seller rejected his first, lowball offer, the agent *was supposed to* pass that info along to the seller. Some actually did pass such valuable tidbits along; others, mistakenly thinking their allegiance should be with the buyers, didn't. But with the advent of laws requiring disclosure about these relationships—and with the rise of buyers' brokers— agents and the general public came to understand that buyers deserve full disclosure: they deserve to know exactly who is being represented by the agent showing them homes. Is the agent representing the buyer or the seller? Many buyers wisely decided they wanted the agent they worked with to actually—and lawfully—represent *them* in the transaction, keeping their confidences safe and helping them bargain for the lowest price and best terms.

Today, most agents require a buyer to sign a disclosure agreement outlining whether the agent represents the seller or buyer. According to a 2005 NAR study, 58 percent of buyers said they had signed a disclosure statement explaining who the agent represented. Unfortunately, 28 percent didn't sign that disclosure form until it was time to write a purchase contract. If any cats were going to be let out of the bag, they could have been long gone by then! For a seller, the bottom line is that you cannot assume that any agent who shepherds a buyer through your home is actually working on your behalf. Assume that the agent is committed to the buyer's interests, and keep offhand comments—such as "We've had a lot of showings; we're pretty confident of selling before our new home is ready"—to yourself. While that sounds as if you're exuding nothing but confidence, such a statement alerts the buyer's agent, and therefore the buyer, to the fact that you have a clock ticking, and tells them you might settle for a lower price.

Buyers today often sign their own contract with a buyer's agent (who will represent their interests) promising that their share of the commission, typically 2.5 or 3 percent, will be paid out of the total commission that comes off the sales price. But if buyers purchase a home from someone who is selling without an agent (more on that later), they may have to cover that commission themselves—unless they persuade the seller to pay it.

So who really pays the real estate commission? It's a very good question, one that's not asked frequently enough. It's certainly reasonable for you, the seller, to believe you're paying it. After all, you're the one who chooses a brokerage company and signs a contract that stipulates the percentage in commission that will be paid when the home sells. Then again, although buyers *think* they're not paying a commission, it can be argued that they are actually paying the whole thing—after all, they're the ones who bring all the cash to the table. In truth, the money comes straight off the top of the deal. Sellers pay it *and* buyers pay it. But you, as the seller, have the opportunity to shop around for real estate services based on price. As long as buyers *think* they're not paying the commission out of their pockets, they have less incentive to shop for reasonably priced service. It's no coincidence that the rise of discount real estate brokerage models focuses on the seller's side of the transaction. Buyers' agents still generally expect the same old 2 or 3 percent, even though buyers these days come to them after already doing weeks of home shopping online.

Your Listing Info: Guess Who Owns It?

Now, you'd think that since you own the home and you're paying a broker to represent you, you should control the information that's presented to the public about your home. Not so fast. Brokers actually think of your for-sale home as *their inventory*. And they think the information about that inventory belongs to them.

This should only really concern you in that brokers make the decisions about where to advertise *their inventory*. They pay the advertising fees, and they decide whether the listing will be posted as widely as possible on the Internet or whether they will try to maintain some control over where their inventory is displayed and sold, thereby limiting the ability of other brokers to lift the listing information from one Web site and display it elsewhere.

Unless you're a Hollywood star or corporate mogul who has to worry about the prying eyes of the public, it's clearly in your best interest to have your home posted—with lots of flattering photos—on every Web site possible. That includes www.Realtor.com (the 3-million-home database sponsored by the National Association of Realtors), your brokerage company's Web site, your agent's personal Web site, and any Web sites run by other agents who care to pick up the listing and post it—even if they offer their own services at a discount and thereby draw the ire of full-price, full-service competitors. It's even in your interest for your property to be advertised outside of the real estate universe, on Web sites such as www.CraigsList.org, a nonprofit advertising/bulletin board site.

A small number of brokers and agents prefer to keep this "inventory" within their own orbit so they don't have to pay fees to discount real estate agents who run their business mainly (or exclusively) over the Internet. That's an inside-the-industry squabble that shouldn't concern you. Just be sure to ask your real estate agent where on the Internet your listing will be posted, and if there will be any restrictions about who may post it. Remember, broad exposure to the greatest number of buyers is the strategy that will net you the highest price and fastest sale.

Full Service or à la Carte?

You may not have to choose between the extremes of listing with a traditional full-service real estate brokerage and going the for-sale-by-owner (commonly known as FSBO and pronounced "fizz-bo") route. The real estate brokerage industry's new term for such go-italones is *unrepresented seller* (and should be pronounced "few-chur kus-te-mer" because many people who try to sell by themselves eventually do list with an agent). A new crop of business models is taking root, giving sellers options for sales help that go beyond the full-service, full-price brokerage model. Services that are aimed at the FSBO market are covered in chapter 10. But if you've decided you want the representation of a real estate brokerage, you still need to decide between the full-service, full-price model and alternatives that provide service at a discount. You also need to decide whether to use a referral service to help find your agent.

Discount Alternatives

We're starting to see more full-service real estate brokerages offering services at a discount. With some discount companies you don't get to choose a particular agent with whom you'll work (in fact, sometimes the bulk of your communication is through a keyboard and the Internet). With others, the choice is all yours. Often, you agree to take on some of the work yourself.

Foxtons, a brokerage that operates in and around the New York City area, covering suburbs in New York, New Jersey, and Connecticut, is a full-service brokerage. Foxtons' brokers and agents belong to the National Association of Realtors, and it charges only a 3 percent commission to sell a home. That's not just 3 percent for the selling side—it's 3 percent total. The company claims it sells 60 percent of its own listings in-house, which means it doesn't have to split its 3 percent with anyone else. But it also pays commissions to other agents who bring buyers. The company does a particularly nice job at photographing homes and preparing layout drawings. For more information, go to www.Foxtons.com or call 800-369-8667.

Progressive Homesellers, a Seattle-based discount brokerage doing business in Washington State (with plans to expand into California) expects you to take on some of the work yourself. Progressive's licensed real estate agents provide most of the usual services to sellers—advising on price, listing the home on the MLS, providing documents—but everything's done via phone, e-mail, or overnight delivery (the company doesn't oversee open houses). You choose between paying Progressive a fee of $3,750 up front (by credit card) or $5,250 at closing. And you decide what commission you will offer a buyer's agent (typically 2.5 percent to 3 percent of the sales price) beyond the listing fee. For more information, go to www.ProgressiveHomesellers.com or call 888-378-7878.

Zip Realty is a full-service brokerage company with local agents in many major metro areas of the country, including Phoenix; Atlanta; Chicago; Boston; Minneapolis–St. Paul; Las Vegas; Dallas–Fort Worth; Houston; Washington, DC; Seattle, and many markets in Florida and California. The company allows you to browse the profiles of its agents working in those communities, and promises discounts of up to 25 percent on your listing fees (it also give buyers rebates of up to 20 percent of the commission). Its services include MLS listing and posting on www.Realtor.com, plus hosting open houses and producing 360-degree virtual tours. For more information, go to www.ZipRealty.com or call 800-225-5947.

There are many companies that charge a flat fee, generally several hundred dollars, to list your home on the MLS. They often offer other services as well, such as providing For Sale signs, lockboxes, contracts, and Web pages. These companies, including www.MLSLion.com, www.KingOffer.com, www.BrokerDirectMLS.com, and www.FlatFeeListing.com are discussed further in chapter 9.

Referral Services and Rebates

Another option is to find a real estate agent through an online referral company. Such companies promise to refer sellers exclusively to pre-screened, licensed agents who are Realtors (members of the National Association of Realtors), and, in states where it's allowed, they offer sellers commission rebates after closing. It's still crucial that you go through the screening steps outlined in chapter 6 before you choose an individual agent through such a service, but it can be a good way to find an agent when you simply don't have much familiarity with the who's who of your local real estate market. The rebates are a nice little benefit, and there's absolutely nothing preventing you from interviewing a couple of agents you find through word of mouth as well.

HomeGain allows sellers to search its roster of participating agents and compare their backgrounds and the commissions they charge. Recently the site was offering product discounts and commission rebates (in states that allow them) of up to a thousand dollars for buyers and sellers who completed sales using their referred agents. For more information, go to www.HomeGain.com.

RealEstate.com, part of LendingTree.com, the online mortgage matchmaker, matches sellers (and buyers) with participating full-service real estate agents. (As with HomeGain, real estate agents pay the company a fee for the referral.) The company offers commission rebates—to buyers and sellers—in the form of Home Depot or American Express gift cards. Recently they offered cards ranging in value from a hundred dollars (for homes that sold for at least $75,000) to over two thousand dollars (for homes that sold for more than $525,000).

Rebate programs are not legal in every state, however, so you won't be offered a rebate if you live in Alaska, Iowa, Kansas,

Louisiana, Mississippi, Missouri, New Jersey, Oklahoma, or South Carolina (the states of Alabama, Oregon, and Tennessee restrict but don't completely prohibit rebates).

Negotiating a Lower Commission

Even if you decide to sell your home through your friendly local real estate agent—the one who's been doing business in your neighborhood forever and seems to know everyone in town—you should feel free to try to negotiate a smaller commission. That agent is certainly aware of all the discount options now available to sellers and may be willing to shave a bit off the commission so you don't take your business to a competitor.

Keep in mind the commission that will be offered to buyers' agents, however, particularly if there are more sellers than buyers in your market. If you negotiate a 6 percent commission down to 5 percent, you might want the usual 3 percent to be offered to buyers' agents, leaving 2 percent to your own agent. (However, a 2.5 percent commission offered to buyers' agents still shouldn't be terribly off-putting.) Real estate remains a sales business, with commissions being a key motivator. If buyers' agents have a choice between showing one listing that will profit them 3 percent versus another that will only profit them 2 or 2.5 percent, some will be quicker to show the more profitable one. With more buyers searching listings on their own, such agents will have less success pushing the higher-profit listing, but the possibility still remains.

There are several situations, as follows, in which you're likely to succeed in negotiating the commission down a bit:

- You're selling an expensive home. If you're selling a home near the top end of your local price range, you have quite an incentive to whittle down that percentage paid in commission. While marketing expensive homes can be costly (they're often advertised with full-color photos in glossy magazines, for example) a 6 percent commission on a $1 million home is 60 grand. On a $2 million home it's 120 grand. Push for a smaller percentage; your agent will still collect a hefty fee.

- You're using the same agent to sell your old home and to buy the new one. This one agent stands to get roughly 6 percent on your sale (which of course will be shared with the broker and the buyer's agent) and 3 percent on your purchase. You should ask for a volume discount.

- Your agent snags an in-house sale. If your agent also finds the buyer, that agent gets to keep the whole 5 or 6 percent commission (which will be shared with the broker). Again, ask for a volume discount.

- Your home is sure to be an easy sale. If you're living in a truly special place—the to-die-for home in the neighborhood, it will sell quickly if you price it reasonably. If there's going to be very little work for the agent, argue for a smaller commission—at least assuming it's sold within the first month.

Razzi's Rules to Live By

⌂ You deserve Cadillac service.

After all, the commission on a $500,000 home is roughly the list price on a brand new luxury car. Kick the tires!

🏠 You pay the buyer's agent.

Then again, it could be argued that the buyer pays everybody's agent. Regardless, the commission comes off the top. And sellers have more incentive to shop for a lower commission.

🏠 Broad exposure is key.

Real estate agents and brokers may think they own your listing information—but you should insist that they publicize it anywhere and everywhere possible.

🏠 Discounters, referrals, and rebates, oh my!

Take a look at the broad array of discount brokers, referral/rebate services, and flat-fee listing companies available to sellers. You could save, especially if you're willing to take on part of the workload.

🏠 Your first negotiation is with the agent.

If you're paying Cadillac prices, you should at least try to get something off the sticker price.

CHAPTER SIX

How to Size Up Real Estate Agents

"Babbitt's virtues as a real-estate broker—as the servant of society in the department of finding homes for families and shops for distributors of food—were steadiness and diligence. He was conventionally honest, he kept his records of buyers and sellers complete, he had experience with leases and titles and an excellent memory for prices."

SINCLAIR LEWIS, *Babbitt*

THEIR SMILING FACES ARE EVERYWHERE. THEY'RE GRINNING AT you from business cards, newspaper ads, bus-stop placards, Web sites, outfield fence banners, For Sale signs, church bulletins, and innumerable free calendars. At last count, there were about 1.2 million members of the National Association of Realtors, the industry's main trade group. That's roughly one Realtor for every 164 adults (twenty-one and older) in the United States. It's a little bit more than the entire population of Rhode Island. Any way you look at it, there are more than enough agents from which to choose. So, what's the best way to go about selecting one?

The best way to find a great agent is the same way you find a great hairstylist, auto mechanic, or babysitter. That is, you have to ask around among people whose opinion you respect. You need the honest viewpoint of people who have actually used the services of a particular agent. Beware referrals to your friend's son-in-law, who just got his real estate license. You might even think long and hard before you do business with your own friend or relative (every family has at least one real estate agent, doesn't it?). Keep in mind that you will be discussing very personal financial information with the agent; you may not want to get into that with relatives. And your friendship might not stand the strain of a difficult home-selling deal. Practice some of the following explanations so you'll be prepared if you decide to pass up the opportunity to be so-and-so's first big break in the real estate business:

- You value your relationship too much to risk bringing the strains of business into it.

- You're afraid you're going to have a difficult transaction, and you wouldn't want to tie up a new pro.

- You've always preferred not to talk about money and contracts with friends.

- You really need to work with someone who has experience selling homes in your idiosyncratic little neighborhood.

- The other agent you've chosen to do business with came so highly recommended by so many of your neighbors that he is simply the best fit for you.

- It was all your husband's decision.

- It was all your wife's decision.

Practice your favorite polite reply so you can deploy it smoothly when someone insists you entrust your home sale to their earnest, but oh-so-green friend or relative. Remember, that commission could be enough to buy a Cadillac, and you deserve to get Cadillac-level service and expertise. And badly handled pricing and negotiating could cost you tens of thousands of dollars beyond the commission.

The Ideal Agent

The ideal real estate agent probably doesn't exist, but we can dare to imagine one. Let's call our vision Special Agent. Special Agent would have the patience of Mary Poppins, the eye for value of Warren Buffet, and the negotiating skills of Donald Trump. But Special Agent would be as truthful with you about your property's deficiencies as Forrest Gump and as well connected as a small-town mayor. Special Agent's sound business practices prevailed through the last real estate downturn, thus they should work in any market. Special Agent would also be fully comfortable with the new technologies transforming today's real estate market. Virtual tours? Special Agent produces the most seductive ones. E-mail? Special Agent lives by it and makes it a point of pride to reply to business e-mail within a day. But Special Agent will communicate by phone or instant messaging if that better suits your style. And Special Agent always has you covered; when off on vacation (or taking real-estate continuing-education courses), Special Agent will see to it that you'll be well taken care of by a qualified assistant. Problems with paperwork, deadlines, and inspections will rarely crop up, because Special Agent will have been on top of the details all the way through.

Team Player or Lone Wolf?

Increasingly, successful real estate agents are hiring assistants, some with their own real estate licenses and some without, to handle parts of the transaction. But others remain single practitioners, handling all the details themselves. Either approach can work, but it's worth having a little discussion with your agent before you sign a listing agreement, so you have a clear idea of just how involved your agent will actually be in the marketing of your home. If you give your listing to a big-time agent who sells multiple millions of dollars of real estate every year, you could very well find yourself dealing mostly with Mr. or Ms. Bigtime's assistants. And that may work out wonderfully; a top-notch team led by a top-notch agent can produce a whole lot of service on your behalf. But you deserve to understand the situation when you're going into it. Ask all potential agents if there are any tasks that are likely to be delegated to an assistant. And if there is no assistant, who will be on duty when your agent is not available? If your primary contact after the listing is signed will actually be a licensed assistant, you should try to meet that assistant, just to make sure you're comfortable working together.

Be wary of any agent who doesn't have some backup plan arranged. Murphy's Law all but guarantees that a buyer will be hot to present a purchase contract on the very day your agent's kid is graduating . . . or getting married . . . or having an appendectomy. You need someone on duty at all times.

Getting the Most from References

Don't sign a listing agreement with any agent until you have had a little chat with two or three of that agent's most recent clients. The reference check is simply part of the due diligence you need to perform before hiring any agent. And good agents should be happy to put you in touch with satisfied clients. Ask for the names and numbers of the most recent clients who sold homes similar to yours; you want to know how the agent is performing *now*, not three years ago. You don't need to find yourself tied down with an agent who used to be the greatest in town, but who hasn't quite kept up with the technology or is easing into semiretirement.

First, if you have the opportunity, drive by and take a look at the clients' homes that the agent helped sell, just for extra perspective. Are the homes like yours in terms of size, price, and neighborhood? If their homes are significantly different than yours—say they're mostly detached homes whereas you're selling a condo—ask the agent for other references.

Then comes the hard part. You need to actually pick up the phone and ask those former clients for an honest assessment of their experience with that agent. Keep in mind that most people want to be polite and uncritical, especially when talking to strangers. Following are some questions to ask when chatting up references, and a little bit of advice on how to read between the lines of a seemingly satisfactory review:

- When did you list your home for sale with this agent? Was it the first listing, or had you listed with another agent or withdrawn it from the market for a while? (You're simply trying to find out if the transaction was more of an ordeal that it appears to have been.)

- How well did the agent stay in touch? Were your questions answered promptly?

- How much of your interaction was with the agent, and how much was with an assistant? Were you happy with that setup? (You want to hear that the assistants or backup agents treated them as well as the agent did.)

- Did the agent give you much useful advice about preparing your home for sale, or staging it? ("Oh, the agent just fell in love with it," isn't necessarily what you want to hear. Instead, award bonus points if the agent recommended an off-site storage rental or a great carpet cleaner who got rid of Fido's aroma.)

- Did you feel like you received good negotiating help?

- Did you like the way the agent advertised the property? Were there a lot of showings? (Keep in mind that it's common for sellers to think their agent hasn't done enough advertising. But if there were a lot of showings, that tells you something was drawing buyers' attention.)

- In your opinion, were the agent's price recommendations on target? (Quietly await the answer, then follow up by asking if the agent recommended any price reductions, and if so, after how many weeks on the market. Ask how the eventual sales price compared to the original listing price. But don't ask how much they got for the home—although they may offer the information.)

- Would you hire this agent again? (This final, simple question is the granddaddy of all questions. Listen carefully to the answer. Unless they had a terrible snafu, most people want to answer yes. After all, nobody likes to admit that they made a mistake when they chose their agent. If there's a long pause, that tells you they're hesitating—and a "probably" is not the answer you're looking for. You want an unequivocal "oh, yes! I wouldn't dream of using anybody else!" If they pause or hedge, you might ask if they had any doubts, and give them the opportunity to vent a little. And if they do give you the enthusiastic "oh, yes!" you might jovially ask if they're related to the agent. Keep it lighthearted, but go ahead and ask. You just might find out their wonderful agent is also their favorite nephew. And if that's the case, give extra credibility to those *other* references the agent provided.)

Designations and Sales Awards

Real estate agents can earn a number of professional designations from NAR and its affiliates. Two of these designations in particular are good indicators that the agent has invested more than the minimum required amount of time and training in the real estate business: CRS (certified residential specialist) and GRI (graduate, Realtor Institute). Earning them requires course work and evidences that the agent has completed a minimum number of sales transactions. Although there's no magic wisdom conferred with these designations, and some successful agents argue that they're too busy actually selling real estate to put the time into earning them, they do signal that an agent has taken the time to get extra training.

Far less impressive are the ubiquitous claims to "multimillion-dollar agent" and "regional sales champ" on agents' business cards.

First, given the price of homes these days, it only takes a couple of deals to launch an agent's sales into the million-dollar ranks. Second, that little sales award tells you nothing about how well the agent performed on the deals in question. The sales could have occurred several years ago (while the agent was still a full-timer), or they could have left behind unhappy clients who would never, ever do business with that person again. These titles are just clutter on a business card.

Following Your Gut

Always give full consideration to the feedback you get from references. But pay even greater heed to your own instincts. If you don't like the agent, for whatever reason, move along until you find one you do like. Selling a home tends to be a very stressful process (especially when you pair it with buying another home), so personal chemistry with your agent really does matter. If you don't like an agent at the beginning of the deal, you will come to loathe that agent by the end of it. Even when your personalities are compatible, there's generally so much fuss involved in home sales that you can find yourself grinding your teeth at the sound of the agent's voice. Hitting it off with an agent is not alone a good enough reason to work with one—but *not* hitting it off is a very good reason to pass one by.

In fact, your agent's personality can work for or against you in dealings with other agents. Even in a big city, the real estate business tends to operate like one big clique. If your agent has a reputation for being disagreeable to work with or for frequently running into transaction snags (due to mismanagement of the tiny details that must be tended to in preparing contracts and shepherding deals to the closing table), other agents may avoid bringing their buyers in to see your home. As always, trust your gut feelings (and if you can get an honest opinion from others in the business, all the better). Hiring an agent who's abrasive or inattentive can cost you time, money, and antacids.

Breaking up is hard to do

Breaking off your relationship with a real estate agent is hard to do — but it is possible. Even the best agents can have trouble moving a home in a slow market. But a dud of an agent can make it nearly impossible to sell at a fair price and in a reasonable length of time.

What makes an agent a dud? Not following through on the promises made during your listing presentation, for starters. Unreasonable delay (more than a few days) in getting your listing information into the MLS or a sign into the front yard. Slipshod MLS entries that lack photos, or include only shots that are unflattering and out-of-focus. Promised 360-degree virtual tours that never happen. Less advertising than promised, or ads that were error-ridden or which placed your home in the wrong neighborhood. Being left out of the local brokers' open-house tour.

There are other transgressions that rightfully irritate sellers. What if your agent is uncommunicative, or even rude to you (if the person you're paying is rude to you, imagine how she might treat others)? What if you get the sense that she decided to "let the MLS sell it," without much effort on her part? What if she failed to make follow-up calls to the buyers' agents who've toured the home? Does she have *any* suggestions about ways you can improve your home's appeal other than lowering the price to an unreasonable level (after all, at a low enough price, any old dog of a house will sell)?

If things go sour with your agent, you may want to switch. But what if there are a couple of months left on your listing contract? Instead of suffering (and seething) in silence while your home grows stale on the market, it would be better to have a little talk with the broker under whom your agent works. Stay calm and unaccusatory, and explain that your arrangement with that specific agent has become unproductive and you would like to work with a different agent within the brokerage. Remember, your contract is actually with the brokerage, and most brokers will seek to keep you a satisfied client by switching your business to a different agent. Insist on it, explaining that it's not in the best interest of the agent or the broker to continue working with a client who is already seriously dissatisfied.

If the broker isn't amenable to changing agents, you *could* just refuse to sell until the clock runs out on your listing, but that's not a terribly viable option if you're under the gun with a job transfer or some other life event that all but forces you to sell PDQ. This is your nuclear weapon! Sure that broker and agent ostensibly keep the listing, and they *could* demand a commission if they produce a ready, willing, and able buyer (although in practice, the commission is usually paid upon completion of the actual sale). But what are the odds of that dud actually finding a buyer? And you *could* make the task more difficult by asking the agent to remove the lockbox and by refusing to leave the house for showings. The specter of this unfortunate-for-everyone scenario is one reason that brokers are usually willing to shift your contract to another agent.

If an agent's transgression goes beyond basic inattentiveness, you should file a complaint with your state's real estate board. Serious transgressions, such as mingling earnest-money deposits (the cash payment that buyers offer along with their purchase offer as evidence of their seriousness about the deal) with the agent's own funds, or failing to present all purchase offers promptly, can be cause for disciplinary measures, including having the agent's license yanked. Agents and brokers are licensed at the state level, and you can file a complaint with the licensing agency. You'll find a list of state authorities in appendix three.

Referral Services

As mentioned earlier, several Internet sites offer free matchmaking services that will pair you up with a real estate agent. These sites act as lead generators for the participating brokers who pay for those leads. You go online and answer a few questions about your plans to sell or buy, including how quickly you intend to go through with a transaction. You supply your e-mail address and phone number so agents can get back in touch with you (expect lots of "special offers" in your email in-box afterward). In exchange for using one of their preselected agents, the sites generally promise a significant discount, or a gift card redeemable at a home-supply store.

When I tried out the service on one of the better-known sites, www.HomeGain.com, I found that my little town is not included in their automated service, so I was unable to take advantage of the free estimate of my home's value. That's not much of a surprise; the community is too small to make it onto most radar screens. However, within ten minutes of filling out the form, I got a phone call from the New Jersey headquarters of Weichert Realtors, which is active in my market, offering to put me in touch with a local agent who has at least one year of experience or $1 million in sales. (As mentioned earlier, given the real estate boom over the preceding few years, $1 million in sales is not that special a benchmark. Just one or two sales may do the trick!) Other referral services include www.RealEstate.com and www.MonsterMoving.com. You also can search the entire roster of local Realtors at www.Realtor.com, though that site makes no attempt to differentiate between the experienced and inexperienced among its ranks.

It doesn't hurt to try one of these referral services. They can be particularly useful if you're moving to an unfamiliar area, and their discounts can save you some money. But I would still perform my due-diligence checkup on any of the agents they refer.

Razzi's Rules to Live By

⌂ Practice saying "no thanks."

Don't let your good manners get you saddled with an inexperienced agent who just happens to be the son-in-law of your neighbor's best friend. Everybody knows *somebody* in the real estate business, but you need to find the one-in-a-million agent who can best represent you.

⌂ Find out who else is on the team.

Before you sign a listing agreement with an agent, ask if the agent will delegate many tasks to an assistant. Find out who will be on duty to help you when your agent is tied up. Teamwork is fine—as long as you know who's in the lineup.

⌂ Chat up the references.

Ask for the phone numbers of the agent's three most recent clients. Then take the time to call them and ask for details about their experience. Give heed to even slightly negative comments; remember, most people want to be polite and positive.

🏠 Ask the magic question:

"Would you hire this agent again?" Then be quiet and wait for your answer. Hesitation or qualifiers like "probably" are *not* what you want to hear.

🏠 Designations aren't magic.

But they're a sign that the agent has invested more than the minimum time and effort in training.

🏠 Personality counts.

If you list with an agent who has a grating personality, or who's inattentive to detail, it will increase your anxiety—and possibly drive away buyers' agents.

🏠 Breaking up is hard to do.

But if your agent is not performing up to reasonable expectations, ask the broker to assign your listing to another agent. Your contract is actually with the brokerage, after all.

🏠 Matchmakers can help.

Online referral services can put you in touch with agents and may even earn you some rebates. But you still need to do your own reference check before signing on with one of the recommended agents.

PART TWO
selling
your
home

CHAPTER SEVEN

The Listing

"The house gave him fresh hope that the life he had longed for was soon to arrive."

GARRISON KEILLOR, *Lake Wobegone Days*

THE LISTING CONTRACT IS THE ALL-IMPORTANT AGREEMENT between you and your real estate agent—technically, with the broker who stands behind that agent. Basically, it's a contract that engages the service of that agent and brokerage to find someone who is ready, willing, and able to buy your home at a price you find acceptable. And if the agent is successful in finding such a buyer, then you agree to pay a percentage of the price as commission.

There are several varieties of listings, which sound confusingly alike. They include the following:

- **Exclusive right to sell.** This is the most common form of listing, and many brokers will work with nothing else. It assures the broker/agent a commission if there is a home sale, regardless of whether that broker/agent is the one who actually finds a buyer. If you, the owner/seller, happen to find a buyer on your own, the agent still gets a commission. Brokers/agents have the greatest incentive to put the work and marketing money into selling a home with this type of listing because they have the greatest chance of earning a commission.

- **Exclusive agency.** This sounds confusingly similar to the above type of listing, and it *is* similar, but with one important difference: you, the seller, don't have to pay a commission if you find a buyer without the help of the broker/agent. Brokers resist working under these conditions because they're actually competing against you. All their time, effort, and marketing money can go to waste if you find your own buyer.

- **Open listing (also known as a nonexclusive or general listing).** With this type of listing, the first broker/agent to reach the finish line earns the payday. You, the owner/seller, can list the home with two or more agents at the same time, but you owe a commission only to the agent who actually finds a buyer. While this may seem like the optimal choice for the owner/seller (wouldn't three agents marketing your property be better than one?), brokers and agents don't quite see the charm. They're less likely to put the time and money into marketing a home if there's a good chance that a competitor will actually take home the commission.

- **Net listing.** This variety is fraught with conflicts of interest between the seller and the broker/agent, and is illegal in many states. With a net listing, brokers/agents are free to set whatever price they choose on the property, and you agree to take away a set amount of money. The broker/agent gets to keep anything over that amount as commission. With this setup, there's an incentive for the broker/agent to mislead the seller about the true value of the property. Even if it is legal where you live, avoid this type of listing.

Deciding How Long to List

There's one important thing to remember when you're sitting at the dining room table and a real estate agent is explaining the terms of the listing agreement she's hoping you'll sign: for now, at least, you are negotiating *against* that agent over the terms of her employment. It *feels* like you're talking about the sale of your property, but for the moment what you're really doing is hiring the rather costly professional services of a real estate brokerage company. And that broker/agent would like to be hired for a good long time.

Often agents will push for a listing that lasts six or nine months. It's in your interest, however, to push for a listing that lasts only three months. After all, you can always renew the agreement if things are going well. Understand that you and the broker/agent have different fears going into this deal. The agent fears that he will spend time and money preparing marketing materials, advertising, hosting open houses, and beating the bushes in search of a buyer, only to have you expect a full-price offer to magically appear at the end of week one. He worries that you'll grow impatient and switch to a competitor when your short-term listing is up, taking away his payday. You, on the other hand, have equally valid fears. You fear that once he has a contract guaranteeing nine months in which to sell your home, he'll skimp on the time and money usually spent on marketing and sit back and wait for a buyer to wander by.

One important thing for you both to consider is the typical time on the market in your community. During the real estate boom in the early part of the decade, people got used to the idea that homes would fly off the market within days of being listed. But historically, it's more typical for a home to remain on the market several weeks to several months. Usually, the most expensive homes in a market sit unsold the longest. After all, there are a lot fewer people in the market for a $3 million home than for a $300,000 home. And those spending $3 million usually don't feel they should have to make a lot of compromises. Your agent should show you sales figures indicating how long listings *similar to your own home* usually stay on the market before a successful sale. That's a reasonable starting point for your negotiation with the agent. Reassure her that you intend to renew the contract if the home doesn't sell within that time frame. But you can expect the agent to dig in her heels and push for a listing that closely matches—or surpasses—the typical time on market.

And if you have a home that's clearly going to be difficult to sell, because it's extremely expensive or it's an oddball in some way (oh, perhaps an old wheat silo that's been converted to a chic living space), you can expect agents to insist on a long listing, or they'll decline to do business with you.

Prepare to Be "Closed"

As you're negotiating the terms of the listing contract, keep your ear cocked for signs that the agent is preparing to reel you in. He's hoping that after his wonderful, professional presentation, you'll agree to sign a listing contract on the spot. If he walks out the door without a signed contract, there's a real risk that you might sign with the next agent who visits. Remember, you're working with a professional salesperson (and, one hopes, a very good one) who's trained to condition people to say yes to the deal, as in "Yes! I want to sign a listing with you, right now!"

A classic sales technique is to get you in the habit of saying yes to a series of small questions leading up to the big yes that really counts. Listen for an agent to run up a string of questions to which the logical answer is yes:

It sure is a rainy spring this year, isn't it?

You're planning to move across town, correct?

You said the refrigerator would convey with the home, didn't you?

This document shows what you could expect to net from the sale if we achieve the price we discussed. Is that in line with what you're expecting?

I'd love to get your home on the market as soon as possible. Would you like to sign this agreement so I can get started right away?

Of course, you *do* want to sign a listing agreement. But just recognize the sales technique and allow yourself the time to hear several listing presentations and to compare the agents' backgrounds, marketing plans, and commissions before you commit. Amazingly, NAR research shows that 64 percent of all buyers interview only one agent before listing. Make sure you're among the other 36 percent!

The Marketing Plan

When interviewing agents for the job of selling your home, you should expect each one to go over the details of the marketing plan they've drawn up. What you *don't* want to end up with is an agent who, once the listing contract is signed, posts the listing on the MLS, plants a sign in the yard, and then sits back waiting for a buyer to appear.

The marketing plan will differ according to the type of home you have. Selling a loft condominium in the city differs from selling a three-bedroom entry-level rancher in the suburbs—which differs entirely from selling a five-bedroom luxury home along the waterfront. However, there are some basic marketing tools, as follows, which you should review with the agent:

- **MLS listing.** This is a cornerstone of marketing any property, and it's almost inconceivable that your agent wouldn't offer it.

- **Brochure.** This is one area where agents can get really creative—or not. Generally, the higher a home's price, the more elaborate the brochure. Ask the agent to show you the type of brochure she plans to use for a home like yours. Make sure there's at least one flattering, focused color photograph of your home's exterior. Additional photos highlighting special features are a plus; if your fabulous in-ground pool and spa is a selling point, it ought to be in the brochure (I've come to expect dull interiors in a home whenever a brochure fails to include interior shots). Does the agent have a way with words? Some can only muster a Jack Friday "just the facts, ma'am" litany of selling points, while others have managed the art of selling romance. The romance thing—it really does work.

- **Sign.** An eye-catching wooden-post-style sign is preferable, of course, to the cheap, short metal sign. For Sale signs really do sell houses. They're best when they include a Take One bin, which you may have to restock yourself (with flyers provided by your agent) if you're lucky enough to draw a lot of attention.

- **Lockbox.** As discussed further in chapter 12, a lockbox allows your agent to leave a key outside, securely attached near your front door. Only other agents working with the local MLS are able to unlock the box and retrieve the key to your door, which allows them to show the home when you and your agent are not available to let them in. Some sellers reject the lockbox and insist on "by appointment only" showings, but it's in your interest to never turn away a buyer who may have fallen in love at the curb!

- **Advertising.** This can be a point of conflict between agents and sellers. Sellers can't get enough of newspaper advertising, while agents sometimes see it as increasingly expensive—and decreasingly effective. Don't be surprised if your agent limits classified advertising to announcements of weekend open houses. But be sure the agent gets those ads on the newspaper's Web site, as well.

- **Internet postings.** Ask all the agents where your home will appear on the Internet. The best answer? Everywhere. You want news of your fabulous for-sale home spread on your agent's site, the broker's site, Realtor.com (the NAR site), Internet-only brokerage sites, CraigsList.org . . . everywhere!

- **Virtual tours and slide shows.** The first place buyers go to shop for homes is the Internet, and you want to catch their eye with the beauty and romance of your home. Photos are a *must* on the Internet (it's just like online dating: you wouldn't date someone without actually seeing a picture of them, and you wouldn't feel the need to tour of a home without first being enticed by an image of it). Even better than a series of still photos is a well-produced virtual tour, which allows buyers to view rooms and even to zoom in on the fireplace. Some of the best tours are set to music. A well-crafted virtual tour can attract buyers all over the world who are looking to relocate. Unless the home you're trying to sell is truly an embarrassment to look at, you'll benefit from a professional-looking virtual tour. And you want it posted as soon as your listing goes on the market, to take advantage of the rush of interest that accompanies a new listing.

- **Open houses.** As discussed in chapter 12, the conventional wisdom in the real estate business is that open houses don't usually sell *that particular* home; they're more of a marketing tool for the agent. That may be true—but open houses are worth a seller's time and effort. Open houses will bring the neighbors in for a look, and that's a good thing. They may know someone who wants to move into the neighborhood. Whenever your agent wants to hold an open house, cooperate by spiffing the place up and getting out of there. You especially want to see your agent hosting an open house for other local real estate agents, and providing some nice finger foods to help draw more in the door. Who knows which of those agents will find your buyer?

Time Is of the Essence

This phrase is used in real estate contracts to indicate that if you miss the deadlines contained in the contract, you haven't met the contract's terms and the whole thing could be nullified. However, it's also a good guiding principle for getting your new listing on the market. You see, there's usually a flurry of interest in a new home when it first hits the market, but the interest can diminish as the weeks go by. So you want to have your home presented in its most favorable light the very day it hits the MLS. That could even mean that your agent should delay posting on the MLS until all the marketing materials are ready to go.

From the very minute your postings appear on the MLS and various Web sites, they should include good color photos and, preferably, slide shows or virtual tours. The photos should reflect the current season; last winter's leafless trees only make your listing look stale. The home and yard should look their polished-up best. The off-site storage unit should, in fact, be off-site by now. (Don't leave it sitting in the driveway. That only advertises the fact that the home didn't always accommodate your belongings so easily. And it looks tacky.)

Beware, though, of the "pocket listing." That's when an agent keeps the news of your brand-new listing confined to his office for a couple of days, hoping that one of his own buyers wants to make an offer—which could double his share of the commission. If another agent within the same office sells the home, that also increases the brokerage's revenue. But that hardly serves your interest, does it? And you're paying a big commission so the agent will represent *your interests*, not his own or the broker's. Clarify with your agent exactly when the listing will be posted on the MLS and the Internet. The listing should go live as soon as all the marketing materials are put together, to take best advantage of that surge of interest in a new listing. Like a big adventure movie that kicks off at a gala premiere, your home should launch on the market with a ready-for-prime-time debut.

The Dream Seller

Just as we sellers talk about real estate agents, real estate agents talk about us sellers. And not all of us have a good reputation. If you insist on an inflated price, refuse to dejunk the house, let Spot scare the daylights out of buyers, turn down a lockbox, or insist that showings happen only between 2:00 and 4:00 PM on Saturdays, you'll be talked about, and not in a good way. Difficult sellers make it difficult to sell the home, and good agents won't waste too much time on them.

Your best strategy is to put a lot of energy up front into finding a skilled real estate agent and to stand your ground when negotiating the listing contract. But then, once you've got this pro on board, *listen* to the agent's advice, and act on it. If the agent tells you the house smells, take care of the odor. If the agent says your lovely red paint in the dining room needs to become taupe, grab your paintbrush. Do everything you can to accommodate all but the most unreasonable requests for showings. Even the best agent can't sell a house if the seller doesn't cooperate.

You can help your agent by arming her with some sales ammunition. Dig out some of the following documents to help your agent prepare marketing materials (give her the copies and be sure to keep the originals for yourself):

- Utility bills for gas, oil, electricity, water, and sewage.

- Your latest property-tax assessment.

- The land survey.

- Simple architectural drawings prepared by the builder or remodeler.

- A professional appraiser's report (perhaps done as part of a mortgage refinancing).

- Copies of contracts for major repairs, remodeling jobs, a new air conditioner, and so on.

- Documentation of any repairs you've made for conditions that might concern a buyer, such as waterproofing the foundation or mitigating an old asbestos hazard.

- Receipts and condition reports from maintenance to your septic system or well.

- Copies of warranties that may convey to buyers (including a whole-home warranty and those covering a new roof, windows, or major appliances).

- The home-sale-document package prepared by your homeowners' association, condo association, or co-op board. This should include copies of the codes, covenants, and restrictions (CCRs), and the financial statements and minutes of recent meetings. If you have copies of recent newsletters, make them available as well. And if any special assessments are pending, make sure to provide this documentation.

- Photographs through the seasons. If you have snapshots of your home looking particularly fetching after a snowfall, or in the midst of brilliantly colored autumn leaves, or when the garden flowers were at their peak, offer them to your agent. They might be included in a video presentation or printed on a special flyer for buyers to see when they tour the home. You might even consider framing three or four seasonal shots and making a grouping out of them.

The Big What-ifs

Circumstances change, as do minds. What will you do if things don't go according to plan? You should discuss these points with the agent before you sign the listing, just to be sure of that company's policies. But for common what-ifs, here's how you can expect things to unfold:

- **What if you change your mind about selling?** The agent can't force you to sell your home, but if he has actually produced a buyer who is financially qualified and ready to buy it, you may owe a commission, even if you don't go through with the sale. If it's clear that you don't really intend to sell, only a foolish agent would continue to look for buyers. But you will probably be prevented from listing with another agent until the listing period expires.

- **What if you find a buyer on your own?** That depends on the type of listing you signed. As outlined at the beginning of this chapter, if you've signed an exclusive right to sell, you still owe a commission. If you've signed an exclusive agency or open listing, you don't.

- **What if you and the buyer strike a deal shortly after the listing expires—will you owe a commission?** Face it, dragging your feet with a buyer until the listing expires in hopes of avoiding the commission would be pretty dirty pool on your part. An agent deserves to be paid for work done in good faith. And listing contracts usually protect agents and their brokers on this point. If within a month or so after the listing expires you reach a deal with someone the agent originally found during the listing period, you will still owe that agent a commission. Agents are also usually protected in this way if you relist with a different agent.

The original agent would still be paid if she was the one who actually found the buyer.

- **What if the agent comes up with a buyer you don't like?** Be careful there. If your reasons for not liking a buyer are related to that buyer's race, color, national origin, religion, sex, family status, or disability (and in some areas, sexual preference), and you refuse to sell that buyer your home, you (and your agent) could be sued for a violation of fair-housing laws. Even if you really don't intend to discriminate against someone on these points, your actions are what count. Your best bet is to let money talk. If the buyer can qualify for the loan and wants to buy . . . then sell that buyer your home. You'll find more on the topic in chapter 16.

- **What if the deal falls apart between contract and closing—will you owe a commission?** Usually not. Sometimes the buyer can't actually come up with the money or the buyer and seller can't agree on who should pay for necessary repairs revealed during the home inspection, and the deal falls apart. Usually you don't owe a commission, but this is something you should discuss with your agent. Of course, if the clock hasn't run out on your listing contract, the agent should resume the marketing effort.

- **What if you become dissatisfied with your agent and want to end the listing early?** It happens. Things aren't working out as you expected with that agent, but you still need to sell your home. You should meet with the broker under whose auspices that agent works and ask to have your listing assigned to a new agent. The broker doesn't have to agree—but that's the wise move for everyone concerned.

Razzi's Rules to Live By

🏠 The listing isn't really about selling your home.

It's about engaging the services of a real estate agent. At its heart, the listing is an outline of what the agent is supposed to do and what you're supposed to pay.

🏠 You're not on the same side yet.

When the agent presents you with a listing contract awaiting your signature, keep in mind that you're actually in negotiations with him over the terms of his employment. You want a low commission and a short commitment; the agent wants a high commission and a long commitment. Negotiate from there.

🏠 Some homes sell quickly, some sell slowly.

Expensive, unique properties typically take longer to sell, even in a strong market. You can expect the agent to insist on a longer listing period for them.

🏠 Nail down the marketing plan.

Thoroughly review exactly how the agent plans to go about selling your home before you sign a listing. Get specifics, including examples the agent has used for homes similar to yours.

🏠 Romance sells.

Some agents are better than others at recognizing the special qualities in a home and selling the romance. You'll see it in their brochures, ads, and online presentations.

🏠 Good photos are a must.

Most buyers start shopping over the Internet. Insist on good quality, in-focus photos in all the marketing materials, and virtual tours whenever possible.

🏠 Look pretty for your debut.

Insist that all the marketing materials, photos, virtual tours, and flyers be ready to go the minute your home is placed on the MLS. "Photo coming soon" is never a good first impression.

🏠 Beware the pocket listing.

It does you no good for the agent to keep news of your new listing confined to the office for the first few days, hoping to score a profitable in-house sale. Don't tolerate it.

🏠 Be a dream seller.

Once you've found your top-notch agent, follow her advice. Do whatever you can to spiff up your home and accommodate showings. Make copies of all important records available to her.

🏠 Talk prenup before the wedding.

Sometimes sellers change their minds and don't want to go through with the deal. Before you sign the listing contract, ask what would happen if, hypothetically of course, you were to change your mind and want out of the deal.

CHAPTER EIGHT

What's the Right Price?

"Not a flock of wild geese cackles over our town, but it to some extent unsettles the value of real estate here, and, if I were a broker, I should probably take that disturbance into account."

HENRY DAVID THOREAU, *Walking*

WHAT IS THE RIGHT PRICE FOR YOUR HOME? THAT IS *THE* question—the one that really matters; the one likely to keep you awake at night. And it's the question that's most difficult to answer. Even after you've sold your home and moved on, you may still wonder if you really sold it for the right price.

Even experienced real estate agents sometimes struggle with price estimates. Licensed appraisers are paid to determine a *value*, but that isn't exactly the same thing as a *price*, which is a marketing decision, a bargaining point, and something negotiable. Your *asking* price is your starting point in negotiations. But it will be the market, the unseen waves of supply and demand tugging at each other, that sets the *selling* price. The right asking price is the number that attracts at least one buyer ready and able to buy. You need to make a well-informed guess at the right price if you're going to sell promptly—and at the highest price. If you err by asking too high a price (and not immediately adjusting once the lack of buyer interest tells you the price is askew), you won't attract buyers, and your home listing will grow stale, possibly driving your eventual sales price down below its true value. Of course, if you err by asking too low a price, you may soon find a buyer ready to snap up that bargain—but you will leave money on the table; you'll never really know what your home might have sold for.

Setting the asking price is critical in achieving a successful sale. Just remember, it's an art more than a science—and some real estate agents are better artists than others.

Ways *Not* to Set the Price

First let's go over how *not* to price your home. Don't even waste your time trying to work up an asking price from the following starting points:

- The profit you need to afford a move-up home. It's all well and good that you need to clear $200,000 profit from your home sale to afford the move-up home you'd like to buy. But buyers really don't care. They're not going to pay a dollar more than what it's worth compared to the competition.

- A sufficient amount to recover the investments you've made in remodeling. Remodeling doesn't *always* pay for itself, although it usually improves your comfort and enjoyment while living in a home. And if that remodeling project happened five or ten years ago, keep in mind that you're now reselling a five- or ten-year-old kitchen or bathroom, and it won't fetch full price.

- The price your neighbor got last year. Last year's market was last year's market. Prices today may be surprisingly different—higher *or* lower—than just a few months ago.

- Your tax assessment. Even when they purport to assess home values at 100 percent of market value, tax assessments are usually lower then current market value (when they're higher than market value, homeowners are pretty quick to appeal for a readjustment).

- An online estimate. Various online calculators offer free estimates of a home's value. While these sites offer some valuable information, they're not yet accurate enough that you can unquestioningly use their estimates as your asking price. For example, some of the estimates offered by www.Zillow.com only claim to get within about $100,000 of the true price. Well, a Magic 8-Ball has that kind of precision. ("Is $435,000 the right price?" Shake, shake, shake. *My reply is no.* "How about $535,000?" Shake, shake, shake. *You may rely on it.*) Estimator sites can be useful for the data they give you—and we'll get to how you should use the sites shortly—but don't adopt their price suggestions without question.

Talking Price with Your Agent

One of the most valuable services a real estate agent offers is help in setting your price. Unfortunately, some agents have a better knack for it than others—and some are not above playing games with sellers in hopes of snaring that listing contract. The truth is, it's *your* job to set the asking price on your home. Agents can give you valuable advice, but the decision is ultimately yours to make.

Let's look at a couple of unsavory games that some real estate agents play. By no means do all agents behave this way; the really good ones wouldn't dream of it. In fact, they usually have enough steady business that they won't accept a listing if they think the seller is insisting on an unrealistically high price. They don't waste their time and money on listings they know aren't going to sell. But one of the reasons you must ask for listing presentations from at least three reputable agents is that doing so will help reveal if any one agent is trying to win your business with a fanciful price estimate.

Usually the first thing you'll do when an agent comes into your home for the listing interview is to lead the agent on a tour of your home. You'll point out its special features, and the agent will gush about how lovely it is, overflowing with compliments about your draperies, or the kitchen layout, or your furniture, or your landscaping. Agents are trained to do that—it's good salesmanship. And, besides that, real estate agents *love* looking at homes; otherwise they'd be in another business. And they usually love people, too, so they tend to be friendly and not above a little flattery. Just see it for what it is, pleasant social banter, and not a sign that buyers are going to stampede your door the day they spot a For Sale sign.

However, if a full-fledged Eddie Haskell (that notorious kiss-up on *Leave It to Beaver*) insists that your home is so wonderful and special that it should be listed 10 or 20 percent higher than other, similar homes currently on the market, step back and reconsider.

Honestly, Mrs. Cleaver, your home *is* lovely, but it's a very rare one that is so charming that it commands such a premium over similar homes. Unless you're in a roaring seller's market, or your home truly has some feature that adds *real* value (like extra rooms, a corner lot, or a view of the water), it's not going to sell if it's priced much higher than the competition. That real estate agent could either be clumsy at making estimates or *deliberately* trying to "buy" your listing with an inflated price. Such agents figure they can always recommend lowering the price after a few weeks, when lack of interest convinces you that the asking price is too high (they will be *shocked* that it didn't sell at the higher price). But, meanwhile, that agent has beaten the competition and secured a three- or six-month listing contract.

Such chicanery can really cost a seller valuable time. Interest in a home is highest when it's fresh on the market, and if buyers skip your home because you listed at too high a price—based on the deliberately misleading recommendation of a "professional"—you've lost valuable market exposure, and that so-called professional has done you real harm. And if you need to sell quickly (honestly, who doesn't?), you could eventually feel pressured to sell for less than you would have. Bottom line: Avoid agents whose price estimates are significantly higher than those proposed by their competitors.

Making It Up on Volume

Believe it or not, you also have to be on guard against agents who lowball your home's price. Despite the fact that their commission is directly tied to your home's selling price, some agents can't be bothered putting in the time it takes to sell a properly priced home.

They'll lowball it a bit, get a quick sale, and move on to the next deal. They see a small cut in their commission, but they can pull off more deals in a given year—and they more than make up for the smaller commission with the higher number of sales. Yes, they make it up on volume, just like Wal-Mart.

For real estate agents, having their commissions tied directly to the sales price isn't always as motivating as you'd expect it to be. In the book *Freakonomics* (Gardners Books, 2005), economists Steven D. Levitt and Stephen J. Dubner point to studies revealing that when agents sell *their own* homes, they tend to let them stay on the market ten days longer, on average, and they sell at a price that's about 3 percent higher than that of other sellers.

Tax Assessments and Online Databases

Property taxes are the lifeblood of local governments. And because it's in the public interest to make sure that the mayor's mother (or whoever is owed a favor from local politicos) isn't getting an unfair break on her property taxes, the tax assessor's records of home values throughout town are public information. Accessing the information used to require a trip to city hall to page through the records yourself, but increasingly communities make these detailed records available for online searching. The records contain plenty of statistics useful to potential home buyers, including each home's lot size, square footage, legal owner, and assessed value. Since it's possible to review records of neighboring properties, you can see how a particular home compares to the Joneses' in size and price.

A number of online services have taken tax records a step further, embellishing them with their own price estimates, maps, satellite photos, and even surprisingly detailed photographs taken from a low-flying aircraft. So far the sites aren't accurate enough on price for you to rely on them to determine your list price, but you should familiarize yourself with their data as part of your research. You can bet any potential buyer will have looked up the price estimates for your home, and you will need to be able to justify any higher price that you think is more accurate.

Take www.Zillow.com. The site's name is rapidly becoming a verb. Just as people "Google" a job applicant or prospective date, people are starting to "Zillow" homes. At last count, the site offered price information on more than 67 million homes, and it is all freely accessible. You don't have to register with your name or answer questions about your intentions to buy or sell. For many of the featured homes, Zillow offers not only tax records (minus the owners' names) but its own "Zestimate," or price estimate. It even helps you adjust the price estimate to reflect remodeling—a very useful feature. I asked some of the homeowners whose homes appear on the site whether the "Zestimates" reflected remodeling and if they were at all close to the price estimates real estate agents had offered them. The numbers were in the ballpark—but not very close to home plate. As it collects more data and refines its processes, Zillow may become an increasingly reliable starting point for negotiations. But, for now, at least, you should treat it as only one tile in the mosaic.

Another new site, www.RealEstateABC.com, offers price estimates and links to homes for sale in the community. Like Zillow, it features maps and satellite photos (but none of the low-altitude fly-by photos that Zillow boasts).

Because they were created by Internet entrepreneurs in California and the Pacific Northwest, many of the innovative real estate sites focus robustly on those areas. However, for the home I know best, namely my own—in the Washington DC area—they didn't prove very close to the mark. RealEstateABC.com's price estimate didn't take into account remodeling done years ago, and so it grossly underestimated square footage and the number of bathrooms. The site's estimate was $45,000 less than my most recent tax assessment. Zillow didn't offer a "Zestimate" for my home, and its tax records also erred. While it got the square footage and the bathroom count right, it pegged the assessed value $75,000 lower than the current assessment. The moral of the story? By all means check these Web sites out; have fun with the maps and fly-by photos. "Zillow" your boss's home or your old flame's place, just for kicks. But you need more information than these sites currently provide when you're trying to set a realistic price on your home.

Your Market: Is It Changing?

Your home-selling strategy will change depending on whether prices in your community are going up, staying somewhat stable, or—hate to say it—headed down. An experienced, forthright real estate agent is invaluable in helping you figure out where prices are headed in your market. Increasing times on the market, a growing inventory of listings, and (naturally) price reductions are unmistakable signs that the market, and prices, are weakening. Decreasing times on the market, a shrinking inventory of listings, and increased occurrence of full-price offers or multiple offers on homes are indications of a strengthening market and rising prices.

The first thing for you to do is to close your ears to news stories about nationwide real estate market trends. They don't matter a whit; you're concerned strictly with your local market, which very well may be moving in a different direction than the nationwide trend. And by local, I mean *local*. I'm talking about your town and your neighborhood. You're concerned with what's happening to prices on homes in your price range, in your community, and in other nearby communities that appeal to the same buyers. For example, prices may be slipping for condos in your town, or for luxury homes priced above $1 million. But if you're selling a charming entry-level home that's in good condition and in a great neighborhood you could find that strong demand is still driving prices up. A good agent will understand which neighborhoods compete for the same buyers that your neighborhood does and will tell you what's happening with prices there.

If you see that prices are rising, or even that nice homes are drawing multiple offers, you have two strategies to consider: price the home right (maybe even a tad higher than the most recent comparable sale) and hope for a reasonably quick sale, or *slightly* underprice it, and hope to spark a bidding war among buyers attracted to a good deal.

If you see that prices are falling, you also have two choices: price the home at the level you *think* is right and wait patiently for a sale (if prices go down, you may have to lower your asking price before you lure an offer) or—gulp—*underprice* it just a bit to get ahead of the market, especially if you need to sell quickly. Here's the logic: falling prices scare buyers at least as much as they scare sellers. After all, sellers will get their money (even if it's less than anticipated) and move on with life. Buyers, on the other hand may end up owning a home whose value is still falling. They're terrified that their big investment will *lose* value, and that makes them even more determined to drive a hard bargain. If you can convince buyers that you're offering them a good deal, you may attract more offers and actually end up selling at a reasonable price. And you won't have to endure the drip-drip-drip water torture of repeated price reductions as you chase the market down.

Doing Your Own Market Research

You *must* do your own market research. Get in the car and visit the neighborhoods that your real estate agent says appeal to the same buyers who'll be interested in your home. Go through a couple of open houses. Check out any new construction in the area (new construction doesn't always make the radar screen of real estate agents who handle resale homes; builders typically sell their homes through their own in-house sales staff). Pretend that you're shopping for a home just like yours, and then go out and see what the market offers. Be as objective as possible. Even though it's natural to think your own home is more stylish or in better repair than others, try your best to look at it with a stranger's eyes. And then price your home competitively.

Razzi's Rules to Live By

🏠 There are two prices for your home.

And you set only one of them—the asking price. The market will set the sales price.

🏠 Setting the asking price is an art.

And some agents are better artists than others. It's actually your job to set the asking price, with their advice.

🏠 Some pricing approaches are worthless.

Don't use these as your basis for an asking price: the profit you need to clear; the amount you spent on remodeling; the price your neighbor got last year; your tax assessment; an online estimate. The only thing that matters is *today's* supply and demand.

🏠 A Magic 8-Ball could set your price.

But "signs point to yes" isn't very specific advice. Nor are the price estimates offered by online services such as www.Zillow.com and www.RealEstateABC.com. But check them anyway, if only so you can negotiate intelligently with a buyer who has already "Zillowed" your home.

🏠 Flattery sells.

Enjoy the real estate agent's flattery, but don't put too much stock in it. Compliments help agents sell you on their services. Buyers will be more critical.

🏠 Don't let an agent "buy" your listing.

Some agents may try to secure your listing by suggesting that your home will sell for significantly more than the price other agents recommend. Be wary if one agent's suggested price is out of line with competing agents' estimates.

🏠 Don't swing at low balls.

Some agents aren't willing to put the time into marketing a properly priced home. If they lowball the price and sell it fast, they can move on to other listings. That's another reason to seek out several listing presentations.

🏠 Fresh sells fastest.

Setting the right asking price is critical because interest in your home peaks when it first appears on the market. Catch the buyers right away with the right price.

🏠 Tailor your strategy to a changing market.

Find out from your agent whether prices are rising, falling, or stable, and plan your pricing strategy accordingly.

🏠 Close your ears to nationwide trends.

You're not selling nationwide. The only thing that matters is supply and demand for homes in your town, your neighborhood, and your price range.

🏠 Falling prices scare buyers as much as they scare sellers.

Buyers worry that prices will continue to fall after they've made their investment. You have to convince them that they're getting a bargain.

🏠 Do your own market research.

Get out and visit open houses and new-home developments that represent your competition. That's the best way to get a good feel for prices.

CHAPTER NINE

FSBO—Are You Cut Out for It?

"There were so many things to attend to—so much gathering and throwing away; and after gathering and throwing away, saving what was salvageable; and after saving what was salvageable, cleaning; and after cleaning, washing down with soapy water; and after washing down with soapy water, dusting; and after dusting, something else; and after something else, something else. So many little things to do. Hundreds of millions of them."

JONATHAN SAFRAN FOER,
Everything Is Illuminated

OF COURSE YOU CAN SELL YOUR HOME BY YOURSELF without the help of a broker. This is America! We have the right to own property and to sell it whenever and however we see fit. Somehow, though, a significant number of people who make their living as real estate agents and brokers seem to believe it is an act of betrayal for people to sell their own home without the help of an agent. I'm often shocked at the vituperative response a good number of real estate pros have to the very subject of FSBO. In fact, the industry is adopting the term *unrepresented seller* as a replacement for the term FSBO. The new term implies that there's something lacking in the transaction, doesn't it?

There is *serious*, deep-seated dislike for the whole notion of selling without an agent. I'm certain that a fair number of real estate pros picked up this book, searched the table of contents for *FSBO* and tossed the book aside just because it devotes a couple of chapters to the topic. That would be unfortunate, because I think there's plenty in this discussion with which they can agree. FSBO isn't always easy—but it is always an option.

So if you do attempt FSBO, you can expect some local agents to go out of their way to discourage you. It's peculiar; some agents don't seem to mind losing a listing to a competitor nearly as much as they mind losing one to the very owner of the property. The truth is, you do not owe any agent his supper.

But not all agents will go the negative route. The savvy ones see a FSBO seller as a potential opportunity. They know that many—if not most—homeowners who start out trying to sell on their own eventually decide to list with a brokerage, and they want to leave a favorable impression so they're the ones who get that business. They may even offer a FSBO seller helpful advice in an effort to build goodwill and demonstrate their expertise. They're smart businesspeople, and you want to hang on to their business cards, just in case you decide to list.

FSBO: Who Succeeds at It?

About 13 percent of the people who sold a home between August 2004 and July 2005 did so without the services of a real estate agent, according to an NAR survey. And more than half of them (about 53 percent) said they would do it again (another 14 percent said they would use an agent the next time, and roughly 34 percent weren't sure what they'd do).

That survey also showed that among home sellers who did hire a real estate agent, the most important reason—cited by 28 percent—was to get help finding a buyer. But a significant share of the FSBO sellers didn't need help with that major task; they already had a buyer lined up. Some 22 percent sold their home to a relative, friend, or neighbor, and an additional 9 percent sold it to a buyer who approached them directly. If you already have a fish on the line, it's tough to come up with a compelling argument for paying 5 or 6 percent to a full-service real estate brokerage for use of their rod and reel.

An additional 4 percent of people who sold a home during that year tried the FSBO route first, but ended up joining the 81 percent of the home-selling population who listed with a real estate agent.

How should you decide if it's worth your valuable time and effort to try selling your home without a broker? First you need to look at yourself, to see if you actually have the time, skill, and temperament to make a successful go at it. Then you need to look at your home: is it likely to be an easy sell—or would it be a challenge even for a skilled agent to market? Having the undeniable right to sell a home by yourself doesn't necessarily mean you will be very good at the task.

FSBO: How Much Can You *Really* Save?

Of course, saving money is the big reason homeowners go through the trouble of FSBO. But taking on the job also means taking on the marketing and transaction expenses that would otherwise be covered by the real estate agent and brokerage company. And you could still end up paying a commission to a buyer's agent. And, not least, there's the worry that you might not be able to fetch as high a price as a skilled agent could on your behalf. You certainly will hear that last point—cast as a dire warning—repeatedly from the real estate pros!

Ten signs you're cut out for FSBO:

1. You make your living selling things.

2. You have a peach of a home to sell.

3. You've been through a few home-sale deals already and understand the process.

4. You can't understand why people get so attached to houses.

5. You make car dealers cry.

6. You're a lawyer, accountant, marketing pro, or entrepreneur.

7. You have the time to handle the job.

8. You *never* trade in your car because you know you can get a better deal on your own.

9. You already know a couple of people who want your home.

10. You turned to this chapter first.

Ten signs you're not cut out for FSBO:

1. Your pizza-delivery guy slows down when passing by, out of habit (who has time to cook?).

2. You can't stand all that chitchat that passes for small talk.

3. Your idea of vacation: poolside service, room service, turndown service.

4. You've ever uttered the words, "Just show me where to sign the *%#* form."

5. You can't wait to show buyers the textured paint you applied by hand in the dining room and your NASCAR-themed family room.

6. Directions to your doorstep: From the main road, take the gravel road to the fork in the road. Proceed to the first development on the left. Look for the pipestem behind 222 Forlorn Lane.

7. You: "After my business trip to London, I'll have a full month to devote to the home sale . . . Oh, wait, where's my BlackBerry?"

8. You're a whiz at time management. Buyers will simply have to arrange their visits between 7:00 PM and 8:00 PM on weekdays and 10:00 AM and 2:00 PM on Saturdays.

9. You: "Strangers, in *my* house? Looking *inside my closets*!?"

10. You just couldn't pass up the great deal last time you bought a car (at sticker price) on the extended warranty, rustproofing, pinstriping, and credit-insurance package.

In fact, NAR-sponsored national advertising has warned that homes sold by a Realtor can sell for 16 percent more, on average, than those sold without an agent. With today's prices, that's a lot of money! And it certainly seems to be more than enough to justify the 6 percent or so commission that's paid to the real estate agent. But before you get alarmed, let's look at what that figure really means.

Does it mean that your home, which is realistically worth about $350,000, will actually sell for $406,000 (16 percent more) if you use an agent? No, it doesn't. An agent cannot make a home sell for more than it's really worth.

Does it mean that your home, realistically worth about $350,000, will actually sell for only $294,000 (16 percent less) if you go it alone? Not necessarily. While it certainly could sell for less than its value if you do a bad job of pricing and marketing it, that is not what the statistic tells us.

The statistic simply tells us that, among the 90,000 people who NAR surveyed, the median—or the mid-point—selling price of a home sold with an agent was 16 percent higher than the median price of a home sold without an agent ($230,000 versus $198,200). But that doesn't necessarily tell us that the real estate agent affected the sales price. It simply tells us that the FSBO sellers overall sold homes at a more moderate price than the sellers who hired agents. Consider this: The same report notes that the median age of a homeowner who sold with an agent was forty-six, and the median age of a FSBO seller was forty-eight. Does selling on your own magically make you two years older than selling with an agent? Of course not! Likewise, selling FSBO doesn't magically cut 16 percent off your sales price.

Expenses You Face

The attraction of the current system of paying a real estate agent's commission out of the sales price is that you never have to reach into your pocket to pay for marketing expenses. The agent pays those expenses and recovers the cost only if and when the property is sold. You, the owner, don't have to come up with a penny for marketing. And if the home doesn't sell, it's the agent who's out that marketing expense, not you.

When you sell by yourself, you bear those expenses up front. Consider the following expenses when putting together a FSBO marketing plan:

- color brochure, produced on your PC

- printing

- For Sale sign

- classified ads

- display ads, with photo, in community newspaper

- MLS posting

- personalized Web page

- temporary cell-phone account dedicated to the home

- attorney's fee for preparing documents

Paying Buyers' Agents

You may also face the prospect of paying a commission to the buyer's real estate agent. In fact, that's a decision you need to address right at the beginning of your marketing effort. Will your advertising offer brokers a 2½ or 3 percent commission if they bring you a qualified buyer? Will you agree to pay the commission out of the sales proceeds if the buyer is already being represented by a buyer's agent? Or will you put your foot down, refuse to pay a brokerage fee, and tell that willing buyer to pay his agent out of his own pocket? Of course, this strategy means you risk losing the sale entirely, or will very likely reduce the amount the buyer will be willing to pay for your home, seeing as he has a big commission check to write . . . probably out of his down payment funds.

Be aware that some buyers' agents deeply dislike working with FSBO sellers; they say there's extra work involved when sellers don't have their own agent to handle paperwork and other tasks, and they end up having to perform double duty for their commission. If things go awry and the deal leads to a lawsuit, the buyer's agent—the professional—may catch the blame. So, even if all your advertising promises a 2½ or 3 percent commission to the buyer's agent, you can expect some agents to cross their fingers and hope their clients don't take a liking to your home.

Dealing With Agents

Agents will be among the first in your neighborhood to notice that your home is being sold FSBO. And the astute ones among them will see that as an opportunity to impress you with their helpfulness and market savvy, so they will be at the top of your list if you decide to switch to an agent. Keep an open mind. You may just do that if the FSBO process doesn't go as smoothly as you'd hoped.

Actually, even if you're planning to list with an agent, you might consider offering your spruced-up home FSBO for just a week or two before you list. You'll have to do some serious market research and price it fairly, of course, and have the time to juggle phone calls and showings. But a week or two as a FSBO seller could let you find out if there are some eager buyers out there who have had their eye on your home for years, just hoping it would go on the market someday. You never know!

Pricing a home right is critical for any home sale, whether you're doing it with the help of a broker or all by yourself. Agents have an edge here; they learn about recent sales prices from their colleagues, and they have access to price information on the MLS. That's one of the valuable things they give you for your commission dollars.

Should you try to tap into that knowledge as a FSBO seller? Before you put your For Sale sign in the yard, should you invite local agents in to give you a listing presentation? You know, just call two or three to tell them you're thinking about selling your home, and see what they suggest as a listing price? Although I know homeowners do it all the time, I think it's bad form to invite agents in for a presentation under the guise of preparing to sign a listing agreement. After all, a good agent puts hours into preparing an analysis of the competing properties on the market, digging up tax records, and otherwise delivering a sales pitch. I believe it actually pays off in goodwill to be forthright about your plans: Go ahead and phone any real estate agents who specialize in your neighborhood, or who have helped you with transactions in the past. Explain that you're seriously considering selling without an agent, and ask if they would be willing to give you any advice on your asking price. Explain that you will consider them for a listing should you change your mind. And tell them that you intend to offer 3 percent to a buyer's agent. Some will decline to offer any price advice, and will

instead tell you to give them a call if and when you decide to list.
Fair enough. Others may get downright frosty, and try to suggest
that somehow you're undermining America, mom, and apple pie by
selling FSBO. But some may chat with you about other properties
currently on the market, sales times, and price ranges (you'll find
more on setting your price in chapters 8 and 11). They'll appreciate
your honesty—and will want to establish themselves in your mind
as the go-to person for local real estate. Of course, if you do change
your mind and decide to list, you'll know who to call.

Flat-fee Services

Until recently, a big drawback to selling a home on your own was
that you couldn't get your home included in the local MLS and on
www.Realtor.com, the big kahuna of listings sites, which draws its
listings from MLS organizations across the country. That's
changing—much to the dismay of the traditional real estate
industry.

Thanks to the Internet, there are a multitude of companies that
charge only a couple of hundred dollars to post your listing on the
local MLS and on Realtor.com. They don't charge any additional
commission for selling the home—but you certainly can't expect
the handholding that you'd get with a traditional real estate agent.
You offer any agent who brings the successful buyer a commission
of up to 3 percent, but if you find a buyer on your own you don't
owe any commission at all.

Traditional real estate agents and brokers dislike these flat-fee
outfits as much as they dislike FSBO sellers—perhaps even more.
The traditional brokerage industry, after all, created the MLS and
pays for its upkeep; brokers dislike its being used as a marketing tool

by homeowners who aren't paying full freight for a traditional listing. What can't be ignored, though, is the fact that many of the agents and brokers offering the flat-fee services are themselves Realtors. Some in the real estate industry are trying to fight the rise of flat-fee services, and prodded by Realtor organizations, several states have enacted laws requiring that real estate brokerages offer sellers a minimum level of services. That's one reason you won't find flat-fee services offered everywhere. But a quick search on Google for "flat-fee MLS" will show you the many, many organizations offering these discount services, and you may find one that serves your area.

Consider what's being offered by www.MLSLion.com, a flat-fee company that does business (over the Internet) in forty states, at last count. For a flat rate of several hundred dollars, homeowners can get their home listed on their local MLS, on Realtor.com, and, sometimes, on databases maintained by individual real estate agents. Many of the featured packages include copies of the contracts and disclosure forms you'll need for your transaction, a For Sale sign, a personalized Web page dedicated to your home, and even a lockbox for the door, which allows local agents access to show the home. You agree to pay a commission of 2 or 3 percent to any agent who brings you a buyer, but if you find a buyer yourself, you don't pay any commission. That's not a bad deal for a few hundred bucks.

Another prominent site, www.ForSaleByOwner.com, offers a full menu of services—starting at less than a hundred dollars—for owners selling FSBO. You can advertise your home in the site's magazine; each month 1.2 million copies are distributed to readers in the largest real estate markets in twenty-six states. You can also post your home on the FSBO-only Web site (at the above address), purchase For Sale signs, and for an extra fee, get help from ForSaleByOwner's affiliate real estate agents. The site's menu includes a flat-fee listing option for placing your home on the MLS and on Realtor.com. If you go this route, you're expected to offer a 3 percent commission to buyers' agents.

Other Web sites offering flat-fee services include the following:

- www.KingOffer.com (costs about six hundred dollars for the first six months; five hundred for the second six months)

- www.BrokerDirectMLS.com (refers you to flat-fee brokers in your state)

- www.FlatFeeListing.com (refers you to flat-fee brokers in your state)

In sum, you may succeed at the job of selling your home without an agent. But you need to approach it as a job and pay for whatever help you need along the way.

Razzi's Rules to Live By

🏠 You don't owe any agent her supper.

You have a right to sell your home without a real estate agent. Don't let miffed agents dissuade you.

🏠 Judge agents by how they treat you.

Savvy agents are kind to FSBO sellers because they know that many of them end up listing with an agent. Keep in touch with agents who are helpful when you're on the other side of the fence.

🏠 Ask yourself if you're really cut out for the job.

Be honest when assessing whether you have the time, skill, and temperament to take on the work.

🏠 Be open-minded about commissions.

Are you really going to turn away a buyer who expects you to pick up his agent's 3 percent commission?

🏠 Be skeptical about horror stories.

Selling on your own will *not* cut your price by 16 percent—at least not if you do your homework.

🏠 Don't play bait and switch with agents.

Don't fib about your intentions to list just so you can get price opinions from agents. Do be up-front and tell them you intend to sell FSBO, and then accept any help they offer.

🏠 Buy the services you need.

Signs, contracts, advertising, and even MLS postings can be obtained without signing on with a full-service agent.

CHAPTER TEN

A FSBO Marketing Plan

"Home is a place not only of strong affections, but of entire unreserve; it is life's undress rehearsal, its backroom, its dressing room, from which we go forth to more careful and guarded intercourse, leaving behind us much debris of cast-off and everyday clothing."

HARRIET BEECHER STOWE, *Little Foxes*

Y OU KNOW THE GUY WHO CLIMBS THE STANDS AT THE STADIUM, hawking food and drinks? *Ice-cold beer! Hot dogs! Peanuts!?* Well, that's you now, marketing your home—shamelessly. As an owner selling by yourself, you need to do everything you can to make sure that buyers discover your lovely home. You have to make sure it's priced appropriately. And then— this could be the hardest part of all—you have to close the deal once you get a good, solid nibble.

The first step is to gather your tools. The previous chapter directs you to resources and online services that can help you obtain many of them, or you can buy what you need locally.

You'll need the following basic items:

- **Temporary cell-phone account.** Do you really want to blast your home phone number all over the Internet and newspaper? Not likely. A good alternative is to buy a pay-as-you-go cell-phone service, such as Cingular's GoPhone, which offers phones starting at about thirty dollars, and monthly service ranging from thirty to seventy dollars. You get voice-mail service and don't have to sign a long-term contract. A competitor, Virgin Mobile, offers phones starting at about twenty dollars, with monthly service ranging from fifteen to sixty dollars. If you make this your only contact number regarding the sale of your home, you can check your dedicated voice mail frequently and field inquiries anytime, anywhere.

- **Dedicated e-mail address.** Similarly, you don't want to publish your workhorse e-mail address all over the Internet, lest you be buried in spam. Set up a special, free e-mail account with Yahoo! or AOL for managing messages related to the home sale.

- **Web page.** Because most buyers now start their home search on the Internet, you want to give them plenty to look at. That means you need a Web site. Either use one of the Web site templates offered through various FSBO or flat-fee listing services, or set up your own through your Internet service provider. An inexpensive source for Web pages and e-mail alike is www.GoDaddy.com.

- **Digital camera.** You absolutely, positively must have attractive, well-focused digital photographs of your home online (home shopping online is just like using online dating—nobody's interested if they can't see a photo). Use a camera with at least four megapixels—the more, the better. If you can get your hands on a wide-angle lens, use that. Take your time, and get good shots of the exterior, the kitchen, the main living space, the master bedroom, and any other focal points, such as the luxurious bathroom, the garden, or the view of the lake. If you don't have a knack with cameras, pay someone to get good photos for you. A local camera shop can put you in touch with a photographer who may be willing to take on the job; a hobbyist who'd like to earn an extra couple of bucks may be just what you need.

- **For Sale sign.** Signs sell homes, and cheap signs imply that you're selling a cheap home. Either obtain a professional-looking sign from one of the FSBO/flat-fee services or invest in your own custom sign. Get the best you can afford. You want attractive, eye-catching colors and bold type. The sign must say "For Sale" and should include your special cell-phone number. If you're willing to pay a commission to buyers' agents, include "Buyers' Agents: 3 Percent." (If you've signed on with a flat-fee service, be wary of writing "FSBO" on your sign; it could get you booted from the MLS. That's why many of these services provide you with their own sign to use.) If you're making a custom sign, include your Web site's URL. Make sure your sign has a weatherproof tube containing a stock of color flyers with all the details about your home, including the price. Tie fresh balloons to your sign frequently, especially on weekends. Consider putting an inexpensive, portable spotlight in the garden to illuminate your sign at night.

Making the Most of Advertising

Classified advertising in newspapers is expensive, especially in big-circulation metro dailies, so you need to make sure every dollar of your advertising budget is spent wisely. If there's a weekly community newspaper published in your area, that could give you great value; buyers who are hoping to move into a community often follow these papers just for the real estate ads. Consider announcing your home sale with a display ad that includes a photo of your home from the street. Publicize the open house you plan to hold within the following week. Include your price, the number of bedrooms and bathrooms, your address, your special phone number, and your Web site's URL. Since the ad won't have room for too many words, remember the advertising adage "Sell the sizzle, not the steak." (They can learn all about the nutrition content once they visit.)

If your community is included on www.CraigsList.org—an online bulletin board and chat arena—post your for-sale ad there, too. It's a great way to reach young buyers and people from out of town.

Ad-writing as Haiku

Study some of the ads in your newspaper's weekend real estate section. Circle the ones that sound like attractive homes, just as an exercise. Odds are they hook you with just a few well-chosen "images." Remember the writer's credo "Don't tell, show." Paint a picture with your words.

What's your hook? Look around your home to see if any of the following apply: stately colonial; storybook Tudor; single-level comfort; clapboard classic; wooded refuge; sturdy Craftsman cottage; bucolic retreat; Williamsburg charmer; Mediterranean villa; cozy cottage; sheltered cul-de-sac; lock-and-go condo; breezy end unit; impeccably maintained classic; blond-wood Scandinavian style; doorman lifestyle; maintenance-free living; embassy-size entertaining; indoor-outdoor living; two-chef kitchen; sumptuous spa; barefoot-on-the-porch swing; stone-walled hearth; window-seat dormers; off-street parking; sunlight-flooded foyer; four-season garden; workshop/oversize garage; patio kitchen; Tuscan kitchen; breathtaking cityscape; private, paneled den; nanny/in-law suite; landscaped pool/spa; oversize windows; gracious entry; charming window boxes; enduring slate/tile roof; master-bedroom retreat; comfy home theater; painless commute.

The point is that you need to emphasize the emotional hook of your home. And even the plainest residence has some particular distinction (beyond low price). Take a good look around your home, single out the one or two hooks, and emphasize them. Window boxes really can transform a plain, little house into a cozy cottage. Of course, if you're calling attention to a particular attribute, you want to feature it in a photo on your Web site and in your brochure.

You must be careful not to violate fair-housing laws with your ads. Generally, the way to stay safe is to talk about *the property* and not about *the people* who you think might want to buy it. You can learn more about those laws in chapter 16.

Things to Keep On Hand

You'll want to assemble a little staging point for buyers just inside your front door, especially if you've obtained a lockbox through a flat-fee broker and may have buyers stopping by with their agents while you're not at home to receive them. Leave a lined sheet of paper or an open journal there for them to sign in with their name, address, phone number, and whether they are represented by an agent. Prime the pump by writing in the contact information for one visitor, so they can see where the information should go—and they won't feel like they're despoiling your pretty blank book. (It's not a fib. Surely your sister-in-law or neighbor has visited the home, right?) Put a little dish or tray out where real estate agents can leave their cards behind. You'll want to follow up with each visitor a day or two after their tour and see if there are any questions you can answer, or if they would like to arrange a second visit.

You (or the friend you will recruit to be on hand during your showings) should invite visitors to sign your contact book; buyers often skip this step if they're not specifically asked. You can't force them to sign in, but you can make it harder for them to decline.

Be sure to keep a stack of brochures/flyers with color photos available on your little stage set. These might be more detailed than the flyers you keep stocked in the tube attached to your For Sale sign, including more pictures and information on nearby amenities, such as the local swim club or golf course.

Technique counts when you're leading prospective buyers on a tour of your home. Essentially, you want to allow buyers to discover the home's charms on their own and to keep the focus off yourself. Allow them to walk ahead of you, or even to go upstairs and wander around without you hovering. (You locked away all the valuables, right?) Give couples the opportunity to chat with each other without you overhearing. Call their attention to one or two highlights of your home ("please feel free to explore the garden; it's full of perennials"), but don't prattle on about the obvious ("this is the bedroom, and that's the bathroom . . ."). Before they leave, offer to answer any questions.

FSBO: Got Contract?

If you're selling completely on your own, it's wise to have a good purchase contract on hand, ready to supply to buyers who are not working with their own agent. It can be very awkward for buyers who might be interested in your home; they may not know how to start the process. It's your job to make it easy for them. If anyone expresses interest in your home, you can simply let them know that you have a blank contract on hand that they might consider using—or that you would welcome a document prepared by their own real estate attorney. If you're selling on your own, you will need the services of a local real estate lawyer—and this is one of the services that lawyer can provide. You can generally expect to pay about a thousand dollars for the lawyer's fees.

You also need to have a full set of disclosure documents ready to give any buyer who expresses interest in your home. You can get help figuring out what's required in your community from your lawyer, an escrow agent, or a fixed-fee broker; some local real estate agents may be willing to help, perhaps for a small fee (requirements change from community to community, but you'll find an overview of disclosure requirements in chapter 16). Having all these documents ready will reassure a buyer that the deal won't be strained and uncomfortable. For good measure, print out a simple statement outlining all the documents you've presented to the buyer, and ask the buyer to sign and date it. That prevents any legal squabbling—"you didn't tell me!"—in the future.

Protecting Yourself

One of the risks a real estate agent undertakes, often without appreciation, in marketing your home is that of touring empty homes with absolute strangers. As a FSBO seller, you assume that task yourself, and you need to be careful. Think about it: you'll be leading strangers on a tour of your home, into the dark basement, the bedrooms, and the bathrooms; you need to do everything you can to minimize the risk that you'll find yourself alone with an intruder who has posed as a serious buyer. The risk is real; every so often, professional real estate agents are harmed—even killed—while trying to show homes. You need to take some reasonable precautions—and stick to them even if a prospective buyer balks.

Always check out buyers' identification before you show your home. When buyers phone or e-mail you, ask for a full name, address, and phone number; check the number against your caller ID—and if they have obscured their number on that service, be particularly insistent about obtaining a number. Be very pleasant about your routine, of course! In fact, you should force yourself to smile when you ask for this information, to ensure that your tone of voice over the phone remains pleasant. If you're communicating by e-mail, simply explain that you need the contact information so you can properly arrange for a showing. Explain that you'd like to be able to get in touch if something comes up that forces you to postpone the showing (after all, you wouldn't want to waste their time!).

If a buyer's agent calls to arrange a showing, she'll be forthcoming with phone numbers for home, cell, and office. Just for good measure, you can discretely phone the office to confirm that the agent is who she claims to be.

Google the names and phone numbers of buyers not represented by an agent. A reverse-lookup feature on www.anywho.com can give you an address if you plug in a phone number, but it doesn't work with cell phones or unlisted lines. If a caller only offers a cell-phone number, push hard for more information. Explain that you simply need to be careful about who you allow into your home. The night before your showing, or earlier the same day, phone the prospective buyer to confirm your appointment—and to confirm that the phone number is valid.

Of course, knowing addresses and phone numbers won't tell you whether a person is a decent individual. What's valuable is finding out whether someone is resistant to letting you know his identity. Asking for the info puts any potential bad guy on notice that you're looking out for yourself.

Never show the home while you are there alone (that includes days you host an open house). Enlist a spouse, friend, neighbor, or your affable neighborhood lacrosse/football/rugby player to stay there with you during the fifteen to thirty minutes of a showing. They shouldn't get involved; they simply should be present. Have your cell phone and house/car keys in your pocket, just in case of trouble. However, even if the family dog is a wonderful protector, you should confine him to his comfy crate in the garage or, better yet, have someone walk him while you show the home. Some buyers are afraid of dogs, and you don't want to scare *them* away.

Buyer-proofing

Be particularly diligent in buyer-proofing your home before you show it to strangers. Lock away (or remove to your bank's safe-deposit box or to a friend's home) spare keys, cash (including the kids' piggy banks), financial documents, jewelry, handbags, small electronics (like digital cameras and iPods), collectibles, artwork, guns, and prescription drugs.

And finally, at the end of an open house, enlist your buddy and go through the home with you to make sure all the lights are turned off—and that everybody has gone home. Just for good measure, check all the closets and dark spots in the basement. You'll sleep better if you do.

Walking Through the Finances

It's useful to have a written outline on hand of just how affordable your home can be—especially if your home is likely to attract first-time buyers. You definitely want to give prospective buyers a copy if you're offering to buy down their interest rate by paying points on their behalf (more on that in chapters 11 and 13).

Contact the lender you used when you last took out a mortgage and request that an illustration be prepared, on company letterhead, outlining what the payments would be on your home at its current asking price. Get details for two or three types of loans: Show a thirty-year fixed-rate loan with a 5 percent down payment and with a 10 percent down payment. Also show a 5/1 hybrid (a fixed rate for five years that later converts to a one-year adjustable rate mortgage [ARM]) and a one-year ARM. If the loan officer is promoting any special loans, include those as well (naturally, the loan officer will include her contact information). Then hand out copies of the sheet to any serious buyers who tour your home.

Turning Nibbles into a Bite

The day after their visit, follow up with a phone call or e-mail asking buyers if they have any questions about your home. If the buyers are represented by an agent, however, you should only address the agent; take the opportunity to ask for feedback on your home. You might glean some valuable advice, disguised as criticism. Keep the conversation pleasant (smile on the face, now!) and let the buyers know you'll be happy to arrange for another tour at their convenience (no trouble at all!). Buyers can sometimes be shy about asking you to go to the bother of showing your home, especially if they're on the fence. You don't want to make it easier for them to simply go ahead and buy another house, one that's listed with an easy-to-approach real estate agent who won't take it personally if they decide not to buy.

If ever you lower your price or decide to throw your garden furniture (or some other extra) into the mix, be sure to let anyone who has expressed *any* interest in your home know about your new, improved deal, via a quick phone call or e-mail (one more good reason to collect that contact information). Include a new photo with the e-mail, just to remind them of how sweet a place it is.

Razzi's Rules to Live By

🏠 Be a shameless promoter.

You're trying to sell an item with a price tag in the hundreds of thousands of dollars. This is no time to be shy.

🏠 Go disposable.

Protect your privacy by using a pay-as-you-go cell-phone number and setting up a special e-mail account for publicizing your home.

🏠 Get all over the Internet.

The vast majority of buyers start their home search online, so you *need* to have a Web page—with lots of gorgeous photos.

🏠 Signs still sell homes.

And cheap signs make your home look cheap. Spring for the best-looking sign you can afford, and keep it stocked with flyers.

🏠 Sell the sizzle.

Find your home's emotional hook, and stress it in all your advertising.

🏠 Set up your home-sale reception area.

Have a little spot just inside the door where buyers can sign in and gather information.

🏠 Give that guy a contract!

Have a blank contract, prepared by your lawyer, on hand to offer to buyers. It will reassure them that you know how to handle the deal.

🏠 Disclose, disclose, disclose.

Make sure buyers receive all the disclosures (regarding property condition, lead paint, and so on) required by law. Disclosures protect you from legal woes.

🏠 Don't talk to strangers.

Don't lead them on a tour of your home, anyway. Get good contact information for every buyer who asks to see your home. A cell-phone number and e-mail address aren't enough to protect you.

🏠 Home alone? Not you.

Always make sure someone is at home with you when you're showing the home to buyers.

⌂ Buyer-proof the place.

Easily pilfered valuables, prescription drugs, handguns: get them out of the house before you let buyers in.

⌂ Smile.

Force yourself to smile when you talk with buyers over the phone. It helps keep your tone light and friendly.

⌂ Follow up obsessively.

Contact buyers promptly after they make an inquiry or tour your home, and anytime you sweeten the deal.

CHAPTER ELEVEN

Hot Market versus Cool Market

"When he came up the hill like this, toward the tall
house with its lighted windows, something always
clutched at his heart. He both loved and hated to
come home. He was always disappointed, and yet he
always felt the rightness of returning to his own place."

WILLA CATHER, *One of Ours*

S OMETHING BEYOND YOUR CONTROL, NAMELY THE
temperature of the overall housing market, will have a
dramatic effect on how easy it is to sell your home.
Practically any hovel with a roof managed to sell quickly in the
roaring housing market in the early part of the decade. But that was
a very unusual market. It's more common for sellers to have to work
a little to get their houses sold. You'll be forced to compromise
somewhere along the line, whether it's on price or closing date or

what you leave behind for the new owners. And usually a sale takes a few weeks to a few months.

However, the good news is that even if the balance of power in your market is solidly in the buyers' hands, you can still manage to sell for a reasonable price and in a reasonable amount of time. Doing so requires discipline and, usually, the help of a top-notch agent.

What's the trick? Well, the best trick is to have a very desirable home in a very desirable location. Remember, just because it's cliché doesn't mean it isn't true: the three most important things about real estate value are (1) location, (2) location, and (3) location. Neighborhoods that are popular because of their convenient location, easy commute, top-notch schools, history, architecture, prestige, views, or landscaping remain the most popular neighborhoods even in slow real estate markets. Homes there will always command a higher price than similar homes in less-desirable neighborhoods.

As for the desirable home, we can assume that your home is desirable to *you*. After all, you chose it, and you decorated it. Now that you want to sell, however, it's important that the home be as desirable as possible to the largest number of strangers, one of whom will be so smitten as to offer to buy it. The rigorous cleaning, repairing, and decluttering regimen outlined in chapters 3 and 4 will help make your home as desirable—to as many people—as possible.

Markets Can Shift Quickly

A market can shift from favoring sellers to favoring buyers, and back, with surprising speed. A major layoff announcement by an important area employer, a big jump in interest rates, or a faltering stock market can convince buyers to put off their house hunting until better days come along. On the other hand, a decline in interest rates or a big company relocating to your town can bring a ton of new buyers into the market—and shift the negotiating advantage to sellers. (Ironically, though, sales almost always jump up—temporarily—when interest rates start to rise. Rising rates scare fence-sitters into the market; they look to buy something *quickly* before rates go even higher.)

Watch for signs of a changing market. Frequently, when a local housing market is starting to cool and the advantage starts to shift toward the buyers, prices stop accelerating for the most expensive homes first. They simply reach a price level where buyers cannot afford to follow.

Often condos are the first to get the chill; they can reach a state of oversupply very quickly, as builders are able to put hundreds of units onto the market seemingly overnight. Sometimes it's the market for brand-new detached houses that weakens first, thanks to a glut of new construction. Developers, who have expensive loans of their own to pay back, quickly grow desperate to unload already built homes. They'll cut prices or, more commonly, offer free incentives such as interest-rate subsidies. One of their trusty sales tools is to load on significant freebies like a finished family room or a granite-countertop upgrade. Condo developers may even offer to pay a year's worth of maintenance fees or throw in home theater equipment. In so doing, these builders and developers drive down prices for all their competitors—and that includes you, trying to unload a resale home. Builders' incentives can be particularly brutal on owners trying to resell their not-quite-new homes in the same development. It's terribly difficult to compete with the lure of brand-new everything, even in the best of times.

Basically, the way you compete with builders who offer such free upgrades is to lower the price of your home, even if it means getting less than you paid. All the listings, advertisements, and brochures for your home should stress the many conveniences that come with buying a nearly new home from you—versus buying new construction. Stress the value of the tasteful window coverings that will convey with the sale; the extra landscaping you've done; the professionally decorated rooms; the already-installed satellite TV dish or security system. Make sure buyers understand that all they have to do is to flip on the light to make themselves at home in your ready-to-go abode, whereas a brand-new home always requires finishing touches–which *they'll* have to pay for.

Experience Pays in an Agent

A good real estate agent will help you spot market shifts. But be aware that, in a tough market, some agents may hedge their opinions a bit, especially *before* you've signed the listing contract. They're still hoping to land you as a client, and they don't want to scare you away with news of a cooling market. Award bonus points to any agent who levels with you about tough market conditions— or about your home's deficiencies compared to the competition.

It's in your interest to be hard-nosed about your own prospects for selling *before* you sign the listing agreement. Ask each agent you interview for current statistics on the local market—and local means your neighborhood, or as close to it as you can get to it. Make sure your prelisting interview covers the following questions:

- How does the number of homes currently listed in the MLS compared to last month and the month before? To a year ago at this time? (If the number of available listings and the time on the market is starting to inch up, the market is cooling.)

- What's happening with homes like mine right now? How long are they staying on the market? Are price reductions common? Are any homes attracting multiple offers?

- How did the eventual sales price of homes you've listed in recent months compare to the listing price? For homes you've successfully sold over the last two or three months, did you have to reduce the asking price during the listing period? How many times? How long were the properties on the market before they sold?

- How much experience do you have selling homes that are similar to mine in price, neighborhood, and amenities? (If the agent hasn't handled many homes similar to yours, you'll want to seriously consider looking for a different agent.)

In a tough market, there can be a particularly big payoff to working with a real estate agent who has years of experience. Give due respect to an agent who survived the *last* tough market—and in many parts of the country, that extends all the way back to the early 1990s. (Make sure, however, that such an experienced agent has kept fully up-to-date with the recent flood of technology. If you find an agent who's been hardened by a tough market who also swears by e-mail, virtual tours, and the Internet, you've hit the jackpot.)

Following the boom years in the early part of the decade, the country was flooded with a gross oversupply of real estate agents.

Just one kind of real estate market

In the minds of the people who make a living selling real estate, there's only one type of market: "a good time to buy a home." Every market twist translates to this one, ever-optimistic message. Of course, that also makes it a good time to sell a home, doesn't it? Here's a translation guide:

Seller's market: A good time to buy because property value may increase as soon as you get in.

Buyer's market: A good time to buy because prices are low and there's lots of selection.

Dead-of-winter market: A good time to buy because you have little competition from other buyers.

Height-of-spring market: A good time to buy because the supply of homes is greatest.

Booming stock market: A good time to buy because your down payment has grown.

Lousy stock market: A good time to buy because it's crazy to put your money into something as volatile as the stock market.

Falling interest rates: A good time to buy because your dollar goes farther.

Rising interest rates: A good time to buy because mortgage loans could get even more expensive if you wait.

Professionals who lost their jobs in downsizing industries saw a lifeline in the easy-to-acquire real estate license. Membership in NAR, the main trade group representing real estate agents and brokers, reached 1.25 million by 2005 (although that number is expected to decline). In some communities, there were more licensed real estate agents than homes being sold. No doubt a good number of these newcomers are fine, smart, hardworking pros. But they haven't been battle-tested by a tough market. An agent or broker who made it through the last downturn—and stayed in business—knows a few tricks that can benefit you.

Boosting Your Odds in a Cooling Market

Your goal is to make *your* home the one that sells, even in a tough market. To do so, you'll have to have a top-notch marketing plan. And it wouldn't hurt to consider throwing some incentives in to sweeten the deal.

As previously discussed, it's more important than ever to have your home scrubbed and repaired and looking its best. It's to your advantage to have a seasoned agent who knows how to handle a buyer's market. It's critical that your price be on target for *today's* market, not last year's, or even that of six months ago. Even with all that covered, you may have to push a bit harder to make a deal happen.

Buyer Incentives

There's no reason you can't offer buyers a subsidized interest rate just like the builders selling new homes do. And you don't have to have any kind of arrangement with a mortgage lender to pull it off, either. Simply let it be known in your listing, brochures, and advertisements that you're willing to buy down the buyer's interest rate, which you do by paying points on the buyer's loan. Points are prepaid interest, paid when the borrower closes on the mortgage. Points lower the interest rate on the loan, and thereby make the monthly payment more manageable. One point equals 1 percent of the mortgage amount, and each point shaves about one-eighth to

How points cut payments

Consider how paying points will make your home more affordable for a buyer:

Loan amount	Points	Interest rate
$200,000	0 points	7 percent
	1 point ($2,000)	6.875 percent
	2 points ($4,000)	6.75 percent
	3 points ($6,000)	6.625 percent
$300,000	0 points	7 percent
	1 point ($3,000)	6.875 percent
	2 points ($6,000)	6.75 percent
	3 points ($9,000)	6.625 percent
$500,000*	0 points	7.25 percent
	1 point ($5,000)	7.125 percent
	2 points ($10,000)	7 percent
	3 points ($15,000)	6.875 percent

*"Jumbo" loans carry rates ⅛ to ⅜ percentage points higher than smaller loans

one-quarter of a percentage point off the buyer's interest rate. Therefore, the more points paid, the lower the interest rate will be. Typically, loans are quoted with zero to three points, but you can pile on more points, if you want to.

From your perspective, there's absolutely no financial difference between cutting $6,000 from your home's price and agreeing to

Monthly payment	Monthly savings (compared to 0 points)	Yearly savings
$1,331	—	—
$1,314	$17	$204
$1,297	$33	$396
$1,281	$50	$600
$1,996	—	—
$1,971	$25	$300
$1,946	$50	$600
$1,921	$75	$900
$3,411	—	—
$3,369	$42	$504
$3,327	$84	$1,008
$3,285	$126	$1,512

subsidize the buyer for up to two points on a loan for $300,000. But frankly, some sellers prefer to pay points so they can brag to their neighbors that they got "their price" for the home. (Keep that in mind when you hear others brag about the price they got for their home. Did it include points, or other closing costs the sellers paid on behalf of the buyer?) And there's one little extra benefit that you and your agent should point out to buyers: they'll get a tax deduction for those points, even though you pay them. It's a quirk of the tax laws, but buyers always get the tax deduction for points. What a deal!

Other incentives may appeal to buyers. Consider allowing any of the following perks to convey with your home:

- Window coverings (would they really fit in your new place, anyway?).

- The refrigerator (in some areas, it's expected to convey with the home; where it's not, you can choose to throw it in).

- A decorating allowance.

- Lawn or porch furniture.

- The gas grill.

- The satellite dish, plus one year's worth of prepaid service.

- A year's worth of prepaid lawn or pool service.

- A one-year prepaid warranty on repairs.

- A year's worth of condo or homeowners' association fees.

- A one-year prepaid swim or tennis club membership.

Agent Incentives

Of course, real estate agents don't work for tips like taxi drivers or pizza-delivery guys. But you might be able to draw a little more of their attention if you sweeten the deal they stand to get for showing and selling your home over the competition's.

Start with the commission offered to any agent who brings in a buyer. Typically, commissions are split fifty-fifty between the agent representing the seller and the agent representing the buyer. So, with a 6 percent commission, the selling agent typically receives 3 percent (which is shared with the agent's broker). The remaining 3 percent goes to the buyer's agent (and is shared with that agent's broker). But what happens if you're successful in negotiating a commission discount with the listing agent? Let's say you drove that commission down to 5 percent. With the typical fifty-fifty split, that means buyers' agents are offered 2.5 percent if they bring the successful buyer. But what if most of the other homes in your area offer them 3 percent? Your home doesn't look quite so attractive to all those faceless agents out there working with buyers. Keep this in mind when negotiating a reduced commission from your agent, and keep the reduction on the selling agent's side. For example, you might ask your agent to accept a 2.5 percent commission and to offer 3 percent to all buyers' agents. Or, in consultation with your agent, you might simply promise a cash bonus to the agent who succeeds in bringing a buyer.

You also could consider other incentives. You could offer a buyer's agent the use of your pro basketball season tickets for one year. You could offer use of your time-share or vacation home. Of course, agents aren't going to twist their clients' arms and talk them into buying your home just because of an incentive, and they should disclose the bonus to their clients. But an incentive could help you get greater attention from more agents, and thereby help the sale.

Selling in a Hurry

Sometimes you just need to get rid of a home *now*. It could be because you suddenly landed a job in another town or because you lost your job and you need to sell the house before your mortgage goes into foreclosure. Maybe you've come upon a fantastic business opportunity, and you need to sell your vacation home to raise the cash. Whatever the reason, you need to move this deal along as fast as possible.

Unfortunately, haste usually translates into a low selling price, and desperation always does. The best way to unload a property quickly is to price it under the market. Talk with your real estate agent and come up with a fair selling price, then undercut it by 5 percent or even more. And then advertise the fact that it's priced to sell. Your neighbors will hate you, because you're chipping away at the value of their homes, but you don't have much choice if you really need to get out in a hurry. (An alternative is to sell your home at auction. You'll find more on that in chapter 14.)

Stay clear, though, of the guys who post We Buy Houses Today! signs around town or advertise that on the Internet. They're sharks, pure and simple. Consider the sales pitch posted on one such Web site (which I won't name, because I don't want to give them any publicity). The information comes from the part of their Web site dedicated to signing up "local affiliates," who will use their system for snatching deeds away for pennies on the dollar: "You see, what I like to do is buy houses at a discount—and I don't mean a few thousand dollars off retail either—no, I'm talking about buying a beautiful $180,000 house for $70,000, no money down, getting the deed and taking home a check the day I buy it kind of deal." Nasty, huh?

How little do these sharks intend to pay? Less than 65 percent of true value, at least according to information posted on the same Web site. Don't trust anyone who promises to rescue you from foreclosure, magically bring you current on the loan, or allow you to continue living in the home—as long as you sign the deed over to them.

In fact, the first place you want to contact when you're running behind on mortgage payments is the mortgage-lending institution itself. Foreclosures cost mortgage lenders a lot of time and money, and they may be willing to help you rework your payment plan to avert it. The second place you should contact is the National Foundation for Credit Counseling, through the foundation's Web site at www.debtadvice.org. The high-quality, free guidance just may help you get back on track.

Razzi's Rules to Live By

🏠 Buyers won't bother with a home they think is over-priced.

They don't like to haggle with someone who's unaware of going prices—or too stubborn to care.

🏠 Markets can shift quickly.

A big shift in interest rates, layoff announcements, or a turnaround in the stock market can draw buyers into the market or keep them away.

🏠 Buyers aren't logical about rates.

At least not always. When rates start to rise, there's a temporary increase in home sales—from buyers who are startled off the sidelines by fear of increases yet to come.

🏠 Builders' incentives are tough to beat.

But you have to try. Builders throw in interest-rate subsidies or free upgrades to hurry along sales in a slow market. You may have to offer your own incentives to compete with them.

🏠 Nearly new homes have benefits, too.

Everyone seems to love the fresh, new thing on the housing market. Point out to buyers that your nearly new home can make their lives easier thanks to the little improvements you've already made.

🏠 Offer cheaper interest rates.

You can pay points to lower a buyer's interest rate. They'll get the tax savings, too.

🏠 Find a battle-tested real estate agent.

Look for an agent who survived the last tough housing market in your area. That agent may know some hard-learned tricks that can get your home sold.

🏠 Sweeten the deal for buyers' agents.

A healthy share of the commission or a bonus can help your home attract attention.

🏠 Desperation drives away dollars.

If you need to sell fast, the surest way is to slash the price.

CHAPTER TWELVE

Showings!

"The farmhouse was built of wood, a board outer-covering over a framework of logs. It was in reality not one house but a cluster of houses joined together in a rather haphazard manner. Inside, the place was full of surprises."

SHERWOOD ANDERSON, *Winesburg, Ohio*

IT'S MIGHTY INCONVENIENT TO LIVE IN A HOME THAT'S UP FOR SALE, at least if you and your real estate agent are marketing it right. You need to keep the entire house—including the places houseguests should be ashamed to snoop—in company's-coming shape.

The Open House

Real estate agents often say that open houses don't usually sell *that* house. So why do agents spend their weekends holding them? Because open houses tend to sell real estate *agents*. They're a great opportunity for them to meet buyers, some of whom will engage their services. Because open houses tend to market the agents more than the specific homes, some people recommend skipping the whole routine. But I think that's a mistake.

Simply put, you want your home to be seen by as many people as possible. And if you can get two, three, a dozen, or more people walking through on a Sunday afternoon, then that's a day well spent. Sure, many of the lookers will be nosy neighbors, but you should welcome them; they may have a friend who's dying to move into your neighborhood. I've even known people to buy a house only a few doors down from their current home. Also, during an open house your agent can get feedback from visitors (often just by eavesdropping on their conversations) that may illustrate a drawback you need to correct. An open house (or several of them, over the course of several weeks) certainly doesn't hurt your marketing, and it just might lure a buyer who falls in love with the place.

Even more important, though, is that your agent holds a brokers-only open house as soon as the place goes on the market. Typically, a pack of real estate agents caravans from one broker's open house to another's, to see what's fresh on the market. Agents usually put out a little buffet to help draw their colleagues in. These can be very effective; you want as many agents as possible to get excited about the prospect of selling your beautiful home!

Lockbox or Not?

For all but the most expensive homes, a real estate agent is going to want your permission to place a lockbox on the door, which gives all the local real estate agents access to your key for showings when you are not home. (Luxury homes are often shown on an appointment-only basis, partly to discourage gawkers. They also take longer than average to sell.) Your agent does *not* have to be present at these showings. It's in your interest to say yes to the lockbox, even though you may be uncomfortable at the idea of strangers traipsing through your home unaccompanied by you or your agent.

Remember, *it's not your home anymore.* By now, you should have locked up your most precious belongings in anticipation of strangers wandering through the place. And you can take comfort that many lockbox systems now keep a record of exactly which agent accessed your home and exactly what time they entered. Most agents are conscientious about keeping an eye on the buyers they take through a home; their reputation among other agents is at stake. And for their own physical safety, they are supposed to get contact information from prospective buyers before they enter an empty house with them. Corporate transferees, in particular, are likely to want to see a home in the middle of the workday, when your agent may be occupied. These are very motivated buyers—they may have three or four days to find a home, and they're not horsing around. If they like the looks of your home, they'll be ready to buy it now—or will move on to something else.

If you decline the lockbox, other agents will have to call your agent and request a showing. They'll have to coordinate schedules, or maybe drive across town to your agent's office to pick up a key. If you require your agent to attend all showings, in the hopes of finding an opportunity to point out special features and answer questions, it'll cut down on showings, including some of the best ones—those in which a buyer is out with an agent, passes by your home . . . and falls in love right there on the curb. They'll want to see it *now*. And *you* want them to see it now, while they're still in the thrall of infatuation. If they drive away, they may never be back.

Short-notice Showings

With or without a lockbox, you can expect to get some last-minute phone calls from agents asking your permission to show the home, *right now.* They might even be calling from their cell phone as they

Additions to your morning routine

As long as your home is on the market, you never know if *this* is the day that a buyer will discover it. It has to be showing-ready every day when you leave for work. Add the following steps to your morning routine while your home is up for sale (some can be done the night before, and it'll be easiest if you enlist the whole family):

• Clean the cat's litter box; spray air sanitizer around the area.

• Run the hand vacuum through all bathrooms still in use.

• Rinse and squeegee or towel-dry the tub and shower.

• Using a premoistened cleaning wipe, swab any used sinks.

• Give toilets a quick wipe and a swoosh with cleanser and a disposable brush.

• Stash shampoo bottles, toothpaste, mouthwash, and other toiletries in a basket and store it in a nearby cabinet.

• Replace family towels with a set of fresh, for-show-only towels (and then reverse the process when the family comes back home).

• Load and run the dishwasher.

sit in their car at the curb. If at all possible, you should welcome them, perhaps asking for twenty minutes or so to tidy up. They can go get a cup of coffee while you dash through the house, freshening. It could just be a demanding, self-centered (and

- Toss a lemon wedge (keep a bowlful in your fridge) into the garbage disposal, and run it for a few seconds.

- Store the dish-drying rack under the sink.

- Gather the napkin holder, vitamin bottles, dish soap, hand lotion, spoon rests, and other clutter from countertops and place in a basket in a closet.

- Make all the beds.

- Lock up jewelry, prescription drugs, and other valuables.

- Put away loose mail, stray shoes, credit card statements, and so on.

- Quickly vacuum anywhere necessary.

- Open the blinds and curtains.

- Leave the lights turned on.

- In winter months, turn on exterior lights before you leave in the morning so passersby see your home illuminated on their way home at dusk.

- Replenish the stack of property-listing flyers, including those in the canister attached to your For Sale sign.

halfhearted) buyer turning your evening topsy-turvy, but it could be an infatuated buyer—and you want to welcome those. Of course, there will be times when you simply can't accommodate a buyer wanting a look—say just after you've wrangled a squirming toddler into the bathtub—but, if you can reasonably accommodate a request for a showing, you should do so.

What if someone, unaccompanied by an agent, knocks on your door and asks for quick look? You'll need to disappoint them, and ask that they contact your agent. Allowing them in is much more likely to lead to trouble than to a successful sale. One of the reasons you're paying good money to an agent is so you don't have to take the very real physical risk of opening your door to strangers, not to mention escorting them, all by yourself, from bedroom to bedroom. You have no way of knowing who this person really is, and whether he or she is a qualified, legitimate buyer—or a criminal looking for an easy entrée to someone's home. Even if it is a legitimate buyer, do yourself a favor and leave showings to the professionals. They know how to ask a few questions and find out if there's serious interest, and, not insignificantly, whether the person who would like to buy your home actually has the money and credit rating necessary to do so. If the person at the door isn't willing to talk with a professional agent, you can be pretty sure that person is not a real buyer. Even if you're selling FSBO, without an agent, you should decline an on-the-spot showing. Be friendly and welcoming, but firm. Tell them you'll be happy to take their contact information and set up an appointment for them to tour the home. Anything else is simply too dangerous.

How to bail out of the house for a showing

The more you manage to leave untouched following your morning cleanup, the fewer steps you'll have to take for a last-minute showing after you've returned home from work. Doing the following should help you get out in a hurry:

- Assign a job to everyone in the family. Younger children might cooperate more if you turn it into a contest—whoever gets through their chores fastest wins a Hot Wheels car, for example. Good kids' jobs include getting the leash on the dog or putting the kitty into her cozy carrier and loading the pets into the car (or wherever you plan to keep them), putting shoes in the closet, packing toys into a toy box, or turning on lights.

- Limit the family to using no more than two bathrooms for the duration of your marketing effort. That way you'll have fewer to freshen at the last minute.

- Store packages of premoistened bathroom, kitchen, and glass wipes near each sink, so you can touch up those rooms, as necessary, before you leave. Keep lightly scented air fresheners there, too, so you can give each area a quick spray.

- Return shampoo bottles, dishwashing soap, and other toiletries to their convenient hiding places.

- Replace the family towels with your for-show-only towels.

How to bail out of the house for a showing

- If various real estate agents have left their business cards in the dish near your stack of listing brochures, leave them visible. It doesn't hurt for prospective buyers to see that others have shown some interest in your home.

- Quickly vacuum any areas that need it. You might even consider buying an extra, inexpensive vacuum so you have one stored on every floor, just to facilitate last-minute sweeps.

- Take out the trash, and give that area a quick spray with your air freshener.

- Turn on the stereo, at low volume, to a jazz or classical music station.

- Double-check that you've turned the burners off on the range and oven. Dinnertime showings are admittedly a nuisance, but that could be *the* buyer knocking at your door.

- For the duration of your marketing effort, keep the car stocked with bottled water, snacks, books or magazines, children's stories, handheld video games, and other items to keep you occupied for the fifteen minutes to an hour that a showing may consume. Otherwise, you may find yourself eating way too much fast food for want of anything better to do.

Getting Lost for Showings

If at all possible, get out of the house while it is being shown. You may think that you'd be the best one to point out all its lovingly crafted details, but that's a job best left to the real estate agents. The fact is, buyers get very uncomfortable looking around a house when the sellers are right there. If they have any manners at all, they'll use them—and that's the problem. They won't poke around in closets and open the oven door. They won't linger in rooms they like, for fear of inconveniencing you—or for fear that they'll wreck their bargaining position if you get an inkling they really like the place. They won't criticize the home if you're within earshot, and that's a very bad sign. Real estate agents get excited when buyers start to criticize a home, at least to a point. It means that they're really considering their life there. To the trained ear, "there's not enough room for Grandma's credenza" translates to "I'm laying my furniture out already." "Hmm, the kitchen only has laminate countertops" translates to "it will be gorgeous when we replace it with granite." That won't happen if you're there. Most mannerly buyers will look around awkwardly, compliment you on your lovely home, and simply leave. So, get out of the way and let the real estate agent earn her commission.

Razzi's Rules to Live By

🏠 Welcome the open house.

Even though most open houses don't actually yield a buyer for that particular home, they remain a good way to get people looking at the place. You want as much exposure as possible; you never know who has a friend who has a friend who'd like your home.

⌂ Get on the brokers' tour.

You definitely want to be included in the special open house for local real estate brokers and agents as soon as your home comes on the market. Make sure your agent provides an attractive spread to entice them.

⌂ Love the lockbox.

It gives local brokers and agents a way into your home even if you and your agent aren't available to let them in. It's one way to snare the best kind of buyer—the one who falls in love right at the curb, and who needs a home *now*.

⌂ Every day is *the* day.

You never know if this is the day your buyer will discover your home. Leave it in ready-for-company shape every morning, with the drapes open and the lights on.

⌂ Lock it or lose it.

With all these strangers traipsing through your home, make sure your valuables are locked up safely.

⌂ Forget about manners.

Try your best to accommodate agents' last-minute requests to show the house. You don't want to let a buyer slip out of your hands . . . and into someone else's.

⌂ No escort, no showing.

Say no to unaccompanied buyers. It's simply too dangerous to allow someone in who hasn't been screened and accompanied by an agent. They're not likely to be serious buyers, anyway.

⌂ Find somewhere else to be:

Get out of the house while an agent is showing it. Otherwise, if prospective buyers have any manners at all, they'll be uncomfortable poking around your home—and they won't start to imagine themselves living there.

⌂ Warm up to criticism.

When buyers start noting drawbacks to your home, they're starting to envision life there. It's actually good news, though it's tough to hear. That's another reason you want to leave for showings . . . the criticism will be less restrained.

CHAPTER THIRTEEN

Sweetening the Deal

"Their neighbor house on the other side, across two cement sidewalks with a strip of grass between them, where lived the old Methodist Mom used to fight with about who would mow the grass strip, has had a FOR SALE sign up for a year. People now want more air and land than those huddled hillside neighborhoods can give them."

JOHN UPDIKE, *Rabbit Redux*

I DON'T KNOW IF ALBERT EINSTEIN EVER TRIED TO SELL A HOME, but if he did, it might explain how he came up with his theory of relativity. Time actually seems to slow down the longer a seller goes without a nibble. Fortunately, there are ways of getting the clock back up to speed.

Listen to what the market has been telling you. Maybe you've had a steady stream of lookers, but few buyers returning for a second visit. That tells you the price may be OK for the number of bedrooms and bathrooms and the neighborhood, but there's something about the home that's not capturing buyers' hearts. Your real estate agent should be collecting comments from some of the buyers' agents, which may hint at the problem. It could be out-of-style carpeting, dark rooms, a dated kitchen, lingering pet aromas, or a suggestion of whole-house disrepair. Take the criticisms very seriously, and consider whether it's time to buff up your product a little bit more. You may have to spend a couple of thousand dollars to rip out the carpeting, improve the lighting, refinish the floors, or even spiff up the kitchen with new appliances, cabinet doors, and a countertop. Of course, everybody hates to put money into a home they're getting rid of, but spending it yourself can actually be cheaper than lowering the price enough to attract buyers who are willing to do the work after the sale. Tread cautiously, though. You aren't fixing up to suit your own tastes; you're simply doing what's necessary to move a product off the store shelves.

Remember, *everyone* feels pressed for time these days. The great majority of buyers are only interested in a home that's in move-in condition; they don't have the time or inclination to redecorate or repair after closing. Plus, they may be stretching their finances so far that they won't have anything leftover to spend on additional work. Those who don't shrink from taking on such jobs are usually hunting for a property they can nab at a deep discount. So, what's your preference: selling cheap, or carefully upgrading your home so it appeals to more buyers?

On the other hand, maybe you've only had a few people stopping by for an initial look, despite professional-looking online presentations (with photos), some advertising, and a couple of open houses. Unless your whole market is grinding to a halt, that indicates that you may have significantly overpriced your home for

175

the neighborhood. Give serious consideration to a meaningful price reduction.

Psychology of Price Reductions

There's no firm rule on how long you should stick to your original listing price. I've seen price reductions occur after only two or three weeks on the market, when the sellers and their agents apparently realized that their home was just a bit overpriced comparatively. And, remember, the competition is always changing. You need to keep an eye on what comes on the market after you've listed and adjust downward if there are better deals out there. The buyers will certainly be making those comparisons!

Just as a Sale! sign at a clothing store attracts the attention of mall goers, your price reduction should kick up a flurry of new interest among buyers. It'll attract new buyers who were looking only in that lower price range, and returning buyers who had already taken a look but concluded that it was more than they were comfortable paying. Your agent should be sure to notify all the buyers' agents who've shepherded people through the home that you have lowered your price. A Reduced sign should be added to the For Sale sign on the lawn. And buyers should feel a little bit of urgency—just like when there's a markdown at the mall. What if another savvy shopper snaps up the great deal first?

You want to capitalize on that sense of urgency. While you certainly don't want to throw money away, keep in mind that one $20,000 reduction (just as an example) has a bigger effect than two $10,000 reductions. One big price cut makes buyers fearful that they'll miss out on the deal. Two price cuts make them wonder if there's going to be a third; buyers start to suspect that you're desperate and that you might accept a lowball offer. Once again, you should take a hard look at the competition on the market and offer a deal that's just a tad more compelling than the rest.

Alternatives to Price Cuts

Beyond simply lowering the price, there are some other ways to sweeten the deal on your home. These won't magically sell an overpriced or shabby home, but they can help make a good deal irresistible.

- Goose the commission. Sweeten the pot for buyers' agents by offering an extra incentive if they bring a successful buyer. An extra couple of thousand dollars in commission, or a free weekend at a resort may help make your offer stand out from the others.

- Give buyers a bonus. It *shouldn't* sway their decision on such a big purchase, but marketing is marketing, and you've got a product to sell. Consider offering buyers a yearlong paid membership to the local swim club, or pay their first year of dues in the condo or homeowners' association. Offer a free stay at your vacation home or time-share. Some sellers throw in the big-screen TV or patio furniture along with the home, particularly if it wouldn't work well in their new home.

- Pay for a warranty. When I advise buyers, I always warn them against giving too great a value to home-repair warranties, because they have significant exceptions that limit their value. But for sellers, warranties can be a useful marketing tool; they can be reassuring to cash-strapped new homeowners, particularly if the home is older, or one in the price range that attracts first-time buyers. For a few hundred dollars, you can buy a warranty that promises to repair or replace covered items during the buyer's first year in the home. Warranties typically cover heating, cooling, plumbing, and electrical systems, plus major built-in appliances such as the range, dishwasher, and refrigerator. If something breaks due to normal wear and tear during that first year, the new owners simply call a toll-free number to arrange for service, and pay a nominal fee for the visit.

- Buy down their interest rate. As discussed in chapter 11, you can pay extra to save your buyers some money. Points, or interest prepaid at closing, reduce the interest rate over the term of the loan. One point is equal to 1 percent of the loan amount, and each point reduces the interest rate by about one eighth to one quarter of a percentage point. For simplicity's sake, let's look at how buying down a borrower's interest rate would affect a thirty-year fixed-rate mortgage for $200,000. When it comes to your bottom line, there's no difference between cutting $4,000 off your home's price and agreeing to subsidize the buyer for up to two points on a loan for $200,000; you're out $4,000 either way. Those two points could cut the borrower's interest rate by one quarter to one half a percentage point. On a thirty-year fixed-rate loan, that would save 33 to 66 dollars per month. The savings could be enough to help the buyers qualify for a mortgage. Also, thanks to a quirk in the tax laws, the buyer would be entitled to the tax deduction on those points, even though you actually paid them. Buying down the interest rate makes the deal more affordable for a cash-strapped buyer and gives you one more thing to crow about in advertising. And buyers get an extra bonus—the tax deduction.

- Pay closing costs. The biggest obstacle for many first-time buyers is coming up with the cash for a down payment. Even if they take out a mortgage with very little down, buyers still face paying a couple of thousand dollars in closing costs. If you offer to credit them, say, two thousand dollars toward those costs, it makes the sale that much easier. Once again, this is a way to set yourself apart from the pack.

- Offer the chance to rent with an option to buy. If you don't *have* to get all of your equity out of that home right away, you might consider making would-be buyers a very attractive offer. Allow them to rent the home with an option to buy it later. Typically, owners charge a bit more in rent than the going rate and credit the excess toward the down payment if the renters decide to buy the home. You can set your home price at the beginning of the lease. This can be a very appealing offer to first-time buyers who fear that rising home prices will outpace their ability to save for a down payment. Of course, you should only offer such a deal to buyers who have a good credit history. A local real estate attorney can help you draw up the rent-with-option-to-buy agreement.

- Offer seller financing. That's right, *you* become the mortgage lender. With interest rates creeping up again, sellers may be able to offer buyers a better deal than regular mortgage lenders can—and earn some nice income to boot. A seller-financing deal can be an attractive way for retirees, in particular, to get some ongoing cash flow from their real estate sale. Again, you'll need the help of a good real estate lawyer to draw up your loan agreement (the IOU for the money they're borrowing) and the mortgage (the buyers' pledge to give up the home in foreclosure if they fail to make timely mortgage payments).

Taking a Time-out from the Market

If the seasons have changed since you listed your home and you don't see any good prospects for a deal, consider taking your home off the market for a few weeks or longer when your listing contract comes to an end. A home that stays on the market endlessly grows shopworn. People stop looking at it; they assume there must be something wrong with it. And buyers tend to give the most attention to the new-listing notices that pop up in their e-mail boxes, anyway.

A market sabbatical is especially compelling if you're heading into one of the real estate market's traditional slow seasons, from November through January and during the peak vacation weeks of summer. Agents will tell you, of course, "you can't sell it if it's not on the market." Just keep in mind that they're scrounging for business at that time of year. And while it's true that the relatively few buyers who remain in the market during the off-season do tend to be very serious buyers, they also know that their scarcity gives them extra leverage. You can expect them to play hardball.

You can use the sabbatical to reassess your marketing plan. Talk to some more real estate agents to see if they have any fresh marketing ideas that would make it worth signing a new listing agreement with them. You may end up relisting the original agent, but it never hurts to look. You can also use the time to freshen up the landscape for the new season, or to make repairs that the market is telling you are needed. And when you do start fresh with another listing, your home will once again pop up as a "new listing" on other agents'—and homebuyers'—computer screens.

Would a different agent do better?

If your home isn't selling as quickly as you thought it would, and especially if other nearby homes seem to be finding buyers, it's inevitable that you will wonder if maybe you chose the wrong agent. This is why it's in a seller's interest to sign a short, three-month listing agreement. But if there's still plenty of time left on your agent's clock, and you're convinced the agent is hindering your sale, ask the broker to assign your listing to another agent. The broker (not to mention your agent) won't be overjoyed at your request, but the broker will probably comply, just to keep you a satisfied client.

Razzi's Rules to Live By

⌂ Listen to the market.

If your home lingers on the market with few showings, few follow-ups, and no offers, the market is telling you that your home isn't competitive with others—at least not at its current price.

⌂ Get the most out of price reductions.

A significant price reduction on your home should spark some urgency among buyers, just like a one-day sale at the mall.

⌂ Cutting the price isn't your only weapon.

You could offer extra incentives to buyers' agents, throw in a bonus to buyers, offer a home-repair warranty, buy down the interest rate, subsidize closing costs, or offer seller financing or a rent-with-option-to-buy contract.

🏠 Take a sabbatical.

If there's been minimal interest in your home, consider taking a break from the market when your listing contract expires. Rethink your marketing plan, and polish the property. Then give it another go with a fresh, new listing.

🏠 Consider shopping for a new agent.

Three-month listing agreements are great because they don't tie you down seemingly forever to an agent who is less capable than you'd thought.

CHAPTER FOURTEEN

When You Need It to be Going, Going... Gone

"... Most of the houses of the Midland town were of a pleasant architecture. They lacked style, but also lacked pretentiousness, and whatever does not pretend at all has style enough."

Booth Tarkington, *The Magnificent Ambersons*

REAL ESTATE AUCTIONS ARE NOT JUST FOR SELLING HOG FARMS and foreclosures these days. They're a realistic alternative for any sellers who are interested in getting a home off their hands, *now*. In fact, residential real estate is the hottest sector of the growing auction business, according to the National Auctioneers Association. Part of that growth comes from developers selling unneeded building lots and unsold condominiums, but it's also built upon an increasing number of individual homeowners looking for a quick sale.

Certain types of homes are particularly well suited for auction. Expensive vacation homes that might appeal to buyers flung across half the country and properties that are notable because of their architecture or history have always been good candidates for auction. Homes that are unusual, such as a former bank that was converted to a residence, may benefit from the concentrated publicity that goes with an auction sale. But you might even consider the technique for a typical three-bedroom ranch-style home on a quarter-acre in the suburbs. Announcing to the world that *this* house is going to be sold on *this* date sets it apart from the pack, and in a market where sellers far outnumber buyers, anything you can do to draw attention to your property is a plus. If you're saddled with a home that has grown stale on the MLS as it bleeds money out of your budget month after month, an auction might be just the way to cut your losses.

Shaking off any stigma

Unfortunately, there still is a bit of cringe factor involved in putting a "To be sold at auction!" sign in your front yard. You'll probably feel like adding a couple of additional signs for the neighbors' benefit. How about a sign saying, "I've Paid All My Taxes!!" Or maybe you'd prefer "The Mortgage Has Never Been a Day Late!!" Qualms are certainly understandable; they come up because auctions have been traditionally used by government agencies and lenders to sell off property after the owners couldn't keep up with their obligations. But that's not necessarily so these days. You can tell the neighbors, your relatives, and your co-workers that you're

How it unfolds

- The seller hires an auction company, paying all advertising expenses and some closing costs up front and in cash.

- With advice from the auction company, the seller sets all terms for the sale, including whether there will be a minimum, "reserve" price that must be met for the sale to occur.

- The auction company launches an intensive marketing and advertising campaign for four-to-eight weeks, to drum up interest and attendance at the auction.

- Interested bidders present a cashier's check for several thousand dollars in order to be allowed to register as bidders. Wise bidders will already have had any desired appraisals or property inspections performed and will have obtained a lender's commitment to giving them a mortgage.

- The highest bidder wins the auction and must immediately present the auction company a cashier's check (or other specific, verifiable source of funds), typically for 10 percent of the full price, including any buyer's premium charged by the auction company.

- The bidder is required to complete the sale within 30 days.

- The seller vacates the home before the closing date and transfers ownership to the buyer.

going cutting-edge with your home sale, and trying the hot, new thing: a live auction. Tell them that your financial history remains sound, but you simply want to get the property sold. And then invite them to stop by and watch on auction day. The more warm bodies present, the more excitement that will be drummed up among those registered to bid.

What's in it for you?

There are some pretty attractive benefits to selling your home by auction. They're the same things that have always appealed to banks and other organizations that have no emotional attachment to a property and simply want to minimize their holding costs and to unload real estate quickly and with minimal fuss. Among the attractions:

- You know when the sale will happen. Especially if you don't set a minimum or "reserve" price, you can be pretty sure *someone* will buy your home on the auction date. You don't have to wonder if your home will sell next month . . . or in nine months, as you do with a traditional listing. The terms of the auction will state that buyers are expected to close within a specific timeframe, typically only 30 days after the auction. And the big chunk of cash that buyers are required to put down on auction day gives them a very big incentive to close on time, lest they forfeit the cash.

- The marketing period is compressed into a span of no more than a month or two. A good auction company makes a big splash of advertising during that brief period to drum up interest in the big event. Marketing can include notices on auction Web sites and newspaper classified ads, more extensive advertising in local,

regional, or national magazines and newspapers, direct mail,
custom-printed brochures, yard signs, and possibly radio
advertising. An expensive resort-area home, for example, might
require lots of advertising in glossy real estate magazines and in
major national publications such as the *Wall Street Journal*, the
New York Times and *USA Today*.

- You won't be expected to have the home ready for showings at
  the ring of the telephone. Showings are typically offered only on
  a few specific dates leading up to the auction. If a prospective
  bidder wants to have a home inspection or professional appraisal,
  that should be arranged before the auction date.

- Homes are offered for sale as-is. Once the gavel comes down, the
  high bidder is committed to the purchase—and he has to hand
  over a down payment, typically 10 percent of the price, on the
  spot. If that bidder fails to close on the deal, he forfeits the cash.
  There are no contingencies for home inspection, sale of the old
  residence, appraisal or mortgage qualification that can sometimes
  trip up a traditional home-sale deal before closing. If, for
  example, before the auction, a bidder paid to have the home
  inspected and the report said the chimney needs repair, you
  wouldn't be expected to make those repairs. The bidder can take
  that information into consideration when figuring his or her
  maximum price. However, the "as-is" nature of an auction
  doesn't mean you're off the hook when it comes to your duty to
  reveal significant defects, such as a leaky roof. And you still have
  to comply with government-mandated disclosures, such as the
  lead-paint disclosure required for any home built before 1978.

187

- You don't have to negotiate over special requests. Buyers at auction can't place conditions on their offer such as "I'll buy, but only if you throw in the patio furniture." The seller sets the terms of the deal. The only thing the buyer sets is the price.

How much can you get?

Keep in mind that most buyers are attracted to auctions by the chance that they could walk away with a bargain. Despite that motive, competitive bidding could drive the price very close to what you would have set as an asking price in a traditional real estate listing. (If you doubt that, search eBay for an inexpensive trinket that you'd really like to have. Go ahead and enter your bid . . . and see how tough it is to bow out when someone else threatens to win the prize!) Then again, if your local real estate market is just flooded with properties, or your auctioneer's efforts were sub-par, or bad weather drives down attendance on auction day, you might *not* attract a crowd of spirited bidders. The gavel could come down on a price that's lower than you expect. That's a disappointment, of course, but you should remember that, at least that gavel price is firm. You won't find your bottom line being nibbled away at in the period up to closing as a buyer continues negotiating over flaws found in the home inspection, or if the appraisal comes in lower than the buyer expected.

However, if you've already offered your home for sale the traditional way with a listing posted on the MLS, that could effectively cap the price you will get at auction. After all, if home buyers were able to get your home for $350,000 last week, why would they volunteer to pay more at auction? Unless for-sale properties are growing scarce in your market, and bidding wars are starting to break out spontaneously, you probably shouldn't expect to get as much at auction as you had asked through an MLS listing. But a successful auction could allow you to move on with your life and possibly garner a bottom-line dollar amount (after all expenses are added up) that is close to your old asking price.

Minding your reserve

Buyers may go to antique auctions or shop for trinkets on eBay just for amusement. But buyers go to real estate auctions to score a bargain. That's why "absolute" auctions, in which the high bidder that day is sure to win the prize because the seller has not set a "reserve" or minimum price, tend to generate larger attendance and more spirited bidding. In fact, all that bidding may even drive the sales price higher than it would have been at a less heavily attended reserve auction.

However, while it can be just dandy for the bankers down on Main Street to auction off foreclosed property at a discount so they can minimize their carrying costs, most homeowners have a substantial portion of their life savings wrapped up in a home. What if an absolute auction draws only a couple of flinty eyed investors, and they stop the bidding $50,000 short of what you need to pay off the mortgage? What if you'd rather stay in that old house instead of taking a $50,000 check to the closing table and walking away with nothing but memories of having lived there? These are the very real worries that make it tough for a homeowner to stomach an absolute auction.

You can guard your wealth and help keep your tummy settled by setting a realistic reserve price. The number should be lower than the amount you really expect the property to sell for, but it should be high enough to prevent disaster. That reserve—your very bottom line—should be kept in confidence by the auction company. Bidders will know simply that there *is* a reserve price, but they won't know the magic number until bidding has surpassed it. At that point, the auctioneer can announce that the reserve has been met, and the property definitely will be sold that day. And that is a very happy moment for a seller! A good auction company can guide you in setting a reserve that is low enough to attract bidders, but high enough to protect you.

What if bidding fails to reach your reserve? Then you have a choice to make. You can choose not to sell, or you can accept the top bid. And that may be a wise choice if it's reasonably close to your bottom line and you really do need to sell. Keep in mind that if your auction has been advertised and promoted adequately, the market has, in fact, told you what your home is worth. It might be much less than you thought it was; it might be less than it was a year or two ago, or it might even be less than you owe on your mortgage. But you could have to wait a good long time for another buyer to come along who is willing to pay a higher price. Remaining in the home or offering the place for rent may be your only realistic alternatives to accepting the top bid.

Calculating the costs

The cost structure involved with a real estate auction is completely different from a traditional listing with a real estate agent. With a traditional real estate listing, the seller pays nothing until a buyer is found and the deal closes. Only then is the traditional agent paid out of closing funds. Any advertising is paid out of the agent's pocket, and if the home doesn't sell, the agent doesn't get that expense back. In a weak real estate market, in which agents may find themselves working on a growing number of listings—which remain unsold month after month, agents who want to stay in business will parcel out their advertising dollars very judiciously. Unfortunately, that's not to your benefit.

With an auction, however, you're the one who writes the check to pay for pre-auction advertising. And, since you're footing the bill, you can expect the auction company to be more lavish with the advertising than if he or she had to pay for it. The amount you will have to pay varies dramatically depending on the price of your home—and on the number of other properties being offered at the same auction. If you're selling a $3 million waterfront home that's likely to appeal to vacation-home buyers up and down the East Coast, you can expect to pay tens of thousands of dollars in marketing fees. For that money, you should expect to see photos (in color, when possible) of your beautiful home published in specialty real estate magazines and in national newspapers. A good auctioneer might send glossy brochures to a select group of potential bidders.

Your tab for marketing a more affordable house or condo would, of course, be significantly lower, especially if your home is one of several that will be auctioned on the same date. Another benefit to a multi-property auction, besides sharing the advertising cost, is that it may attract more bidders than a single-property auction held on your front lawn. With a multi-property auction, there's always the chance that someone who was originally drawn by the opportunity to bid on another property might take an interest in yours, especially if she loses the bidding on the other one!

You also may be expected to pay for a title search, land survey, and perhaps other common closing costs before the auction, so this vital information can be made available to prospective bidders. The list of expenses to be paid by the seller varies according to local custom, so be sure to get full details about these expenses when interviewing different auction companies.

Buyers share the costs

Auction companies typically tack a "buyer's premium" onto the winning bid. The amount can vary, but 10 percent is not

Auction lingo

Absentee bid: A bid submitted by someone not attending the auction. Often bids are submitted to the auction company before the auction begins. Some will accept bids from pre-qualified buyers by telephone or over the Internet.

Absolute auction: An auction in which there is no minimum or "reserve" price set for the property and no other conditions that have to be met. The high bidder wins, no matter what.

Auction listing agreement: The document by which you hire someone to auction your home. It details the rights and responsibilities of the seller and auctioneer.

Auction with reserve: An auction in which the seller reserves the right to accept or decline a bid within a specified time.

Buyer's premium: A percentage of the sale price that will be added to the final bid. That percentage is noted in the uncommon. That will, of course, affect the amount of money that bidders can afford to pay for your home. Typically the auction company's commission, and sometimes a commission to a buyer's real estate agent or a referral fee to an agent are paid out of the buyer's premium.

Some companies list a home on the local MLS as a traditional sale while it is also being marketed for auction. If you choose a company that does such a parallel sales route, you need to clarify

pre-auction documentation so bidders can set realistic budgets for themselves.

Conditions of Sale: The legal terms governing a particular auction, including acceptable methods of payment, buyer's premiums and other conditions that a buyer needs to be aware of before placing a bid.

Minimum opening bid: Some auctions will announce a dollar amount where bidding should begin.

Preview: Specific dates and times when the property will be opened for inspection by prospective bidders. Also called Open House or Inspection.

Reserve price: The minimum price a seller will accept at an auction.

Withdrawal: Failure to reach the reserve price or insufficient bidding.

Source: National Association of Realtors

how much commission that agent stands to earn, and whether a commission will be owed along with the auctioneer's expense.

Sellers may be expected to pay a commission, perhaps 5 to 8 percent of the price, to the auction house as well. Review all commissions and fees in detail with the auctioneer, so you understand how much you have to pay, how much the buyer has to pay, what expenses will be covered by the buyer's premium, and how much cash you need for marketing and other costs. If the auction concludes without your property being sold, perhaps because bidding failed to clear your reserve price, you will still be expected to pay a commission to the auctioneer. Be sure to get all the details before you hire the services of an auction company.

Finding a good auctioneer

Auctioneering, like real estate brokerage, is licensed and regulated by individual states, and so the rules change depending on where you live. In some states, auction sales are covered under the traditional real estate broker's license; in other states, an auctioneer's license is required, perhaps without a real estate license. However, as interest in using auctions to sell non-distressed real estate (that is, sales that aren't prompted by bankruptcy or other financial hardship) grows, more traditional real estate brokerages are starting to work with auctioneers so they can more easily offer both types of sales to their customers.

For example, in the greater Philadelphia area, Prudential Fox & Roach Realtors has linked with Sheldon Good & Company, a major nationwide auction company, to offer auction services to sellers. Under their system, sellers of homes valued at $1.5 million or more may have a single-property auction, while homes worth less than that would be sold at multi-property auctions. If you've already listed with a traditional real estate agent, it could be worth asking if they have a relationship with an auctioneer.

Whether you go with a real estate agent who does auctions or an auctioneer, you can expect to sign a listing agreement—the document by which you hire that person to sell the home on your behalf. It will contain all the details about which services will be provided, and what fees are expected to be paid by the buyer and the seller.

You also can find qualified auction companies (and upcoming auctions) by searching the database kept by the National Auctioneers Association, www.auctioneers.org. Auctions and auctioneers also are advertised on www.auctionzip.com and in local newspaper classified ads. If you're considering selling at auction, it would be reassuring to attend a live real estate auction to familiarize yourself with the process before you make your decision. As always, you need to perform your due-diligence evaluation of auctioneers before you hire one. Interview at least two or three, get details of the marketing plan they propose to conduct (with your money!), compare the fees and services, and speak to three or more recent home sellers whose homes they auctioned.

Razzi's Rules to Live By

⌂ Auctions build urgency.

If buyers know your home is going to be sold at auction on a specific date, that can be enough to drum up interest from buyers afraid to let it slip away from them.

⌂ Squelch the cringe.

Auctions are *not* just for foreclosures and tax delinquencies. Tell the neighbors your finances are fine—and invite them to the auction.

⌂ Auctioneers don't dawdle.

Everything happens on a tight schedule. Advertising lasts only a few weeks, bidding may last only a few minutes, and buyers are expected to close within 30 days.

⌂ Buyers expect a bargain.

Buyers, many of them investors, are attracted to auctions by the chance of getting a below-market price. Setting a low reserve, or forgoing a reserve altogether, attracts more bidders and can boost your price.

⌂ You start with a big check.

You pay all advertising costs up-front, and can expect to pay fees and commissions even if the property doesn't sell.

⌂ You're dealing with a fast-talker, after all.

Before hiring an auction company, talk to clients who've sold homes like yours, review the details of the advertising plan, and get a full explanation of all fees that will be charged to you and to the buyer.

PART THREE

closing the deal

CHAPTER FIFTEEN

Negotiating Your Way to Agreement

"One thing you learn fast, in Corky's trade, in fact
Corky'd picked it up as a kid, nothing's fixed or
permanent or real, in real estate. Everything's
location, context. Ever-changing."

JOYCE CAROL OATES, *What I Lived For*

IT'S ALWAYS EXCITING NEWS WHEN YOUR AGENT TELLS YOU
there's an offer to buy your home. Soon you will dare to leave
for work in the morning without turning all the lights on. You'll
be able to make an offer on that lovely home across town. You'll
finally be able to start packing boxes and moving on with your life.
All you have to do is put your John Hancock on that fabulous
purchase offer and, bingo! You're on the way to the closing table.

Well, curb your excitement just a bit. That offer may need a
little tweaking before it's an agreement that's a good deal for both
you and the buyer. In most cases, there's a round or two of offers

and counteroffers before both parties agree to final terms. Another word for these rounds is *negotiation*.

Keep this in mind throughout the negotiation process: when you sign the buyer's offer, it becomes a binding sales contract (as long as all the contingency conditions outlined in that contract are satisfied in a timely manner). If you make any changes to that offer, you have rejected it and made a counteroffer. And the buyer might choose to simply walk away from your counteroffer.

Usually, buyers don't walk away. At least not if they're seriously interested in your home. And not if your counteroffer is reasonable. Often a seller's changes are simply handwritten onto a purchase offer and returned to the buyer's agent. But if the offer is significantly different, your agent should present a clean, new document to the buyer's agent.

Price is not the only thing that should concern you. Terms are important, too, and during the negotiation process you can refine the terms. Some points you might want to include in a counteroffer include adjusting the buyer's proposed closing date or asking to rent back the home for a week or two after closing so you can move into your new home at a more convenient date (offer to post a sizable security deposit and pay rent at least equal to the buyer's mortgage payment, which usually is significantly more than your old mortgage payment on the same home). The buyer may have requests, too. Maybe you'll agree to accept a price that's lower than your asking price, but you will choose not to pay points on the buyer's mortgage, as he proposed.

Savvy buyers will include with their purchase offer a list of items they expect to convey with the home. These may include appliances you had planned to take with you (who expected them to want that old refrigerator in the garage?) or the one set of window coverings that matches your custom-made bedspread. This could even include items you explicitly said would *not* be included in the sale (like your antique chandelier, which you *knew* you should have replaced before showing the home, but never got around to). If you object to selling such items along with the home, strike them from the contract then and there. It'll be your last chance.

If you heat your home with fuel oil, or if you will leave behind a significant store of good firewood, your contract should include a provision calling for you to be compensated for the value of the fuel that conveys with the home.

Your agent may be of limited help as you evaluate whether to make a counteroffer. He doesn't know what you're truly willing to live with, after all. At the same time, he has a very keen interest in seeing you just sign the darn contract, which brings closing day and a commission check into view—and frees his time to focus on other buyers and sellers.

Don't be surprised if a buyer responds to your counteroffer with yet another counteroffer. It might even lack some provisions you had kind of liked in the first version, and it's likely to include another nibble on the apple.

Seasoned negotiators say you always should get a little something for every concession you make. Not only does that strategy net you more, but it sends a message to the other side that there's a price to be paid for every request—and that tends to curtail requests (you might agree, for example, to pay two thousand dollars toward closing costs, but then decline to leave the requested sound system behind). There's always a chance you could kill the deal, but some people simply don't know how to quit nibbling away at negotiations. Curtail the nibbling by insisting that all counteroffers be made in writing; that way you'll get something in your hands that you can sign quickly, so you can move on.

Remember, the best negotiations leave both sides feeling satisfied. That doesn't necessarily mean triumphant—both parties should be satisfied that they've achieved their most important objectives and are being treated fairly. Remember, you still face several weeks of working together to get to that closing table. Problems can still crop up (maybe involving the title search or scheduling a home inspection by the deadline set in the contract). You even could wind up reopening negotiations if the home inspection reveals the need for costly repairs. If you've bargained the other party into a corner already, you can't expect much cooperation if trouble crops up later. And buyers these days may be closer to their last dollar than ever. They may reach a point where they can't budge another bit—even if they want to.

Holding Out for a Better Deal

There's a chestnut in the real estate business that the first offer you get is usually your best offer. That one's pretty hard to prove or disprove. After all, if everyone accepted the first offer, how would anyone know what subsequent offers would be? But you can get a feel for how likely it is that a second offer might be forthcoming. Did offer number one come after only a week or two on the market? Have there been many people looking at the home? Have a few been back for a second look (a very good sign that they're giving it serious consideration)? Ask your agent if other buyers have requested additional information about your home, like how much you spent on utility bills last winter. If there's still strong interest in your home, don't feel compelled to jump at a weak offer. Try to negotiate a weak offer into a form that's closer to your liking, of course, but don't alienate the would-be buyers; you could eventually reach a deal.

Check to see whether there's an expiration date on the purchase offer. If there isn't, that offer remains live until the buyer withdraws it (of course, that can happen at any moment). While I think it is terribly bad form to actually shop an offer around among other potential buyers, it doesn't hurt for your agent to give serious prospects word that it's last call for offers on your home. There's no need to disclose the price or terms of the offer in hand, but a phone call to buyers' agents representing people who've shown serious interest is not out of line. In fact, your agent might place the call as soon as there's word of an offer in the works. Consider it the auctioneer's "going, going . . . " before you say "gone!"

Bonanza! Multiple Offers

You may even find yourself in the enviable position of fielding two or more offers to buy your home. A quick flurry of full-priced offers can be a sign that you set your asking price too low, but skillful handling of the situation can ensure you still get the true value of your home. Your agent may notify the buyers' agents representing the interested parties that there have been multiple offers and invite them to come up with their last, best offer within the next twenty-four to forty-eight hours. This is how a little bidding war sometimes breaks out. But some buyers may withdraw their offers on the spot, choosing not to be bid up higher (or perhaps they only want your home if it's a steal).

Another course of action is to pick the strongest bid and enter negotiations solely with that buyer. You and your agent actually need to be careful not to sell your home more than once. You have only one home to sell, of course. And putting out two or more counteroffers is asking for trouble. What if more than one buyer accepts? How would you prove which one was accepted first? Who gets the home? Who gets the commission? This is the stuff of lawsuits, and you want to steer clear of it. Deal with one buyer at a time, or ask all the buyers to submit their best offers at once, and then choose one from that bunch to negotiate with.

Contingencies to Expect

There are several contingencies commonly found in purchase offers; they give buyers important protections, and they can help protect you, as a seller, by minimizing the risk of lawsuits after closing. You need to review these contingencies and make sure they're not so open-ended that they offer buyers an escape hatch right up to closing day. It's also in your interest to ascertain that the contract details how and when each of these contingencies will be satisfied—and removed as a potential stumbling block to closing.

Home Inspection

This contingency makes the purchase offer hinge upon the buyer receiving a satisfactory home-inspection report. Make sure it specifies how many days (or weeks) the buyer has to get the inspection report (the standard purchase contract produced by the California Association of Realtors, for example, allows buyers to request a standard seventeen days or an alternative period to get the inspection). During peak season for real estate sales (generally the springtime), inspectors can get booked up, so more time may need to be allotted.

Make sure the contract also specifies what will happen if the inspector finds flaws; it's in your interest that the contract allow you the opportunity to make repairs in response to the inspector's report.

A more open-ended inspection contingency could allow the buyer to slip out of the deal on a whim. ("The inspector found loose doorknobs, so we'll pass on the house. Please return our earnest money.") But with a contract that gives you the chance to make repairs, if something significant turns up in the inspection that truly affects the livability or value of the home—such as a foundation problem—negotiations are still open with the buyers. You can offer to make the fix before the sale closes or to credit the buyers with enough money from the sale proceeds that they can have the work done to their satisfaction. But the buyers might choose to call off the purchase altogether. You don't have a really firm deal until the inspection has been done, you've resolved how to make or pay for necessary repairs, and the buyers have removed this contingency.

Lead-based Paint Evaluation

If your home was built before 1978, it may contain lead-based paint. All sellers of homes built before that year, when lead-based paint became illegal to use in homes, are required to disclose to buyers any information they have about the presence of lead in the home. If your home is that old, federal law requires you to allow buyers up to ten days to get an inspection or a risk assessment for the presence of lead. Buyers and sellers can agree (in writing!) on a different period for inspections, or buyers can waive the requirement altogether. If they do so, be sure to get a signed, written statement to that effect.

Lead is a big deal. It's especially hazardous to children and pregnant women. It's particularly hazardous if the paint is obviously chipping and peeling, but intact lead paint still presents risk. And renovations can unleash a lead hazard. It can cost thousands of dollars for a qualified lead-mitigation company to come in and remove lead-based paint or to encapsulate it in another, special type of paint. The presence of lead paint can reduce the value of your home. Let's say a young couple makes an offer to buy your place, and the inspection reveals lead-based paint. They were planning to do some renovations—and to start a family—and the thought of dealing with lead sours them on the deal. They withdraw their offer and ask for their earnest-money deposit back. That deal is gone—and you now have information to add to your disclosure: you have a legal duty to disclose to all subsequent buyers that your home was found to have lead-based paint. You might choose to pay for the remediation work yourself, to remove the stigma. If you do so, be sure to show all prospective buyers documentation of the remediation work done by a qualified contractor, including that contractor's documentation showing that the house is now free of a lead hazard. For more information, contact the National Lead Information Center at 800-424-5323. You can also research the U.S. Environmental Protection Agency's regulations and recommendations online at www.EPA.gov.

Radon Gas

The EPA and the U.S. surgeon general recommend testing all homes for radon before they're bought or sold. Radon is an invisible, tasteless, odorless, radioactive gas. Radon in indoor air is estimated to cause about 21,000 lung cancer deaths annually in the United States, according to the EPA, making it the number-two cause of lung cancer (smoking remains the number-one cause). The only way to find out whether radon is present is to test for it. Qualified radon testers can conduct quick tests, taking as little as forty-eight hours, which include measures to prevent or detect any tampering by the home's occupants that could result in an artificially low reading.

Radon tests typically measure the level of the radioactive gas in the lowest occupied floor of your home over the course of a few days to a few weeks. It's very important that you not interfere with the test or try to distort the readings. There are anti-tampering devices that attempt to track such behavior—and, besides, you wouldn't really want to put someone at risk for lung cancer, would you?

Testing for radon is part of the home-sale routine in some parts of the country; in others, it's not. If you already know there's an elevated level of radon in your home, you are duty bound to reveal that to buyers before the price is set. If a buyer makes the sale contingent on a presale test, and elevated levels are found, you can expect some negotiating over who will pay for a qualified contractor to install ventilation or another type of system that will lower radon levels. According to the EPA, the cost for such a system typically ranges from $800 to $2,500. You can find more information, including advice on hiring a qualified tester, at www.EPA.gov.

Extra Inspections

The professional home inspector might find some conditions that warrant further investigation. Wall cracks or sagging floors might be cause for an inspection by a licensed structural engineer, for example. Or suspicious-looking insulation might warrant an inspection for asbestos. These extra inspections are permitted under a well-written home-inspection contingency clause.

The buyer may add other contingencies for additional

inspections. If there are a lot of trees on the property, especially if they tower over the home, the buyer may want to call in an arborist to find out if they're in danger of falling, or if having them trimmed will cost thousands of dollars. If the swimming pool looks like it's in disrepair, savvy buyers will add a contingency that the pool be inspected by a qualified pool company, as well. If the home has a septic system, that merits a look from a septic company, too.

You may be able to head off some of these requests by putting buyers' minds at ease about the overall condition of your home. Dig out recent receipts for tree work, septic-tank cleaning, pool maintenance, foundation waterproofing, roof work, and any other work you've had done in the past few years, and make them part of the information packet available to buyers.

Finance Contingency

Most people need a mortgage to buy a home. And an astute buyer will want to make sure they can get out of the deal—and get their earnest money back—if they can't actually qualify for a mortgage at a decent interest rate. They should want this safeguard even if they've given you a lender's mortgage-preapproval letter (you never know when a job might be lost). Such a contingency simply states that the deal is dependent on the buyers qualifying for a mortgage with a reasonable interest rate, which they should specify. As the seller, though, you need some assurance that this deal won't fall apart the night before closing. Make sure the contingency also requires the buyer to apply for the mortgage within a week or two after you've accepted the contract. And you and your real estate agent should follow up to make sure that happens on time.

Appraisal Contingency

Lenders always require that a property be appraised before they'll make a mortgage loan. Typically, the buyer's real estate agent will schedule an appraisal; it must be with an appraiser who is acceptable to the lender. The cost is a few hundred dollars, payable at closing. An appraisal contingency specifies that the deal hinges on the appraiser saying the home is worth at least as much as the buyer has agreed to pay. Without this contingency, if the appraisal should come in lower than the agreed-upon price, the buyer would still be committed to buying the home and would face having to raid her savings to come up with the difference between the purchase price and the amount the lender will approve as a loan amount, given the appraised value of the home. If the buyer can't (or won't) come up with the extra cash, she might have to walk away from the deal and forfeit her earnest money. An appraisal contingency shields buyers from this risk; they can choose to get out of the contract. But you may find yourself agreeing to lower the price to make the deal happen anyway. After all, what are the odds you'll find another buyer who's willing to pay more than the appraised value?

Homeowners' Insurance Contingency

If you live in an area that's experiencing a troubled homeowners' insurance market (and that's plenty of places these days, particularly along the coasts), it's not a certainty that new owners will be able to secure a reasonably priced policy. They may include a contingency that pegs the deal on availability of insurance. Again, you want to see that they look for a policy right away, and that "reasonably

CLUE-less? Not you

The CLUE report is a product of the insurance industry's centralized database for homeowners' insurance claims. Officially named the Comprehensive Loss Underwriting Exchange, it tracks the history of claims submitted by an individual *and* the history of claims filed for a specific property. Both records go back five years. If frequent claims have been filed for your home (or if you have a record of submitting claims on other properties), insurance companies may decline to offer coverage (and some of them consider *two* claims in a couple of years to be frequent). This might force the new buyers to get a policy from a company that sells super-expensive coverage to borrowers at high risk of submitting claims.

There might be more of a claims history on your home than you remember. There have been instances in which a simple phone call to an insurance agent inquiring whether some hail damage to the roof would be covered was reported on the owner's claims history, even though the owner never followed through by filing a claim. Or, if you've only owned for a couple of years, the previous owners' claims may still show up on the record.

A buyer cannot get a copy of the CLUE report for your home without your help. But it may be in your interest to get a copy for them, especially if it contains good news. Request one online at www.ChoiceTrust.com or by phone at 866-312-8076. Everyone is entitled to one free report per year. Additional reports cost about twenty dollars.

priced" is defined in the contract. And get that contingency removed as quickly as possible. You might help set buyers at ease by requesting a copy of your home's insurance-claim history, called a CLUE report, and showing it to prospective buyers.

Setting a Closing Date

Your contract also should stipulate when you need to vacate the home, and when the new owners are entitled to move in. Usually, you hand over the keys and the garage-door openers right at the closing table. But buyers might ask you for access to the home before closing so they can paint or make repairs, especially if you've already vacated it.

You should be a little wary of accommodating their request. What if they break something, or get hurt, or the deal falls through? You might want to stick to the typical arrangement (and detail it in the contract, of course) which requires you to leave the home in broom-clean condition. (There's more on that in chapter 18.) Broom-clean means you will have removed all your belongings and swept the floors. The contract should allow the buyers to walk through the property a day or so before closing to verify that everything that should stay has been left behind and that everything that should be removed is gone.

Put Down the Screwdriver

Don't even think about removing fixtures from your home while the sale is pending. In fact, you ought to leave things alone once the home is put on the market. After all, to a prospective buyer who visits on Sunday afternoon and then returns Wednesday evening for a second look, it hardly inspires confidence to discover that the sconces have been removed from the hallway. Anything that has been screwed or bolted in to the structure is supposed to convey with the home. If you start tinkering with it after agreeing to a sales contract, you're asking for trouble. While you're at it, don't dig up any plants in the garden, either. Although you may have the legal right to remove plants, it's very bad form. Take out anything you want *before* you put the home on the market. Once the For Sale sign goes up, leave everything as is.

Get It in Writing

These words ought to be embroidered in a cross-stitch sampler, framed, and handed down through the generations: *Get it in writing.* Absolutely everything involved in a real estate deal must be in writing. If your agent tells you there's an offer to buy your home, believe it when you have the paper in your hands. When the buyer's agent says his client is satisfied with the home-inspection results (or with the repairs you made upon the buyer's request), make sure your agent gets a written document removing that contingency. Remember, paper is your friend in a real estate deal— and time is your enemy. Whatever needs to be done, make sure you do it as promptly as possible. Get the details in writing, and file the documents in a big accordion file so you can get your hands on everything quickly should any questions arise.

At some point, you will finally have it: a purchase contract, signed by both seller and buyer. The Contract Pending sign will go atop the For Sale sign in your yard. Go out to dinner, celebrate, call the movers . . . and leave for work with the lights off and your toothbrush left on the bathroom counter. You've sold your home!

Razzi's Rules to Live By

🏠 Prepare to tango.
It takes two to negotiate a final deal that's acceptable to all concerned. A round or two of offers and counteroffers will help you work out the finer points.

🏠 The offer could disappear.
A buyer can withdraw an offer anytime before you sign it.

🏠 Terms are as important as price.
Details like closing dates and rent-back agreements can be as important as dollars.

🏠 The agent wants to see you sign a contract.
Agents may be of limited help when you're trying to decide whether to make a counteroffer. After all, they have a vested interest in seeing you and the buyer come to terms before the deal slips away—and their payday with it.

🏠 Get as good as you give.
In negotiations, try to get a little concession for every concession you agree to. That may help end the other party's tendency to keep nibbling at the deal.

🏠 Don't go in for the kill.
The best negotiations leave both parties feeling satisfied. Remember, you still face several weeks of working together to get to closing.

⌂ Announce "last call."

Before you jump on an offer, give other serious buyers one last opportunity to get their offers in.

⌂ Don't sell your home twice.

All that gets you is a lawsuit. Either ask all bidders to make one final best offer, or choose one buyer to negotiate with.

⌂ Get rid of contingencies promptly.

The deal is not done until all the buyer's contingencies have been satisfied—and removed.

⌂ Say no to early occupancy.

It's too risky to allow a buyer to work on the home (or to actually move in) until that buyer officially owns it.

⌂ Put the screwdriver down.

And no one gets hurt. Anything that's screwed in or bolted to the building is supposed to convey to the new owners.

CHAPTER SIXTEEN

Laws All Sellers Must Heed

"Home is the place where, when you have to go
there, they have to take you in."

ROBERT FROST, *The Death of the Hired Man*

S TRIKE THE PHRASE "BUYER BEWARE" OUT OF YOUR
vocabulary. Buyers these days have a right to any
information you have that would affect their decision to
buy your home—and the price they would be willing to pay for it.
And if you fail to disclose such important information, you might
find yourself wrapped up in a lawsuit. That's true whether you're
working with a real estate agent or selling on your own. Seller
beware—not following the laws could get you in a heap of trouble.

Property-condition Disclosure

Most states require that sellers fill out a detailed form noting any
significant flaws with their home. Hot spots on disclosure forms
include roof damage, water leaks, asbestos, cracks in the structure,
mold, and problems with the septic system. Some, however, allow

sellers to opt to sell the home "as is," which is a signal to buyers that they really should be thorough in their own inspection. Even if you are able to choose an "as is" sale, that doesn't relieve you from liability if you were to hide flaws from buyers. That fresh coat of paint to hide water stains on the ceiling—where you *haven't* fixed the leak above—could still land you in court after the deal has closed.

As discussed in the previous chapter, most buyers will put contingencies in their purchase offer that allow them to have inspections performed for possible problems such as the presence of lead or radon gas. Whether or not they ask for those inspections, sellers have a duty to disclose problems along those lines—at least if they're aware of any.

Lead-paint Disclosure

If your home was built before 1978, you will need to give buyers a disclosure form revealing any information you have about the presence of lead in the home. You also have to allow them up to ten days to get an inspection or a risk assessment performed. Your real estate agent should provide a copy of the required form. For more information, contact the National Lead Information Center through its Web site at http://www.cpa.gov/lead/index.html or by phone at 800-424-5323.

Radon-gas Disclosure

If you've had your home tested for radon gas, you need to make those results available to prospective buyers. If not, they may wish to add a contingency to their offer that allows them to have a test performed before their contract becomes binding. Remember, radon isn't necessarily a deal breaker; the problem can be fixed for a fairly manageable price.

Environmental-contamination Disclosure

If your property has a history of problems that could have a lingering environmental health effect for future owners, you need to protect yourself by disclosing all the information you have. Let's say you've gone through a landlord's nightmare: you discovered that renters were making the illegal drug crystal meth on the property. Hopefully, the police have dealt with the situation, and your former tenants are now residents of your friendly local correctional facility—but you still have a problem on your hands. The drug-making process leaves behind very harmful environmental contamination, which must be cleaned up properly. For any subsequent sales, you need to disclose this history of contamination, along with documentation attesting to the environmental cleanup. Or, let's say an old heating-oil tank sprang a leak a few winters ago. You paid a contractor to clean up the oil and repair the system, but the environmental problem isn't entirely behind you—you should still disclose the facts about that incident, and the documentation of the cleanup. Keep in mind that environmental problems are not limited to inner-city or low-income areas. In one very posh area of Washington DC, homeowners have discovered old nerve-gas shells that date back to World War I. So far, the U.S. Army has spent more than $90 million cleaning up remnants of the land's wartime history, but people trying to sell a home in that neighborhood need to disclose the issue to potential buyers. Environmental problems can crop up even in the toniest of neighborhoods.

Building Permits and Inspections

You *did* get a building permit before you converted the attic into an extra bedroom, didn't you? And your local government's building inspector actually inspected the work when it was done, right? Even projects tackled by an ambitious, knowledgeable do-it-yourselfer need to get a final approval from local building authorities (and yes, they will use that information to boost your property tax assessment). If you built a deck or did your own electrical wiring in the basement family room, you need to have the building inspector verify that the work was done up to the standards set in the building code. Keep any documentation you get from the building inspector (which may only amount to a signed sticker affixed to your circuit-breaker box).

Buyers wouldn't be happy to find out that the bedroom you added on isn't legal because it doesn't have windows big enough to allow firefighters to get inside. And unhappy buyers file lawsuits when they learn that they'd have to shell out thousands of dollars to make the place safe. You don't want to even think about the liability you'd face if that deck you *thought* you had built solidly were to collapse and injure people. Cover yourself by making sure all the work you've done was permitted and approved *before* you put that home on the market.

Things You Don't Have to Volunteer

Generally, you don't have to divulge information that ought to be obvious to anyone visiting the home. You don't have to volunteer that airplanes heading to the nearest airport make for noisy backyard barbecues. You don't have to volunteer that the neighbors tend to have raucous parties now and then. Noise from a nearby railroad track? They ought to be able to figure that one out as well.

Nor do you have to make public tidbits of the home's history that don't directly affect its livability or value. Let's say the owners before you met an unfortunate end right there in the home. You don't have to volunteer that. Let's say you really believe the neighborhood tale about the old Civil War wife, whose visage is still occasionally seen peering out the attic window, waiting for Johnny to come marching home again. That's hardly a fact, now, is it? However, if buyers specifically ask you about past crimes, deaths, or alleged hauntings, you'd best spill any stories you have about the old missus in the attic. Obviously, they consider it a fact that would affect their decision to buy, and fibbing will only cause you trouble later. You might say it could haunt you.

Fair-housing Laws

Sellers are also obliged to comply with federal, state, and local fair-housing laws. Federal law prohibits discrimination on account of a buyer's race, color, religion, sex, national origin, disability, family status, or on account of the presence of children in the household. Some state and local laws add sexual orientation to the list of protected categories. Penalties can be levied even if you or your real estate agent did not really intend to dissuade a certain type of buyer from choosing your home. What matters is the *effect* of your actions.

Real estate agents are usually attuned to the risks of discriminating, intentionally or unintentionally. They face stiff penalties for violating these laws, and they usually get the rules drilled into them during their training. But, even if you have an agent working on your behalf it's wise for you to be aware of the rules as well. If you're selling on your own, it's a must.

Maybe you'd just love for your home to go to a nice, young family with children, one that reminds you of your own family back when the kids were small. You post an ad on CraigsList.org calling your home a "perfect place for raising children" and highlighting your "family-friendly" neighborhood. Such an ad could be seen as discriminatory against singles. At newspapers, sharp-eyed ad salespeople are supposed to reject such an ad for fear of violating fair-housing laws themselves, but on the Web, you're working without a net. Even advertising a neighborhood as "nice and quiet" can be seen as suggesting that families might not be welcome there.

Your best bet is to stick to the facts about your home and neighborhood. Talk about the number of bedrooms, square footage, accessibility of mass transit, and so on. Leave it to buyers to decide if it's their type of neighborhood. And if you find yourself fielding offers from two or more competing buyers, make your decision based on price, contract terms, and their documented ability to get a mortgage. Stay away from decisions about who would be a good fit with the neighbors. Some buyers may go so far as to include a photo of their lovely family along with the purchase offer, in hopes of swaying a seller. Resist such tugs at your emotions—and stay out of trouble. It's the right thing to do.

Condos, Co-ops, and Homeowners' Associations

If you're selling a home that's part of a condominium, a co-op, or a homeowner's association, you have a duty to help buyers get the information they need about that organization. After all, belonging to one involves financial obligations that directly affect whether they can afford to live in that community—and whether they'll be happy there. In fact, some jurisdictions require that buyers be given from two to five days to review those documents, during which time they can back out of the purchase contract. You don't have a deal until this grace period has elapsed. Even if your jurisdiction doesn't require such a review period, smart buyers will write a contingency into their purchase contracts, so be prepared to deal with it. Community associations typically charge a hundred dollars or more for a set of documents; it's helpful to have a complete, up-to-date set on hand when you put your home up for sale so you don't have to fret about whether the association will get them to the buyer in a timely manner.

Belonging to one of these associations is not all about fees and rules, however. There are benefits, and you want to make sure potential buyers know about them, too. Tell buyers about the reserved parking, concierge services, swimming pool, tennis courts, workout room, golf privileges, lake access, professionally maintained landscaping, or whatever amenities will be theirs if they buy your home. (Even if it's a popular resort community, you can't assume that they know about all the benefits. You never know what little feature is going to ring a buyer's bell.) If your community offers many of these goodies, it's worth compiling a little presentation on paper or CD that prospective buyers can take home. You might include it on your home's Web site. If your association has its own Web site that can be accessed by the public, make sure to provide a link from your home's Web site and to include the URL in all your marketing materials.

Selling a co-op poses additional challenges—namely, the members of the co-op board who will be casting thumbs-up or thumbs-down on anyone who wants to buy your shares and move into the building. Some co-op boards can be ferocious in reviewing prospective members, and their pickiness can make it tough to unload your place, and thus holds down its value. It's in your interest to run as much interference as possible between your prospective buyer and the co-op board. Pass along any tips you can about board members' preferences (maybe they seem to harbor a particular dislike for residents who plan to knock down interior walls) to help your buyer through the gauntlet. And don't neglect to turn on the charm when you run into those all-powerful board members in the elevator! They hold your home sale in their hands.

Razzi's Rules to Live By

🏠 Forget "buyer beware."

These days, buyers have a right to know about anything that will affect a home's value. Protect yourself by disclosing any flaws you're aware of.

🏠 Fix flaws, but never hide them.

Patching the roof is a repair; painting a water stain without fixing the leak is deception. Keep documentation of all the work you've had done.

🏠 "As is" doesn't mean "hide and seek."

Even if your jurisdiction allows you to sell a home "as is" instead of filling out a detailed disclosure form, you must still take care not to hide defects.

🏠 Environmental contamination isn't just a city thing.

Homes anywhere can have problems with lead, asbestos, or other contaminants. Disclose what you know, and allow time for buyers to get the inspections they want.

🏠 Don't state the obvious . . . or conjecture, either.

You don't have to disclose the obvious, such as the fact that the nearby railroad can be a tad noisy. Nor do you have to volunteer information that doesn't directly affect the home's value. But if you're asked a question, tell the truth.

⌂ Even you could run afoul of fair-housing laws.

Even if you start out with the best of intentions, your actions could violate fair-housing laws if the *effects* of those actions are seen as discriminatory against buyers. Stick to the facts about your home and the neighborhood's amenities, and let buyers decide whether it's their kind of place.

⌂ Pave the way for membership.

Help your buyers promptly obtain disclosure-information packages from your homeowners' association, condo, or co-op board. You don't have a deal until they've had the opportunity to review them.

⌂ Boast about the amenities.

Don't assume buyers know all the benefits they'll derive from becoming a resident of your association or development. You never know which amenity will sell them on the deal.

CHAPTER SEVENTEEN

Seller's Remorse and Squirrelly Buyers

> "Aided by the dizzying fumes of paint thinner, I imagined myself an archaeologist digging through the strata of former lives whose histories could be reconstructed by their choice of wall coverings."
>
> AMY TAN, *The Hundred Secret Senses*

B RACE YOURSELF: THINGS ARE ABOUT TO GET WEIRD. Specifically, *you* are about to get weird. And it won't help matters at all that the buyer is also likely to go through his or her own bout of "what-have-I-done?" angst. Just be prepared for some out-of-character behavior, on your own part and the buyer's, and know that this is a natural by-product of a decision as momentous as changing homes.

Let's consider, shall we, the following very sensible reasons why a rational person such as yourself might become just a tad unglued during the course of a home deal:

- It involves a whole lot of money— these days, even an amount that is expressed as a fraction of millions—"a quarter-million-dollar home"; "a half-million-dollar home." Or it's so unspeakably expensive we talk around the big *m* word entirely—it's "one-point-fifteen" or "two-point-four." Who are you kidding? Deep in your mind, you know darn well just how costly this deal is. For most of us, it's the biggest expense of our lives.

- This deal could still fall apart. It's not over until the signatures are on the paper and the money and title have changed hands.

- You may be looking at an interest rate on your new mortgage that is significantly higher than the rate on the loan you had on the old home. Unfortunately, this is the situation facing most buyers these days. We can no longer take advantage of rock-bottom interest rates to take some of the edge off high home prices. If only we could take the old loan along with us, but, alas, lenders don't see it that way.

- You're giving your home up to someone else. You can remember every nail you drove into the walls, every bag of mulch you spread. The new owners will probably let it all go to seed, you imagine.

- You're moving into the unknown. You might not have even found your new home yet. You could be homeless if you don't find a good deal pretty soon (homeless with a ton of cash in the bank— and a key to a temporary rental, but who's being rational?).

- Your daily routine has been shot to pieces. First, there was weekend after weekend consumed with the work of getting the home ready for market. Then there were days on end involving the extra hassle of keeping the home a showplace. And just when you thought you could relax, it's time to start dismantling rooms and packing up for a move.

- The kids are not shy about telling you they'd rather keep everything just as it has always been. Kids can be surprisingly resistant to change. Besides, all they know is that they have to say good-bye to friends and pack up their belongings—for a move that probably wasn't their idea to begin with.

- Moving is going to entail a whole lot of work. The longer you stay in a home, the more junk you accumulate. And now you must lay hands on *every single piece* of stuff you own and haul it somewhere else.

- You'll never know for sure if someone else might have paid a little bit more for your home. Unless your home sparked a spontaneous bidding war, you're bound to wonder if you could have gotten a higher price.

- Your ability to move into your new home without further complications now rests on the ability—and willingness—of practical strangers to follow through on the promises made in the purchase contract. What if the buyers are flakes? What if they can't afford it, after all? Will you be left high and dry with an unsold home?

- A bunch of professionals—most not of your choosing—are now coming into the deal, all seemingly capable of convincing the buyers that they ought to get a lower price. The buyer will pay for a home inspector to go through and find fault—and then expect *you* to pay for it. The appraiser might not think the value is as high as you and your buyers did. The termite inspector might find bugs, and on and on. Anything unearthed will probably cost you—and could threaten the deal altogether.

- Everything in your home looks great and works well since you got it fixed up for sale, and it's difficult to recall why you wanted to move in the first place. It's just like seeing an old sweetheart arm in arm with a new love; suddenly, that old sweetheart is quite the looker. Why didn't you see it before?

Many of us aren't all that comfortable with change. Or with ceding control to others. Combine change with our inability to control all the details and it's enough to keep any hardy soul awake in the middle of the night, rehashing decisions made weeks or months ago.

It may help some to recognize seller's remorse when it hits. You're not alarmed by a leaden belly after Thanksgiving dinner or an aching head after too much champagne, because you knew they were coming. The feeling is uncomfortable—but you know it will get better with time. When you sit up in bed at 2:00 AM with that "what have I done?" feeling, recognize it for what it is— seller's remorse—and remember that it, too, will pass, given a little bit of time.

You can help coach yourself and the rest of your family through it. Go back through the decision-making process that led to placing your home on the market in the first place. What was the basic reason? A promising new job? Better neighborhood? Shorter commute? Roomier home? Milder climate? Better schools? Easier maintenance? Less expensive lifestyle? Keep your mind on that original motive. You're close to achieving it.

What you *don't* want to do is to let these emotions lead you into rash behavior. Maybe you start to wonder what would happen if you called up your real estate agent and said you've reconsidered. You don't want to sell after all! Well, keep in mind that you've signed a contract that says you *will* sell. Maybe you figure you'll just subtly sabotage the deal—dig in your heels and refuse to address any problems discovered by the home inspector, for example. Well, that *might* drive the buyer off—but it will be a mighty nasty process. Maybe you'll just procrastinate—no need to hire movers or start packing boxes just yet. But you know how well that approach usually works. If you think you've got anxiety now, wait until the moving van is twenty-four hours away . . . and closing . . . and you're not ready. *That's* anxiety.

Giving Sentiment Its Due

Why on earth *wouldn't* you be sad about moving out of your home? Put me in a decent *hotel room* for more than three days and I start to get attached to the place. Your home is the place where intimate, dramatic things happen. New couples set up housekeeping together and learn how to mesh the styles and tastes of two individuals into one coherent look. People have babies and not long thereafter get a toddler's-eye view of the place as they go about baby-proofing outlets and stairwells. Santa Claus comes, as does the occasional influenza. We lounge in the tub, paint the walls our favorite colors, and laugh with friends at the table. We're as comfortable in our homes as a dog asleep on the porch with his belly exposed to the sky. Of course you're going to be stressed! It will take time to feel so at home under a new roof.

The Kids' Perspective

This home may be the only place your children have ever lived.
The decision to move almost certainly wasn't theirs. All they know
is that they're moving, they're going to have to make new friends,
and they'll (possibly) have to find their niche in a new school. And
Mom and Dad have been really picky lately about toys left on the
floor and gobs of toothpaste in the sink.

Try to find time for the kids to host one last sleepover. Make
sure to get everyone's pictures—and their instant-messaging names,
e-mail addresses, and phone numbers, so your kids can stay in
touch without a hitch.

If you've already found a new home, you can help your children
manage their own anxiety by focusing on the excitement of starting
fresh. Kids sometimes don't even know that they're anxious, let
alone why. They may just be grumpier, or clingier, than usual.
(Teenagers may be even more aloof, if that's possible. *Whatever.*) It's
up to the grownups to figure out what's really behind their out-of-
sorts mood and to try to help them manage it. Visit the new school,
and spend a Saturday morning on the playground. Get them to
help you locate new Little League teams, ballet classes, Scout
troops, or anything else that supports their passion of the moment
(they can compile folders of the information you find or mark
important dates on the family calendar). Getting kids involved in
organized activities in their new neighborhood helps ease the way
to friendships, and it can be especially helpful if you're moving
during the summertime, when some neighborhoods can be
surprisingly devoid of children, who all seem to be tied up with
summer camps. Older kids may be reassured to know that pretty

much every community has its own mall and multiplex—and good cell-phone service.

Get your kids excited about the move by encouraging them to focus on the spaces that will represent their turf, namely their bedrooms and the family room or playroom. Let them help you choose paint colors, throw rugs, and bed coverings. If they're intent on replicating their old rooms down to the very last poster, give them a camera, a tape measure, and a pad of graph paper. They can draw a diagram of where *everything* went, and figure out how to transfer that scheme to the new place.

Saying Good-bye

Now that you've cleaned up your home so beautifully—and before you start packing boxes—you have a good opportunity for one last celebration. Even if you're just moving across the street, you can salute the old place and toast your good times under the old roof. You might be surprised that your friends would like to have one last look around of their own. Take photos together with your friends in front of the old mantle or around the kitchen table. While you're at it, go from room to room and snap photos of each one (don't even skip the bathrooms, the garage, or the laundry room). Years from now you may enjoy a good gander. (There's a more practical benefit as well. If anything happens to your belongings in transit to the new home, pictures can help document your loss.) Young children, especially, can be dismayed at how quickly they forget aspects of the place where they lived when they were little. Snap some shots of the landscape, as well, and jot down the names of the plants growing there. You might even take a few blossoms and press them between the pages of a book, for posterity. (I've known of some particularly devoted gardeners leaving detailed layouts of their gardens, with names of all the plants for the new owners' benefit. It's a very welcoming gesture for future owners.)

You and your children may also find comfort in leaving a little bit of yourselves behind. You could plant a sapling in the back yard or write your names in an out-of-the-way spot in the basement or garage. These little activities—ceremonies, really—are a way of acknowledging what an important part of your life this home has been.

Squirrelly Buyers

Do you suppose that, while you're experiencing the anxiety of seller's remorse, those bloodless buyers who negotiated such a steal of a deal are sleeping tight, satisfied with the idea that they nabbed the perfect home? Ha! They're likely going through very similar nighttime ruminations. No matter what they paid, they probably think it was too much. They're convinced the housing market is about to collapse. They worry that the furnace will die as soon as they move in. And the big, new mortgage they're taking on will drive them to penury. Few people escape a bout of "buyer's remorse" somewhere along the way. And when they're stricken hard they can be a pain in the neck for you to deal with.

These squirrelly buyers may try to reopen negotiations at every turn. The home-inspection report usually offers the best opportunity for this (ah!—confirmation that the place is going to suck all their money down the drain!). If they really want to back out of the deal, they can become impossible to please at this point. They may even make requests of you that aren't covered in the contract—"We know we didn't ask for it in the contract, but could you leave the draperies behind anyway?" Their loan may get delayed, because they failed to get some papers to the loan officer promptly. Unfortunately, their woes become your woes. If you're in a particularly strong seller's market and have other buyers waiting to pounce on your deal, you might just want to let them walk, rather than deal with their foot-dragging. You might even get more money from a different buyer. Otherwise, you and your agent need to stay on your toes to make sure their contingencies get satisfied and removed from your contract quickly.

There's not much you can do to coax them out of their funk. But you need to protect yourself. Maintain a businesslike posture, making it clear to them and their (probably exasperated) real estate agent that you expect them to abide by the terms of the contract. And by all means, make sure you meet every condition of that agreement on time and to the letter; you don't want to give them any ammunition. But avoid further antagonizing them (as much as you might want to). It simply won't help you get to closing day any faster.

Razzi's Rules to Live By

🏠 That's why you need a contract.

Buyers and sellers commonly hit a rough patch of remorse. Think about why you wanted to sell in the first place, and stick to the terms of the contract.

🏠 Give sentiment its due.

It's only human to grow attached to your home and to feel sad about giving it up. Indulge yourself by taking the time to say good-bye properly. Invite your friends over one last time.

231

⌂ Kids don't always take things in stride.

Your children are in for a lot of changes, and they don't have much say over them. Help them remember their old home—and focus on the excitement of moving to a new one.

⌂ Leave a hint of yourselves behind.

Somewhere in an out-of-the-way nook, have everyone in the family write their initials and the date. Or plant a sapling out back. It helps you say goodbye.

⌂ Go wild taking photographs.

Before you start packing up, take pictures of all the rooms. They can bring back memories later—and help you document insurance losses, if necessary.

⌂ Procrastination only makes it worse.

If seller's remorse has you dragging your feet on moving-related chores, you'll soon discover what stress is all about.

CHAPTER EIGHTEEN

Wrapping It All Up

"A home without a cat—and a well-fed, well-petted
and properly revered cat—may be a home,
perhaps, but how can it prove title?"

MARK TWAIN, *Pudd'nhead Wilson
and Those Extraordinary Twins*

IF ALL GOES WELL—NOT THAT IT ALWAYS DOES, BUT THIS IS AN
ideal scenario—you and the buyer will be equally intent on
making your deal happen without delay. You'll both be attentive
to all the details that need to be wrapped up during the weeks
between contract and closing. And by closing day the only thing
either of you will have to worry about is a temporary case of writer's
cramp, caused by signing and initialing page after page of legal
documents. In a well-managed transaction, there should be no
surprises at the closing table. In fact, in some places, including
California and Hawaii, the actual close of escrow happens without
the parties being physically present at a closing table. Buyers and

sellers sign their respective documents separately and authorize an escrow agent to handle the details on their behalf.

Closing is a simpler transaction on the seller's end than it is on the buyer's, since buyers are typically buying a property *and* taking out a mortgage loan at the same time. All a seller walks away with, usually, is money . . . and a paid-off mortgage.

Nevertheless, the deal isn't done until it's done. It doesn't help that you've probably been living on a diet of take-out for the days leading up to the closing, while all your household necessities were being packed into moving boxes. You very likely have a home purchase of your own to tend to—perhaps even on the same day as your home-sale closing. It's only human to tense up waiting for those dominoes to fall, in smooth succession, so you can move on to the next chapter of your life.

You can take some of the heat off by building a bit of extra time into your schedule. Renting back your old home for a couple of days after closing allows you to schedule the close on your new home a day or two later. That gives you a buffer in case your sale hits a temporary snag (say the buyer's loan documents aren't ready on time for the scheduled closing, or the buyer objects to specious lending fees that were sprung on him at the last minute and wants them removed). If your buyer or the buyer's agent has been operating in a hit-or-miss fashion since first being offered a contract and has been indecisive or slow to get contingencies removed, it's reasonable to think the indecision will continue right to the end. It would be wise for you to build some wiggle room into your own schedule, delaying the close on your new home for a few days, just in case some unexpected drama is brought to the table.

Handing Off the Utilities

About a week before you're scheduled to close and move out, call all of your local utility companies to arrange for service to be turned off. But make sure the utilities remain turned on through the end of your moving-out day! You'll need your electricity, heating or air conditioning, phone, and water. Err on the side of generosity; it won't break the bank to keep the lights on a day or two longer than absolutely necessary. When you check with the utilities, ask about any old deposits you may have placed when you originally set up service. You may be due a refund, which can often be credited to your new account if you'll be using the same utility company.

If you heat your home with fuel oil, you should be credited for the amount of fuel left in your tank at closing; this item should have been addressed in your purchase contract.

Keep your homeowners' insurance in effect for every second that you own the home. In fact, talk with your insurance agent to make sure that, whether under your old policy or a new policy, your belongings remain insured throughout the moving process. Although a homeowners' policy won't cover your belongings while they're traveling across country on a moving van (separate coverage that you can purchase through the moving company covers that), it will cover those precious items that you choose to move by yourself. It will cover you if someone breaks into your minivan at a rest stop and steals the delicate electronics you were moving on your own. Homeowners' policies may even cover you if someone swipes your laptop computer at the airport. In fact, the weeks leading up to your home sale and moving day are a good time to talk about buying any separate riders needed to cover specific high-value items like your jewelry, art, or home-office equipment, which might not be fully covered under your ordinary homeowners' policy.

Preparing for the Big Move

If you have house pets, you should take advantage of the weeks leading up to moving day to get them ready for the transition. Even the calmest pet is going to endure a stressful time and might display some uncharacteristic behavior, such as wandering off or nipping at someone's hand. Make sure your pets are licensed and that their rabies and distemper shots are up-to-date; put the necessary tags on their collars. Keep their vaccination certificates, along with other important papers, handy throughout your move (that tag on the collar is not enough to prove that rabies shots are up-to-date). You might even ask your veterinarian about implanting a tiny microchip just under your dog's or cat's skin. The chip contains an identifying number for your pet. It costs under a hundred dollars to have the chip injected between your pet's shoulder blades and to have the pet's identity registered in a database. Animal-control officers and shelters routinely scan for these chips, which can help reunite you with your lost, stressed-out companion.

If you will be driving any significant distance to your new home, get your vehicles serviced early, so you don't have to worry about them as moving day approaches. Make sure the tires are up to a long trip with a heavy load. If you need to rent a trailer or a cartop luggage carrier, get your reservation in early, particularly in the summertime.

Things to Leave Behind

Don't forget to round up keys to rarely used doors, window locks, or the backyard shed, as well as spare keys left with neighbors, and to turn them over to the new owners (while you're at it, return the neighbors' set of spare keys, so they don't have to wonder what became of them).

Most jurisdictions require that homes be sold with working smoke detectors, and an increasing number of states and cities require carbon-monoxide detectors as well (Massachusetts, Minnesota, and New York City among them). Be sure to leave behind the required smoke and carbon-monoxide detectors, as well as any optional detectors that have been screwed into the wall or ceiling, or which have been hard-wired into the electrical system; those units are now considered part of the building. If you have supplemental carbon-monoxide detectors that simply plug into an electrical outlet and are not required by law, you can take them with you. If you're not sure whether a detector is required where you live, the professional home inspector, your real estate agent, or even the local fire department can tell you.

Buyers will expect you to get rid of old cans of paint and other refuse, particularly difficult-to-dispose-of substances such as pesticides, paint thinner, antifreeze, and the like. But it's considerate to leave behind any good paint that they could use for touch-ups. Just make sure the paint really is in usable condition and that it is clearly labeled, so the buyers don't mistake the yellow paint you used in the kitchen for the yellow paint you used on the clapboard! If in doubt, you might ask their real estate agent if the buyers would like to have the paint.

Leave behind owners' manuals (and purchase receipts, if you have them) for the furnace, air conditioner, water heater, and appliances. A list of names and phone numbers for repair services and contractors that you've used successfully over the years would certainly be appreciated by any newcomer.

It's also a kind touch to leave the bulbs in the light fixtures that you're leaving behind (why some people bother to move these is a mystery to me). And if you can keep an overzealous helper from packing them in your moving boxes, leave behind some paper towels in the kitchen and some toilet paper in the baths. The new owners will thank you on their moving-in day.

Broom Clean?

A sales contract usually specifies that the home will be left in "broom clean" condition when you vacate. Basically, that means that *all* your stuff is gone, and you literally have swept the floors and vacuumed any wall-to-wall carpet. You should, however, take things just a step or two farther.

Of course you will leave in place any window coverings that were specified in your contract (you don't need to have draperies dry-cleaned before the hand-off, as you're sometimes required to do when vacating an apartment). Empty the refrigerator, and wipe down the inside. If the home will remain vacant with the electricity off for more than a day or two, leave the refrigerator door propped open so it doesn't develop a bad smell. Wipe off the kitchen counter and range and quick-mop the kitchen floor. Make sure the inside of the dishwasher is dry, so smells or mold don't develop. And give the garbage disposal one last spin, just to make sure nothing lurks behind. Do a quick wipe-up of the bathrooms on your way out, getting the inside of the medicine cabinets, if necessary. Remove any ashes left in the fireplace. Leave the lawn recently mowed and your trash neatly set out at the curb for pickup (if that's the better part of a week away, you might do your old neighbors a favor and arrange for a quick trip to the dump). The new owners will certainly want to give the home a thorough scrubbing, but you want to leave them *nothing* unpleasant to remember you by. I still harbor not-so-fond memories of the dried-on Jell-O splashes left on the inside of the refrigerator after our last home purchase!

Closing Day

Within a day or two of closing, the buyers will almost certainly request a final walk-through to verify that your home is in the same condition it was in weeks earlier when they decided to buy it. Accompanied by their real estate agent, they will want to ascertain that the items they expect to convey with the home (appliances, window coverings, light fixtures, and so on) are still there. Ideally, the final walk-through will happen after your belongings have been loaded onto a moving truck, but that's not always possible. Do try, at least, to have your moving boxes and furniture arranged neatly, so everyone can get a good look at the walls and floors. If the buyers take issue with the condition of your home, and it's not something you can resolve on the spot ("We thought you'd find those cans of touch-up paint useful, but we'll be happy to get rid of them for you") phone your agent immediately to arrange a get-together with their agent, so the problem gets worked out before it escalates.

Before you head for the closing, make sure you have your photo ID and those of all other homeowners. Also bring your accordion file with all the documents involved in the home sale, so you can get your hands on anything easily should a question pop up. A copy of your pest-inspection report could be handy to have, for example, just in case someone misplaced the one you submitted earlier. Don't forget to bring all your copies of all the keys to the home, and those garage-door openers.

At the closing itself, you and the buyers will receive copies of the HUD-1 form, which is a federally mandated breakout of where all the money goes in a home sale (you'll find a sample copy at the end of this book). Take your time reviewing this document, and ask for explanations of any items that interest you—explaining things is part of the closing agent's job. Although buyers are entitled to an advance look at the HUD-1 before closing (if they request it—and unfortunately, the information is not always available in advance), sellers are not given the same consideration. The first time you see the HUD-1 is probably going to be at the closing.

On the HUD-1 form, the left-hand column details amounts being paid by the buyer; the right-hand column details amounts being paid to the seller, or amounts that will be subtracted from your sales proceeds. Pay particular attention to lines 500 through 520, which detail the fees that will be paid out of your sales

Items to take to closing

- Photo ID for all legal owners

- House keys, including spares and keys for infrequently used locks

- Garage-door openers

- Your forwarding address information (for the closing agent)

- Copies of *all* documuments related to the sale, such as pest-inspection reports and contingency releases

- A dollop of patience

proceeds. Those include any settlement expenses you've agreed to pay for (such as the pest inspection, for example), the amount needed to pay off your mortgage (line 504), and any home-equity loans or lines of credit (line 505). Verify that these are the same amounts that the lender quoted you when you called to ask about your payoff amounts (if you've made extra monthly payments in the interim, adjust accordingly). You'll find the real estate brokerage commission detailed on line 700 (no one will fault you if you whip out your calculator just to double-check that the number actually represents, say, 6 percent of the actual sales price). *Your* bottom line—the amount of cash you walk away with—is on line 603.

The Money: Where Does It Go?

If you are closing on your new home shortly after the sale, you need to keep your funds readily available. Using the same escrow agent, title company, or attorney to handle both transactions will smooth the process, but that decision is not always the seller's. You may ask to have your closing agent arrange for a wire transfer so your sale proceeds go directly to your bank or to the closing agent who will be handling the next transaction. Check with the closing agents involved—and with your bank—to make sure that the funds for your home purchase are available without delay.

If there will be a delay of a few weeks or months between your home sale and the purchase of your new home, arrange for your bank to hold the proceeds in a money-market account, where it will earn a small bit of interest and still be accessible when you need it.

If you have arranged to temporarily rent back your old home, you will get your security deposit back after you have vacated the home and the buyers have verified that you've left it in good condition.

Tying Up the Loose Ends

In the weeks following your sale, keep an eye on the mailbox. Your old mortgage lender should send you a copy of your lien release—a confirmation that the lender has notified your county or city government that it no longer holds a lien against the property you sold. If you don't receive a copy within a month of closing, phone your old mortgage servicer (you'll find the phone number on your old mortgage payment coupons or escrow account statements) and ask when you can expect to receive it. Call your closing agent for good measure, as well. If you don't receive the document within the following two weeks, send a letter to the mortgage company demanding a copy of the lien release. Ask the closing agent to follow up, as well. Stay on top of this easy-to-forget detail, because a lender's sloppiness in recording a release of the lien can cloud the title to that property—and make it more difficult for you to qualify for new credit. Once you get the document, keep it on file with the rest of the papers you signed at closing. Keep that file together with your records dating back to when you first bought the property.

Keeping the IRS Happy

If your profit from the home sale is under that tax-free threshold of $500,000 per married couple/$250,000 per single person, you don't even have to report your home sale to the IRS. Make sure, however, that you're figuring the profit correctly. Reread the rules outlined in chapter 2 for figuring your profit, including how to adjust for profits rolled-over from pre-1997 home sales and for the value of improvements you've made to the home. If your profit exceeds the $500,000/$250,000 threshold, you will need to report the excess as a capital gain.

Filing Address Changes

Don't forget to send your change-of-address information to the IRS. You can't afford to miss any tax refunds—or audit notices! Go to http://www.irs.gov/taxtopics/tc157.html and download a copy of Form 8822, "Address Change Request," which you can mail to the IRS. Uncle Sam *really* hates to lose touch.

While you're at it, you can file a change of address form, effective after moving day, directly with the U.S. Postal Service. Go to https://moversguide.usps.com and enter your personal information so your mail can be forwarded without delay. Of course, you should notify all the people you do business with, including doctors, banks, stockbrokers, and the publishers of your favorite magazines, of your new address.

If you will continue to do business with the same bank after the move, all you have to do is to notify them of your impending change of address and order a new batch of checks with that new address. If your move includes a change to a new bank, set up the accounts before your move, so everything is ready to go as soon as you relocate.

Razzi's Rules to Live By

🏠 Closing should be simple.
Your goal is to have all the details wrapped up well ahead of the actual closing of the deal.

🏠 Build in some slack.
Try to schedule closing so you have a few days between the sale of your old home and the purchase of the new one. Rent back your old home for a few days, if necessary.

🏠 Drama is not a part-time vocation.

If the buyers (or their agent) have been hit-or-miss about the details all through this deal, it's only logical to expect that behavior to continue right through closing day. Brace yourself—and build extra time into your schedule.

🏠 Keep the lights on!

When you arrange for your utilities to be cut off, be absolutely sure they'll remain turned on through the very end of your moving-out day.

🏠 Guard against insurance gaps.

Make sure your homeowners' policy remains in force every second you own that home. And make sure that either your old or your new policy covers your belongings while you're moving them between homes.

🏠 Take a rider.

This is the perfect time to make sure that your homeowners' policy includes any extra riders necessary to cover your most valuable possessions.

🏠 Get the dog, the cat, and the car ready for the move.

Each of them will be bearing more stress than usual—so get them checked out and ready.

🏠 Be kind to your buyers.

Leave your home as tidy as possible, and leave behind contact information for good plumbers and other repair people. If you're lucky, the kindness will be repaid to you by the people vacating your new home!

⌂ Understand the HUD-1.

Take the time to ask questions when reviewing this document, which spells out exactly where all the money goes in the home-sale deal.

⌂ Watch the mailbox.

Keep an eye out for the lien release from your old lender. And make sure the IRS—and everyone else—knows how to get in touch with you.

⌂ Set up checking accounts early.

Have your new, updated checkbook ready to roll by moving day.

CHAPTER NINETEEN

Moving On

"Home is where the heart is and hence a
movable feast."

ANGELA CARTER, *My Father's House*

R EPUTATION IS THE ONLY THING THAT MATTERS WHEN IT
comes to hiring movers. It is far more important than
price. Step back and think about exactly what you are
doing: You are calling in a crew of strangers to load practically
everything you own—your furniture, rugs, books, china, pots and
pans, toys, tools, clothing, electronics—onto a large truck. With
your blessing, they will drive away with all of it, leaving you with
nothing but a piece of paper (sure, it's one important piece of
paper, but it's only as good as the company behind it). They may
even load several homes' worth of belongings into that same truck
before they drive it, perhaps a very long distance, to your new
home. Along the way they may drop off individual loads belonging
to other people, much the same way a bus deposits its passengers at
different corners. And you'd better be ready to receive everything on
moving-in day, or they can put all your belongings in storage and
charge dearly by the day until you can accept delivery.

To top it all off, the law actually allows movers to refuse to unload your belongings if you don't pay up right there at your new doorstep. And the amount you owe can legitimately go quite a bit higher than the amount written on your estimate. Even if you have a written *binding* estimate, extra fees can be added to the bill. If you have a written *nonbinding* estimate, you should assume the final fee will be higher than it states.

The rules outlined in this chapter are issued by the Federal Motor Carrier Safety Administration, and apply only to interstate moves. They don't apply to same-state and local moves (even moves that cross state lines within one metropolitan area, such as a move from Brooklyn, New York, to Hackensack, New Jersey, are considered local moves, and are not covered by the federal rules). Your best bet—whether your move is across town or across continent, is to understand the rules and apply your best consumer vigilance to the entire transaction. You want problem-free, professional service at a predictable price, and that's not too much to ask. The best way to find it is to deal only with reputable movers, whether interstate or local. And give the movers as much information as possible about the weight and value of your belongings and the accessibility of your new home.

Using a Referral Service

Internet-based referral services such as those accessed through www.Move.com and www.RealEstate.com can be helpful for getting *ballpark* estimates of your moving expenses, plus referrals to companies that you might consider doing business with. But that should simply be the starting point for your investigation. You absolutely must evaluate each moving company on your own, and insist that they send someone to your home to prepare a thorough, written estimate of their fees. Ask for references to at least three recent clients, and follow up with a phone call to ask about their experience with that mover.

Educating Yourself

Even the terminology they use tells you that the world of moving companies isn't in sync with the world of consumers. They throw around words that are commonly understood by the guy managing the loading dock of your local Wal-Mart or Home Depot, but not by most people who shop there. For example, you don't have a contract or a receipt for your belongings; you have a *bill of lading*. Your Oriental rug is a *high-value article* because it's worth more than a hundred dollars per pound. When the mover says, "Hey, lady, you didn't tell me there were steps leading to your front door," he adds a *flight charge* to your bill. When you ask the movers to pack or unpack boxes or crates, you're buying *accessorial services* (and you'll be billed for the boxes and Bubble Wrap, too). When the movers tell you the streets in your townhouse development are too narrow to accommodate their big truck, they will bring in a small truck to carry your stuff to the big truck and will charge you for *impracticable operations*.

To learn more about this strange world, go to the Web site, run by the federal government, www.ProtectYourMove.gov, and read the consumer-friendly advice posted there. (Well, they try to be consumer friendly. After all, it's a document about laws written by regulators.) You can download from the site a copy of the sixty-two-page brochure "Your Rights and Responsibilities When You Move," which interstate movers are required to give consumers. Same-state and local movers aren't required to, but understanding it will help you know what kind of service to ask of them. And it helps to have the information sooner rather than later.

Here's what you can generally expect for interstate moves, depending on whether you have a binding estimate or a nonbinding one:

Binding estimate: Just as the name implies, this is a firm price based on the quantity of goods the mover has agreed to ship and the services you've requested. You'll pay more if you request additional services (packing/unpacking, etc.) or if the mover encounters impracticable operations (again, conditions that require extra work, such as a freight elevator being out of service on moving day). You will be expected to pay up to 15 percent extra on the doorstep for impracticable operations; anything beyond that is supposed to be billed to you and payable within thirty days.

Nonbinding estimate: If you get a written, nonbinding estimate from the mover, your actual charges will be based on the weight of your shipment plus the cost of extra services. You have a right to accompany the truck to an official scale and to request a reweigh, if you wish. When the movers arrive at your new doorstep, they can demand payment for as much as 10 percent more than the nonbinding estimate (assuming the weight justifies the charges, of course). Anything above that 10 percent will be billed to you. They will also demand payment, right at your doorstep, for any additional services you requested (packing/unpacking, etc.). On top of that you will be expected to pay up to 15 percent extra for any impracticable operations (those narrow streets) that turn up, with any cost beyond that billed to you and payable within thirty days.

Before you sign a contract for services from a mover, clarify exactly which forms of payment they will accept on moving day.

Some will accept credit cards (verify that they take the one you plan to use), but others require a certified check, money order, cashier's check, or cash. They will *not* generally take an ordinary check.

Scam Artists

Unfortunately, there are some fly-by-night movers out there who take advantage of uninformed consumers by offering cheap over-the-phone or over-the-Internet quotes. ("A one-bedroom apartment? We'll move that for a thousand dollars. Our truck will be there Tuesday morning.") Once their goods arrive at the new doorstep, however, consumers find that the bills are several times higher than the quoted amount. At this point, the owner has two choices: pay the bill or watch the goods go into storage where they will rack up steep daily fees. Some of these movers have been prosecuted for deliberately scamming people with intentionally low-balled quotes, but such enforcement happens after the fact. Calling the local police because the movers are in your driveway, refusing to unload your belongings until you pay their larger-than-expected bill probably won't help; the police may be limited in what they can do at that point (it's not as if a crooked mover won't have a good story about how you added a couple of extra double dressers to your load). Remember, the law allows movers to refuse to unload until you pay.

Keep all of the documentation related to your move with you throughout the process. Your folder should include your written estimate, the bill of lading, your inventory list (signed or initialed by the mover and you), and the insurance/liability documents provided by your mover. Make sure you have the telephone number for your moving company, as well as the identification or registration number the mover has assigned to your load. Above all, don't let this critical folder find its way onto the moving truck!

Insuring Your Load

Never try to economize by skimping on insurance for the belongings you're sending away with a mover. If ever the phrase "penny wise and pound foolish" were appropriate, it's with regard to movers' liability coverage. The bare-minimum version, which movers include at no extra charge, covers you for only sixty cents per pound. That's right, sixty cents per pound. You can't even buy lettuce for sixty cents a pound — maybe cabbage. So, if you would be content replacing your lost or damaged dining room furniture with a load of cabbage, go ahead and skimp on moving insurance. They've gotcha covered. This pennies-per-pound coverage is called "released value protection." Avoid it.

With interstate movers, you only get that cabbage-equivalent coverage if you sign away your right to purchase additional protection. The movers will offer you either "full-value protection" (which might cost $250 on a load worth $25,000, according to a very inexact example published by the Federal Motor Carrier Safety Administration), which requires them to repair, replace, or pay for lost or damaged items. Or the movers will offer a separate insurance policy as an alternative to full-value protection. If you purchase that outside insurance offered through the moving company, the movers are responsible only for the sixty-cents-per-pound value; the insurance policy picks up the rest. Whatever you choose, demand documentation of the policy from your movers. It's also important that you declare any items of "extraordinary value" such as jewelry (which you really ought to carry yourself), silverware, china, furs, antiques,

Oriental rugs, or computer software, so you can be sure it's covered, even if it increases your expense. When it comes to insurance, either you're covered or you're not. There's not much in-between.

Moving Day

On moving day, track every box that goes onto the truck. If the mover does not give you an inventory sheet, make one yourself, and don't let anything slip by. When the movers arrive at your new home, have someone inspect every box that comes off the truck, and direct the movers to the room where it belongs. Movers work in a hurry; keep track of the boxes! And if any boxes or pieces of

Things you cannot send with movers:

- propane tanks used for your gas grill

- fireworks, ammunition, kerosene, charcoal, charcoal lighter fluid, batteries (whether for the car or your flashlight), and other explosive or flammable substances

- pool chemicals, laundry bleach, cleaning solvents, aerosols

- paint (latex or oil-based)

- lawn chemicals, including fertilizers, pesticides, and weed killers

- fire extinguishers

- perishable food

- houseplants

furniture look as if they've been handled roughly, give them a good inspection before you sign off on their receipt. Note damages right on the inventory form, and make sure the movers sign or initial it.

Keep a cooler full of cold soft drinks available for your family and the movers on moving day. And be ready to tip the moving crew when they unload your belongings, especially if they take extra care to avoid dinging your furniture and walls, or if they provide other extra services. Between twenty-five and fifty dollars per person, depending on the size of the crew and the weight of your stuff, is reasonable.

Moving Electronics

If your home is like mine, it could be mistaken for a sidewalk sale at RadioShack. We have multiple computers, printers, televisions, stereos, speakers, and lesser items, plus boxes full of cables and various widgets that make the black boxes talk to each other. Not all of this stuff travels gracefully.

Your first step is to assume the worst will happen. Back up every bit of computerized information that you value. If necessary, invest in an external hard drive for the computer so you can make a backup of your important data. Other options are burning files to CDs or filing them on large-capacity ZIP drives or on small flash-memory drives. However you do it, make sure you have copies of all your digital photos, downloaded music, tax returns, financial records, e-mail address books, and work-related documents. Then be sure to keep that backup away from the machine itself. Store it at your office, your mother-in-law's home, or the bank's safe-deposit box. Only after backing up everything can you begin to prepare your electronic gear for the move. This is plain, old-fashioned, eat-

Things you should not send with movers:

- Keepsakes. The children's baby teeth, their first snippets of hair, Great-grandma's embroidery, home videos, photo albums, your Joe Montana autograph, Grandpa's woodworking tools, and so on. If it would break your heart to lose it, move it yourself.

- Important papers. Cash, bonds, stock certificates, passports, birth/death/divorce certificates, contracts, insurance policies, deeds, car titles, papers related to your recent home sale and purchase, the mover's contract and estimate, and so on.

- Electronics. The big-screen TV may be too unwieldy to move yourself, but you may as well take charge of the portable electronics. Computers (especially laptops), external drives, small televisions, all types of cameras, stereo equipment, iPods, and video games will all travel well in the back of your own vehicle.

- Comfort and convenience items. You may encounter an unexpected wait for your belongings to arrive at your new home. A couple of inflatable mattresses with sheets, blankets, and pillows will help you avoid having to pay hotel bills. Towels, a couple of lamps, a coffee pot, and toaster oven will let you make do for a while. Don't forget the can and bottle openers, corkscrew, and a decent knife. Keep your first-aid kit handy to deal with moving-day cuts and scrapes. Also pack one telephone with an answering machine.

- Children's security items. They *need* their blankie, favorite toy, going-away photo book, Game Boy, favorite clothes, pillow, and medicine whether they're fifteen months or fifteen years old. They just call their comfort items by grown-up names when they get older (go ahead, pack your favorite pillow in the car, too).

- Simple tool kit with hammer, screwdrivers (Phillips and flat heads), pliers, adjustable wrench, masking tape, duct tape, and WD-40 lubricant. Don't forget to add flashlights, scissors, a utility knife, note pads, and waterproof markers. If you have room to haul them, a vacuum and some cleaning supplies would be nice to have *before* the movers arrive.

- Pet necessities. Of course Fido and Fluffy are traveling with you (unless you've arranged for special shipment by airline). But don't forget their food, medicines, carriers, crates, beds, toys, dishes, leashes, immunization records, and so on. This little move of yours may be the most stressful event of their lives, and items that smell like home will help calm them. Just in case the unthinkable happens and they wander off, have a photograph that you could use on a flyer to help get them back.

- Firearms can be carried on moving trucks, but they require special treatment. Make sure you discuss this issue with your movers, so unloaded weapons can be accounted for and kept secure. Confirm that the weapons are legal in the town you are moving to.

your-spinach advice, yet it can take hours to do and is easy to overlook in the rush of preparing for a big household move.

It's safest to transport computer and electronic parts in their original boxes, but if they're not available, your moving company can sell you boxes strong enough to handle the load, along with foam peanuts, Bubble Wrap, and anything else you need to make the gear secure. Talk this over well in advance with your movers. Find out what special hoops they want you to jump through regarding the packing of electronics, so they can't void any claim for damage when the truck arrives at your new home.

Mayflower Transit recommends that you turn off televisions and other electronics for at least twenty-four hours before transport (and keep them off for twenty-four hours after arrival) so the items can reach room temperature, reducing the risk of damage. You may also need to get a pro to help you pack up a plasma TV for shipping. Talk it over with the people who sold you the television, and with the movers, as soon as you start to make your moving plans. Keep any papers *anyone* gives you about moving these items, just in case a dispute erupts over damages.

Large zippered plastic storage bags, indelible markers, and mailing tape can help you keep track of the various remote controls, connector cables, and battery-charging stations that go with your devices. Pack each set of accessories in its own bag, label it clearly, and tape the bag to the back of the device. If you have a particularly intricate web of multicolored cables plugged into the back of a device, take a close-up photo of the arrangement before you start pulling plugs. Tape labels to individual cables if you think you might get confused when it's time to put the web back together again. On second thought, just assume you'll get confused, and label everything.

Razzi's Rules to Live By

🏠 Reputation is all that matters.

You're calling in strangers to load everything you own onto a truck and drive it away. You need to know they're trustworthy.

🏠 Get an estimate in person, and in writing.

Only do business with movers who will come to your home to see your belongings and provide a written estimate of the fee.

🏠 The law is on their side.

It's actually legal for a mover to refuse to unload your belongings until you have paid the bill, in cash or an equivalent, right at the doorstep.

🏠 Insure yourself to the hilt.

Buy all the extra insurance you can get from the moving company, and make sure your homeowners' policy remains in effect to cover the items you move yourself.

🏠 Don't risk heartbreak.

If it has great value—and especially great sentimental value—find a way to move that item yourself.

🏠 Go camping.

Be prepared to rough it, in relative comfort, for a few days in your new home before the moving van arrives.

🏠 Secure the electronics.

Back up *all* your data, make a note of how everything's plugged together, keep track of the accessories, and pack it all with great care.

Afterword

A HOME SALE IS USUALLY TRIGGERED BY SOME OTHER MAJOR transition in our lives—a new job, new family, increased income, the desire to try out life in another part of the country. There are the sales triggered by deep personal losses, as well. I hope that the advice offered in these chapters helps smooth your transition to that new chapter in your life. Here's wishing you wonderful luck with your effort, and all the best in your new home! At any time, please feel free to visit my Web site, www.fearleeshome.com, where you'll find updates and an e-mail link for your questions and comments.

Appendices

Razzi's Rules to Live By

🏠 We can't always time our home sale.

Life events such as marriage, job transfers, divorce, illness, and death dictate when we must sell a home, regardless of whether it's a buyer's or seller's market.

🏠 Selling now may preserve future gains.

If your profit on a home sale would hit $500,000 as a married couple or $250,000 as a single person, selling now would reset the meter and allow future profits to go untaxed as well.

🏠 Buyers bloom in the springtime.

It's the peak season for selling because buyers like to get the deal settled in time for a summer move. Homes also tend to look their best in spring. There's another brief spurt of interest between Labor Day and Halloween.

🏠 Snowbirds are serious.

The few buyers who are out looking at homes during winter tend to be serious buyers who *need* to complete a deal. But they'll drive a hard bargain, too.

🏠 Selling first is safest, financially.

Selling your old home before buying a new one is the safest course for your money. But you may have to compromise on the selection of your new home.

🏠 A bridge will take you there.

If you're truly determined not to give up your current home unless you find the perfect replacement, you may have to buy first. A bridge loan (often simply a home-equity line of credit) can help you make the jump.

🏠 Six months' inventory is key.

That's the dividing line separating a balanced market from a market favoring buyers or sellers. If selling everything on the market would take about six months, it's a balanced market. If it would take less time, it's a seller's market. If it would take more time, it's a buyer's market. Ask your agent for a market reading.

🏠 Watch for signs of a shifting market.

You'll make the most money if you react quickly to a market that's shifting from one that favors buyers to one that favors sellers, or vice versa. Hold out for a better price if the sellers are getting the upper hand; cut your price fast for a quick sale in a market where buyers are gaining an edge.

🏠 It's just an opinion.

Even experienced real estate agents can only give you an educated opinion on an appropriate asking price. The best they can do is to try to read the market, and sometimes they don't get it quite right.

🏠 Real estate agents are optimists.

They have to be, or they wouldn't choose to make a living as self-employed entrepreneurs in a sales-oriented field. Just remember that while they're gushing about the prospects of selling your home at top dollar.

🏠 You need price estimates from at least three agents.

Requesting them is a regular part of the listing interview.

🏠 Sales price doesn't determine profit.

At least not alone. The price you paid for your home matters just as much as the price you sell it for.

🏠 Roll-over, you're dead.

Tax rules no longer force you to trade up to a more expensive home in order to avoid paying tax on part of your home-sale profit.

🏠 Half a million ain't what it used to be.

Even though tax laws allow a married couple to keep up to $500,000 and singles to keep up to $250,000 in home-sale profit tax free, you could find yourself exceeding that thanks to today's home prices. That's especially true if you have old, untaxed home profits from homes sold before 1997.

🏠 Timing counts with the IRS.

That $500,000/$250,000 tax break on home-sale profit is available to you only if you've owned and lived in the home for two of the five years leading up to the sale.

🏠 The IRS sometimes makes exceptions.

You may still qualify for part of the $500,000/$250,000 tax break even if you lived in the home less than two years, under the following conditions: your home sale was forced by major events or circumstances such as military service, job relocation, the birth of twins or other multiples, job loss, divorce, illness, or death.

🏠 The IRS gives you a break on death and taxes.

If you inherit a home, you don't face a tax bill for capital gain that built up over the years before ownership shifted to you.

🏠 Remodeling investments count, too.

Hang on to records, contracts, and receipts for all your remodeling jobs over the years. They count toward your basis in the home—the total amount you've invested—and can lower the amount of home-sale profit that you might owe tax on years from now.

🏠 Save by tracking expenses.

Home-sale expenses such as real estate commissions and lawyers' fees are subtracted from the sales price to arrive at your net proceeds—the number that really counts.

🏠 Don't forget your refinance points.

Now's the time to deduct any points from a mortgage refinance that you haven't already deducted on your income tax returns.

🏠 Moving costs might be tax-deductible.

If you take a new job that's at least fifty miles farther from your old home than your old job was, you can claim an income-tax deduction for moving expenses.

⌂ The minute you decide to sell your home, it stops being your home.

It becomes nothing more than a dolled-up object in a department-store display. Scour yourself out of the picture.

⌂ Fix it, finally.

All those little jobs that you've been meaning to do need to be done now, and all the little flaws that have grown practically invisible to you need to be repaired before fresh eyes examine your home. You don't want those minor flaws sending a major message to potential buyers.

⌂ Keep up with the Joneses.

If buyers shopping in your neighborhood and price range expect to find at least three full bathrooms, but yours has only one or two, spending the money to bring your home up to par could result in a big payoff.

⌂ Don't overdo it.

Don't commit to a major remodeling just in preparation for sale. Usually you won't recover the full investment—but you *will* undergo the full hassle.

⌂ Let kitchens and baths shine.

They're the key to buyers' hearts, and they take the heaviest day-to-day wear. Focus your presale improvements on these areas.

⌂ You can get diplomacy from your friends.

But when you're paying good money to a real estate agent, you deserve the cold truth about flaws in the home you're trying to sell.

🏠 Follow real estate's golden rule:

Disclose unto others as you'd have them disclose unto you. If your home has a flaw that would affect a buyer's decision to buy and/or the price they'd pay, then you must disclose that to the buyer—or risk a legal tussle.

🏠 A new furnace is *not* a hot button.

Don't expect buyers to get too excited about your new furnace, roof, or other utility. They expect these things to be in working order. But putting money into a repair or replacement can remove a flaw.

🏠 Let the buyers do the inspection.

Don't spend a few hundred dollars on an inspection before putting a home up for sale. Savvy buyers will want their own inspection anyway, and you can use that money for any needed repairs.

🏠 A warranty is a sales tool.

Home-repair warranties typically have frustrating exclusions and exceptions, making them a mediocre deal for homeowners. They're better thought of as a sales tool, a little extra that might reassure a buyer.

🏠 Be ready for evening drive-bys.

Buyers often drive past in the evening just to see if your home is a candidate. Leave lights on in the front rooms and outdoors so they can see it at its best. Homes without curb appeal don't stand a chance.

🏠 Green thumbs bring greenbacks.

Put some time and money into making the front lawn look as good as possible, even if all that beautifully manicured green stuff is nothing but weeds.

🏠 Be merciless about clutter.

You need to get rid of junk that isn't worth its keep; store unneeded belongings off-site, and put unsightly necessities out of view.

🏠 Clean with a vengeance.

Clean homes look good and smell good. And they sell faster and for more money.

🏠 Spruce up until you no longer want to leave.

That's the sign that you're ready to invite buyers in so they can fall in love with it, too.

🏠 Notice what's *not* there in magazine pictures.

Homes look best without necessities like dish racks, toothbrushes, and toasters. Put them away.

🏠 Assume that Fido and Fluffy smell.

Visitors will pick up scents that you've naturally grown accustomed to, so be diligent in eradicating pet scents.

🏠 Set the stage.

Remove items that don't add to that glossy-home-magazine setting, and rearrange belongings so they tell a lovely domestic tale. Buy (or borrow) items, if necessary; the investment will pay off.

🏠 You deserve Cadillac service.

After all, the commission on a $500,000 home is roughly the list price on a brand new luxury car. Kick the tires!

🏠 You pay the buyer's agent.

Then again, it could be argued that the buyer pays everybody's agent. Regardless, the commission comes off the top. And sellers have more incentive to shop for a lower commission.

⌂ Broad exposure is key.

Real estate agents and brokers may think they own your listing information—but you should insist that they publicize it anywhere and everywhere possible.

⌂ Discounters, referrals, and rebates, oh my!

Take a look at the broad array of discount brokers, referral/rebate services, and flat-fee listing companies available to sellers. You could save, especially if you're willing to take on part of the workload.

⌂ Your first negotiation is with the agent.

If you're paying Cadillac prices, you should at least try to get something off the sticker price.

⌂ Practice saying "no thanks."

Don't let your good manners get you saddled with an inexperienced agent who just happens to be the son-in-law of your neighbor's best friend. Everybody knows *somebody* in the real estate business, but you need to find the one-in-a-million agent who can best represent you.

⌂ Find out who else is on the team.

Before you sign a listing agreement with an agent, ask if the agent will delegate many tasks to an assistant. Find out who will be on duty to help you when your agent is tied up. Teamwork is fine—as long as you know who's in the lineup.

🏠 Chat up the references.

Ask for the phone numbers of the agent's three most recent clients. Then take the time to call them and ask for details about their experience. Give heed to even slightly negative comments; remember, most people want to be polite and positive.

🏠 Ask the magic question:

"Would you hire this agent again?" Then be quiet and wait for your answer. Hesitation or qualifiers like "probably" are *not* what you want to hear.

🏠 Designations aren't magic.

But they're a sign that the agent has invested more than the minimum time and effort in training.

🏠 Personality counts.

If you list with an agent who has a grating personality, or who's inattentive to detail, it will increase your anxiety—and possibly drive away buyers' agents.

🏠 Breaking up is hard to do.

But if your agent is not performing up to reasonable expectations, ask the broker to assign your listing to another agent. Your contract is actually with the brokerage, after all.

🏠 Matchmakers can help.

Online referral services can put you in touch with agents and may even earn you some rebates. But you still need to do your own reference check before signing on with one of the recommended agents.

🏠 The listing isn't really about selling your home.

It's about engaging the services of a real estate agent. At its heart, the listing is an outline of what the agent is supposed to do and what you're supposed to pay.

🏠 You're not on the same side yet.

When the agent presents you with a listing contract awaiting your signature, keep in mind that you're actually in negotiations with him over the terms of his employment. You want a low commission and a short commitment; the agent wants a high commission and a long commitment. Negotiate from there.

🏠 Some homes sell quickly, some sell slowly.

Expensive, unique properties typically take longer to sell, even in a strong market. You can expect the agent to insist on a longer listing period for them.

🏠 Nail down the marketing plan.

Thoroughly review exactly how the agent plans to go about selling your home before you sign a listing. Get specifics, including examples the agent has used for homes similar to yours.

🏠 Romance sells.

Some agents are better than others at recognizing the special qualities in a home and selling the romance. You'll see it in their brochures, ads, and online presentations.

🏠 Good photos are a must.

Most buyers start shopping over the Internet. Insist on good quality, in-focus photos in all the marketing materials, and virtual tours whenever possible.

🏠 Look pretty for your debut.

Insist that all the marketing materials, photos, virtual tours, and flyers be ready to go the minute your home is placed on the MLS. "Photo coming soon" is never a good first impression.

🏠 Beware the pocket listing.

It does you no good for the agent to keep news of your new listing confined to the office for the first few days, hoping to score a profitable in-house sale. Don't tolerate it.

🏠 Be a dream seller.

Once you've found your top-notch agent, follow her advice. Do whatever you can to spiff up your home and accommodate showings. Make copies of all important records available to her.

🏠 Talk prenup before the wedding.

Sometimes sellers change their minds and don't want to go through with the deal. Before you sign the listing contract, ask what would happen if, hypothetically of course, you were to change your mind and want out of the deal.

🏠 There are two prices for your home.

And you set only one of them—the asking price. The market will set the sales price.

🏠 Setting the asking price is an art.

And some agents are better artists than others. It's actually your job to set the asking price, with their advice.

🏠 Some pricing approaches are worthless.

Don't use these as your basis for an asking price: the profit you need to clear; the amount you spent on remodeling; the price your

270

neighbor got last year; your tax assessment; an online estimate. The only thing that matters is *today's* supply and demand.

⌂ A Magic 8-Ball could set your price.

But "signs point to yes" isn't very specific advice. Nor are the price estimates offered by online services such as www.Zillow.com and www.RealEstateABC.com. But check them anyway, if only so you can negotiate intelligently with a buyer who has already "Zillowed" your home.

⌂ Flattery sells.

Enjoy the real estate agent's flattery, but don't put too much stock in it. Compliments help agents sell you on their services. Buyers will be more critical.

⌂ Don't let an agent "buy" your listing.

Some agents may try to secure your listing by suggesting that your home will sell for significantly more than the price other agents recommend. Be wary if one agent's suggested price is out of line with competing agents' estimates.

⌂ Don't swing at low balls.

Some agents aren't willing to put the time into marketing a properly priced home. If they lowball the price and sell it fast, they can move on to other listings. That's another reason to seek out several listing presentations.

⌂ Fresh sells fastest.

Setting the right asking price is critical because interest in your home peaks when it first appears on the market. Catch the buyers right away with the right price.

🏠 Tailor your strategy to a changing market.

Find out from your agent whether prices are rising, falling, or stable, and plan your pricing strategy accordingly.

🏠 Close your ears to nationwide trends.

You're not selling nationwide. The only thing that matters is supply and demand for homes in your town, your neighborhood, and your price range.

🏠 Falling prices scare buyers as much as they scare sellers.

Buyers worry that prices will continue to fall after they've made their investment. You have to convince them that they're getting a bargain.

🏠 Do your own market research.

Get out and visit open houses and new-home developments that represent your competition. That's the best way to get a good feel for prices.

🏠 You don't owe any agent her supper.

You have a right to sell your home without a real estate agent. Don't let miffed agents dissuade you.

🏠 Judge agents by how they treat you.

Savvy agents are kind to FSBO sellers because they know that many of them end up listing with an agent. Keep in touch with agents who are helpful when you're on the other side of the fence.

🏠 Ask yourself if you're really cut out for the job.

Be honest when assessing whether you have the time, skill, and temperament to take on the work.

⌂ Be open-minded about commissions.

Are you really going to turn away a buyer who expects you to pick up his agent's 3 percent commission?

⌂ Be skeptical about horror stories.

Selling on your own will *not* cut your price by 16 percent—at least not if you do your homework.

⌂ Don't play bait and switch with agents.

Don't fib about your intentions to list just so you can get price opinions from agents. Do be up-front and tell them you intend to sell FSBO, and then accept any help they offer.

⌂ Buy the services you need.

Signs, contracts, advertising, and even MLS postings can be obtained without signing on with a full-service agent.

⌂ Be a shameless promoter.

You're trying to sell an item with a price tag in the hundreds of thousands of dollars. This is no time to be shy.

⌂ Go disposable.

Protect your privacy by using a pay-as-you-go cell-phone number and setting up a special e-mail account for publicizing your home.

⌂ Get all over the Internet.

The vast majority of buyers start their home search online, so you *need* to have a Web page—with lots of gorgeous photos.

⌂ Signs still sell homes.

And cheap signs make your home look cheap. Spring for the best-looking sign you can afford, and keep it stocked with flyers.

🏠 Sell the sizzle.

Find your home's emotional hook, and stress it in all your advertising.

🏠 Set up your home-sale reception area.

Have a little spot just inside the door where buyers can sign in and gather information.

🏠 Give that guy a contract!

Have a blank contract, prepared by your lawyer, on hand to offer to buyers. It will reassure them that you know how handle the deal.

🏠 Disclose, disclose, disclose.

Make sure buyers receive all the disclosures (regarding property condition, lead paint, and so on) required by law. Disclosures protect you from legal woes.

🏠 Don't talk to strangers.

Don't lead them on a tour of your home, anyway. Get good contact information for every buyer who asks to see your home. A cell-phone number and e-mail address aren't enough to protect you.

🏠 Home alone? Not you.

Always make sure someone is at home with you when you're showing the home to buyers.

🏠 Buyer-proof the place.

Easily pilfered valuables, prescription drugs, handguns: get them out of the house before you let buyers in.

🏠 Smile.

Force yourself to smile when you talk with buyers over the phone. It helps keep your tone light and friendly.

🏠 Follow up obsessively.

Contact buyers promptly after they make an inquiry or tour your home, and anytime you sweeten the deal.

🏠 Buyers won't bother with a home they think is overpriced.

They don't like to haggle with someone who's unaware of going prices—or too stubborn to care.

🏠 Markets can shift quickly.

A big shift in interest rates, layoff announcements, or a turnaround in the stock market can draw buyers into the market or keep them away.

🏠 Buyers aren't logical about rates.

At least not always. When rates start to rise, there's a temporary increase in home sales—from buyers who are startled off the sidelines by fear of increases yet to come.

🏠 Builders' incentives are tough to beat.

But you have to try. Builders throw in interest-rate subsidies or free upgrades to hurry along sales in a slow market. You may have to offer your own incentives to compete with them.

🏠 Nearly new homes have benefits, too.

Everyone seems to love the fresh, new thing on the housing market. Point out to buyers that your nearly new home can make their lives easier thanks to the little improvements you've already made.

🏠 Offer cheaper interest rates.

You can pay points to lower a buyer's interest rate. They'll get the tax savings, too.

🏠 Find a battle-tested real estate agent.

Look for an agent who survived the last tough housing market in your area. That agent may know some hard-learned tricks that can get your home sold.

🏠 Sweeten the deal for buyers' agents.

A healthy share of the commission or a bonus can help your home attract attention.

🏠 Desperation drives away dollars.

If you need to sell fast, the surest way is to slash the price.

🏠 Welcome the open house.

Even though most open houses don't actually yield a buyer for that particular home, they remain a good way to get people looking at the place. You want as much exposure as possible; you never know who has a friend who has a friend who'd like your home.

🏠 Get on the brokers' tour.

You definitely want to be included in the special open house for local real estate brokers and agents as soon as your home comes on the market. Make sure your agent provides an attractive spread to entice them.

🏠 Love the lockbox.

It gives local brokers and agents a way into your home even if you and your agent aren't available to let them in. It's one way to snare the best kind of buyer—the one who falls in love right at the curb, and who needs a home *now*.

⌂ Every day is *the* day.

You never know if this is the day your buyer will discover your home. Leave it in ready-for-company shape every morning, with the drapes open and the lights on.

⌂ Lock it or lose it.

With all these strangers traipsing through your home, make sure your valuables are locked up safely.

⌂ Forget about manners.

Try your best to accommodate agents' last-minute requests to show the house. You don't want to let a buyer slip out of your hands . . . and into someone else's.

⌂ No escort, no showing.

Say no to unaccompanied buyers. It's simply too dangerous to allow someone in who hasn't been screened and accompanied by an agent. They're not likely to be serious buyers, anyway.

⌂ Find somewhere else to be.

Get out of the house while an agent is showing it. Otherwise, if prospective buyers have any manners at all, they'll be uncomfortable poking around your home—and they won't start to imagine themselves living there.

⌂ Warm up to criticism.

When buyers start noting drawbacks to your home, they're starting to envision life there. It's actually good news, though it's tough to hear. That's another reason you want to leave for showings . . . the criticism will be less restrained.

⌂ Listen to the market.

If your home lingers on the market with few showings, few follow-ups and no offers, the market is telling you that your home isn't competitive with others—at least not at its current price.

⌂ Get the most out of price reductions.

A significant price reduction on your home should spark some urgency among buyers, just like a one-day sale at the mall.

⌂ Cutting the price isn't your only weapon.

You could offer extra incentives to buyers' agents, throw in a bonus to buyers, offer a home-repair warranty, buy down the interest rate, subsidize closing costs, or offer seller financing or a rent-with-option-to-buy contract.

⌂ Take a sabbatical.

If there's been minimal interest in your home, consider taking a break from the market when your listing contract expires. Rethink your marketing plan, and polish the property. Then give it another go with a fresh, new listing.

⌂ Consider shopping for a new agent.

Three-month listing agreements are great because they don't tie you down seemingly forever to an agent who is less capable than you'd thought.

⌂ Auctions build urgency.

If buyers know your home is going to be sold at auction on a specific date, that can be enough to drum up interest from buyers afraid to let it slip away from them.

🏠 Squelch the cringe.

Auctions are *not* just for foreclosures and tax delinquencies. Tell the neighbors your finances are fine—and invite them to the auction.

🏠 Auctioneers don't dawdle.

Everything happens on a tight schedule. Advertising lasts only a few weeks, bidding may last only a few minutes, and buyers are expected to close within 30 days.

🏠 Buyers expect a bargain.

Buyers, many of them investors, are attracted to auctions by the chance of getting a below-market price. Setting a low reserve, or forgoing a reserve altogether, attracts more bidders and can boost your price.

🏠 You start with a big check.

You pay all advertising costs up-front, and can expect to pay fees and commissions even if the property doesn't sell.

🏠 You're dealing with a fast-talker, after all.

Before hiring an auction company, talk to clients who've sold homes like yours, review the details of the advertising plan, and get a full explanation of all fees that will be charged to you and to the buyer.

🏠 Prepare to tango.

It takes two to negotiate a final deal that's acceptable to all concerned. A round or two of offers and counteroffers will help you work out the finer points.

🏠 The offer could disappear.

A buyer can withdraw an offer anytime before you sign it.

🏠 Terms are as important as price.

Details like closing dates and rent-back agreements can be as important as dollars.

🏠 The agent wants to see you sign a contract.

Agents may be of limited help when you're trying to decide whether to make a counteroffer. After all, they have a vested interest in seeing you and the buyer come to terms before the deal slips away—and their payday with it.

🏠 Get as good as you give.

In negotiations, try to get a little concession for every concession you agree to. That may help end the other party's tendency to keep nibbling at the deal.

🏠 Don't go in for the kill.

The best negotiations leave both parties feeling satisfied. Remember, you still face several weeks of working together to get to closing.

🏠 Announce "last call."

Before you jump on an offer, give other serious buyers one last opportunity to get their offers in.

🏠 Don't sell your home twice.

All that gets you is a lawsuit. Either ask all bidders to make one final best offer, or choose one buyer to negotiate with.

⌂ Get rid of contingencies promptly.

The deal is not done until all the buyer's contingencies have been satisfied—and removed.

⌂ Say no to early occupancy.

It's too risky to allow a buyer to work on the home (or to actually move in) until that buyer officially owns it.

⌂ Put the screwdriver down.

And no one gets hurt. Anything that's screwed in or bolted to the building is supposed to convey to the new owners.

⌂ Forget "buyer beware."

These days, buyers have a right to know about anything that will affect a home's value. Protect yourself by disclosing any flaws you're aware of.

⌂ Fix flaws, but never hide them.

Patching the roof is a repair; painting a water stain without fixing the leak is deception. Keep documentation of all the work you've had done.

⌂ "As is" doesn't mean "hide and seek."

Even if your jurisdiction allows you to sell a home "as is" instead of filling out a detailed disclosure form, you must still take care not to hide defects.

⌂ Environmental contamination isn't just a city thing.

Homes anywhere can have problems with lead, asbestos, or other contaminants. Disclose what you know, and allow time for buyers to get the inspections they want.

🏠 Don't state the obvious . . . or conjecture, either.

You don't have to disclose the obvious, such as the fact that the nearby railroad can be a tad noisy. Nor do you have to volunteer information that doesn't directly affect the home's value. But if you're asked a question, tell the truth.

🏠 Even you could run afoul of fair-housing laws.

Even if you start out with the best of intentions, your actions could violate fair-housing laws if the *effects* of those actions are seen as discriminatory against buyers. Stick to the facts about your home and the neighborhood's amenities, and let buyers decide whether it's their kind of place.

🏠 Pave the way for membership.

Help your buyers promptly obtain disclosure-information packages from your homeowners' association, condo, or co-op board. You don't have a deal until they've had the opportunity to review them.

🏠 Boast about the amenities.

Don't assume buyers know all the benefits they'll derive from becoming a resident of your association or development. You never know which amenity will sell them on the deal.

🏠 That's why you need a contract.

Buyers and sellers commonly hit a rough patch of remorse. Think about why you wanted to sell in the first place, and stick to the terms of the contract.

🏠 Give sentiment its due.

It's only human to grow attached to your home and to feel sad about giving it up. Indulge yourself by taking the time to say good-bye properly. Invite your friends over one last time.

🏠 Kids don't always take things in stride.

Your children are in for a lot of changes, and they don't have much say over them. Help them remember their old home—and focus on the excitement of moving to a new one.

🏠 Leave a hint of yourselves behind.

Somewhere in an out-of-the-way nook, have everyone in the family write their initials and the date. Or plant a sapling out back. It helps you say goodbye.

🏠 Go wild taking photographs.

Before you start packing up, take pictures of all the rooms. They can bring back memories later—and help you document insurance losses, if necessary.

🏠 Procrastination only makes it worse.

If seller's remorse has you dragging your feet on moving-related chores, you'll soon discover what stress is all about.

🏠 Closing should be simple.

Your goal is to have all the details wrapped up well ahead of the actual closing of the deal.

🏠 Build in some slack.

Try to schedule closing so you have a few days between the sale of your old home and the purchase of the new one. Rent back your old home for a few days, if necessary.

🏠 Drama is not a part-time vocation.

If the buyers (or their agent) have been hit-or-miss about the details all through this deal, it's only logical to expect that behavior to continue right through closing day. Brace yourself—and build extra time into your schedule.

🏠 Keep the lights on!

When you arrange for your utilities to be cut off, be absolutely sure they'll remain turned on through the very end of your moving-out day.

🏠 Guard against insurance gaps.

Make sure your homeowners' policy remains in force every second you own that home. And make sure that either your old or your new policy covers your belongings while you're moving them between homes.

🏠 Take a rider.

This is the perfect time to make sure that your homeowners' policy includes any extra riders necessary to cover your most valuable possessions.

🏠 Get the dog, the cat, and the car ready for the move.

Each of them will be bearing more stress than usual—so get them checked out and ready.

🏠 Be kind to your buyers.

Leave your home as tidy as possible, and leave behind contact information for good plumbers and other repair people. If you're lucky, the kindness will be repaid to you by the people vacating your new home!

🏠 Understand the HUD-1.

Take the time to ask questions when reviewing this document, which spells out exactly where all the money goes in the home-sale deal.

🏠 Watch the mailbox.

Keep an eye out for the lien release from your old lender. And make sure the IRS—and everyone else—knows how to get in touch with you.

🏠 Set up checking accounts early.

Have your new, updated checkbook ready to roll by moving day.

🏠 Reputation is all that matters.

You're calling in strangers to load everything you own onto a truck and drive it away. You need to know they're trustworthy.

🏠 Get an estimate in person, and in writing.

Only do business with movers who will come to your home to see your belongings and provide a written estimate of the fee.

🏠 The law is on their side.

It's actually legal for a mover to refuse to unload your belongings until you have paid the bill, in cash or an equivalent, right at the doorstep.

🏠 Insure yourself to the hilt.

Buy all the extra insurance you can get from the moving company, and make sure your homeowners' policy remains in effect to cover the items you move yourself.

🏠 Don't risk heartbreak.

If it has great value—and especially great sentimental value—find a way to move that item yourself.

🏠 Go camping.

Be prepared to rough it, in relative comfort, for a few days in your new home before the moving van arrives.

🏠 Secure the electronics.

Back up *all* your data, make a note of how everything's plugged together, keep track of the accessories, and pack it all with great care.

Handy Web Sites

Change of address

https://moversguide.usps.com
The U.S. Postal Service Web site allows you to enter information for mail forwarding.

www.IRS.gov/taxtopics/tc157.html
At this Internal Revenue Service site, you can download a copy of Form 8822, Address Change Request, which you should send to the IRS to make sure you receive notices about tax audits or refunds without delay.

Discount brokers

www.Foxtons.com
This full-service discount brokerage operates in the New York City metro area, including the New Jersey and Connecticut suburbs.

www.ProgressiveHomesellers.com
This Seattle-based brokerage does business in Washington State and

planned to expand to California. Sellers can choose to pay a flat fee at the time of listing or a higher fee due when and if the home sells.

www.ZipRealty.com
A full-service brokerage company with local agents in many major metro areas across the country. It promises discounted listing fees to sellers and rebates to buyers.

Government information

www.epa.gov/lead/index.html
This site, run by the U.S. Environmental Protection Agency, offers information about lead risks associated with the purchase or remodeling of homes built before 1978, when lead-based paint was outlawed. It also allows users to search for certified abatement and inspection firms.

www.epa.gov/radon
The U.S. Environmental Protection Agency's information about radon gas, including a link to its publication, "Home Buyers' and Sellers' Guide to Radon" and links to state radon authorities.

www.HUD.gov
The main Web site of the U.S. Department of Housing and Urban Development, which offers a lot of consumer-friendly information about the home sale process.

www.IRS.gov
Through the Internal Revenue Service's home page you can search for and download Publication 523, "Selling Your Home," and Form 3903, "Moving Expenses," among other documents.

Real estate brokers and referrals

www.HomeGain.com

Users of this site can register to get referrals to participating Realtors and to get mortgage quotes, search home listings, and obtain home-value estimates.

www.RealEstate.com

Users are asked to input their contact information and answer questions about their plans to buy or sell and are then referred to participating brokers and agents, plus other services. The site is owned by LendingTree, a company that offers internet-based mortgage referrals (www.LendingTree.com).

www.Realtor.com

The official Web site of the National Association of Realtors, it allows users to search more than 3 million home listings nationwide and to search for Realtors by city and state. It also has links that allow you to search for lenders and moving companies. The same database also can be accessed at www.Move.com.

Flat-fee listings and For Sale By Owner services

www.ForSaleByOwner.com

This site caters exclusively to owners who are selling without an agent, offering ads on its Web site and in its printed magazine, For Sale signs and other materials. For an additional fee, sellers can choose to have their listing placed on the local MLS.

Flat-fee listings are also available through the following services, in the states where it is allowed:

www.MLSLion.com
www.KingOffer.com
www.BrokerDirectMLS.com
www.FlatFeeListing.com

Moving information and referrals

www.Move.com
This umbrella site provides the same moving referral services that can be accessed under the names www.monstermoving.com and www.Realtor.com. (It also includes Realtor.com's home listings.)

www.protectyourmove.gov
This site, maintained by the Federal Motor Carrier Safety Administration, which regulates interstate movers, has a wealth of consumer information about hiring moving companies and about avoiding scams.

Miscellaneous

www.anywho.com
This online telephone directory run by AT&T offers free reverse lookups of published telephone numbers which allows you to find a caller's name and address.

www.auctioneers.org
The site maintained by the National Auctioneers Association allows you to search for qualified auctioneers and upcoming auctions.

www.auctionzip.com

A searchable listing of upcoming auctions.

www.ChoiceTrust.com

Before an insurance company agrees to offer a homeowner's policy, it will check for a claims history on the Comprehensive Loss Underwriting Exchange (CLUE) report maintained by ChoiceTrust. Homeowners are entitled to one free copy per year.

www.Craigslist.org

For the metropolitan areas that are covered by Craigslist pages, the Web site's browsers can post and search ads for properties and rentals, and can post questions that may be answered by knowledgeable locals.

www.debtadvice.org

The National Foundation for Credit Counseling offers reasonably priced help in getting out from under troublesome debt as well as in managing lesser debt loads. It also provides counseling for people who plan to become homeowners.

www.FearlessHome.com

The site includes updates to *The Fearless Home Seller* and its companion volume, *The Fearless Home Buyer*, with links for e-mailing the author.

www.remodeling.hw.net

Look up the estimated home-value payback associated with common remodeling jobs in the "Cost vs. Value Report" published by Remodeling Magazine.

www.Zillow.com

At last count, estimated values and tax records for more than 67 million homes nationwide could be searched on this site. Many entries include maps and aerial photos.

State Real Estate Commissions

ALABAMA

Alabama Real Estate
  Commission
1201 Carmichael Way
Montgomery, AL 36106
Phone: 334-242-5544

www.arec.state.al.us/

ALASKA

Real Estate Commission
550 W. 7th Ave., Suite 1500
Anchorage, AK 99501-3567
Phone: 907-269-8197

*www.dced.state.ak.us/occ/prec
  .htm*

ARIZONA

Department of Real Estate
2910 N. 44th St., Suite 100
Phoenix, AZ 85018
Phone: 602-468-1414

www.re.state.az.us/

ARKANSAS

Real Estate Commission
612 S. Summit St.
Little Rock, AR 72201-4740
Phone: 501-683-8010

*www.state.ar.us/arec/arecweb
  .html*

CALIFORNIA

State of California
Department of Real Estate
P.O. Box 187000
Sacramento, CA 95818-7000
Phone: 916-227-0864
www.dre.ca.gov/

COLORADO

Division of Real Estate
1560 Broadway, Suite 925
Denver, CO 80202
Phone: 303-894-2166 or -2185

www.dora.state.co.us/real-estate/

CONNECTICUT

Department of Consumer
   Protection
165 Capitol Ave.
Hartford, CT 06106
Phone: 860-713-6050

www.ct.gov/dcp/site/default.asp

DELAWARE

Real Estate Commission
861 Silver Lake Blvd., Suite 203
Dover, DE 19904
Phone: 302-744-4519

www.professionallicensing.state
   .de.us/boards/realestate

DISTRICT OF COLUMBIA

Board of Real Estate
941 North Capitol St., NE
Washington, DC 20002
Phone: 202-442-4400

www.dcra.dc.gov/dcra/site/
   default.asp

FLORIDA

Dept. of Business and
   Professional Regulation
Customer Contact Ctr.
1940 N. Monroe St.
Tallahassee, FL 32399-1027
Phone: 850-487-1395

www.state.fl.us/dbpr/re/index
   .shtml

GEORGIA

Real Estate Commission
229 Peachtree St. NE, Suite
   1000
Atlanta, GA 30303-1605
Phone: 404-656-3916

www.grec.state.ga.us/

HAWAII

Real Estate Branch
335 Merchant St., Room 333
Honolulu, HI 96813
Phone: 808-586-2643

www.hawaii.gov/hirec

IDAHO

Real Estate Commission
P.O. Box 83720
Boise, ID 83720-0077
Phone: 208-334-3285; toll-free
   in Idaho, 866-447-5411

www.idahorealestatecommission
   .com

ILLINOIS

Division of Banks and Real
   Estate
500 East Monroe St.
Springfield, IL 62701
Phone: 217-782-3000

www.idfpr.com/default.asp

INDIANA

Professional Licensing Agency
Indiana Real Estate
 Commission
402 W. Washington St., Room
 W072
Indianapolis, IN 46204
Phone: 317-234-3009

www.in.gov/pla/bandc/estate/

IOWA

Professional Licensing Division
1920 S.E. Hulsizer Rd.
Ankeny, IA 50021-3941
Phone: 515-281-5910

*www.state.ia.us/government/com/
 prof/sales/home.html*

KANSAS

Real Estate Commission
Three Townsite Plaza, Suite 200
120 SE 6th Ave.
Topeka, KS 66603
Phone: 785-296-3411

www.accesskansas.org/krec/

KENTUCKY

Real Estate Commission
10200 Linn Station Rd., Suite
 201
Louisville, KY 40223
Phone: 502-429-7250

www.krec.ky.gov/

LOUISIANA

Real Estate Commission
P.O. Box 14785
Baton Rouge, LA 70898-4785
Phone: 225-765-0191; toll-free
 in Louisiana, 800-821-4529

www.lrec.state.la.us/

MAINE

Dept. of Professional and
 Financial Regulataion
Office of Licensing and
 Registration
35 State House Station
Augusta, ME 04333-0035
Phone: 207-624-8603

www.state.me.us/pfr/olr/

MARYLAND

Real Estate Commission
500 N. Calvert St.
Baltimore, MD 21202-3651
Phone: 410-230-6200 or -6201

*www.dllr.state.md.us/license/
 real_est/reintro.html*

MASSACHUSETTS

Division of Professional
 Licensure
239 Causeway St.
Boston, MA 02114
Phone: 617-727-3074

www.mass.gov/dpl/

MICHIGAN

Dept. of Labor & Economic
  Growth, Licensing Div.
P.O. Box 30004
Lansing, MI 48909
Phone: 517-241-9288

www.michigan.gov/cis

MISSISSIPPI

Real Estate Commission
P.O. Box 12685
Jackson, MS 39236
Phone: 601-932-9191

www.mrec.state.ms.us/

MISSOURI

Real Estate Commission
P.O. Box 1339
3605 Missouri Blvd.
Jefferson City, MO 65102-1339
Phone: 573-751-2628

http://pr.mo.gov/realestate.asp

MONTANA

Board of Realty Regulation
P.O. Box 200513
301 South Park
Helena, MT 59620-0513
Phone: 406-841-2354

*www.discoveringmontana.com/
  dli/bsd/license/bsd_boards/
  rre_board/board_page.asp*

NEBRASKA

Real Estate Commission
P.O. Box 94667
1200 N St., Suite 402
Lincoln, NE 68509-4667
Phone: 402-471-2004

www.nrec.state.ne.us/

NEVADA

Real Estate Division
2501 E. Sahara Ave., Suite 102
Las Vegas, NV 89104-4137
Phone: 702-486-4033

www.red.state.nv.us/

NEW HAMPSHIRE

Real Estate Commission
State House Annex, Room 434
25 Capitol St.
Concord, NH 03301
Phone: 603-271-2701

www.nh.gov/nhrec/

NEW JERSEY

Real Estate Commission
240 W. State St.
P.O. Box 328
Trenton, NJ 08625-0328
Phone: 609-292-8300

*www.state.nj.us/dobi/remnu
  .shtml*

NEW MEXICO

Real Estate Commission
5200 Oakland Ave., N.E., Suite B
Albuquerque, NM 87113
Phone: 505-222-9820; toll-free
  in New Mexico: 800-801-
  7505

www.state.nm.us/clients/nmrec/

NEW YORK

Division of Licensing Services
84 Holland Ave.
Albany, NY 12208-3490
Phone: 518-474-4429

www.dos.state.ny.us/lcns/
  realest.html

NORTH CAROLINA

Real Estate Commission
P.O. Box 17100
Raleigh, NC 27619-7100
Phone: 919-875-3700

www.ncrec.state.nc.us/about/
  about.asp

NORTH DAKOTA

Real Estate Commission
200 E. Main Ave., Suite 204
Bismark, ND 58502-0727
Phone: 701-328-9749

www.governor.state.nd.us/boards/
  boards-query.asp?
  Board_ID=93

OHIO

Department of Commerce
Division of Real Estate &
  Professional Licensing
77 S. High St., 20th Floor
Columbus, OH 43215-6133
Phone: 614-466-4100

www.com.state.oh.us/real/

OKLAHOMA

Real Estate Commission
Shepherd Mall
2401 N.W. 23rd St., Suite 18
Oklahoma City, OK 73107
Phone: 405-521-3387; toll-free
  in Oklahoma: 866-521-3389

www.orec.state.ok.us/

OREGON

Real Estate Agency
1177 Center Street NE
Salem, OR 97301-2505
Phone: 503-378-4170

www.rea.state.or.us/

PENNSYLVANIA

Real Estate Commission
P.O. Box 2649
Harrisburg, PA 17105-2649
Phone: 717-783-3658

www.dos.state.pa.us

RHODE ISLAND

Department of Business
    Regulation/Real Estate
233 Richmond St.
Providence, RI 02903
Phone: 401-222-2246

www.dbr.state.ri.us/real_estate.html

http://www.rilin.state.ri.us/

SOUTH CAROLINA

Department of Labor, Licensing
    & Regulation
P.O. Box 11329
Columbia, SC 29211
Phone: 803-896-4643

*www.llr.state.sc.us/POL/RealEstate
    Commission/INDEX.ASP*

SOUTH DAKOTA

Real Estate Commission
221 W. Capitol, Suite 101
Pierre, SD 57501
Phone: 605-773-3600

www.state.sd.us/sdrec/

TENNESSEE

Real Estate Commission
500 James Robertson Pkwy.
Nashville, TN 37243-1151
Phone: 615-741-2273; toll-free
    in Tennessee: 800-342-4031

*www.state.tn.us/commerce/
    boards/trec/*

TEXAS

Real Estate Commission
P.O. Box 12188
Austin, TX 78711-2188
Phone: 512-459-6544; toll-free
    in Texas: 800-250-8732

www.trec.state.tx.us/

UTAH

Division of Real Estate
P.O. Box 146711
Salt Lake City, UT 84114-6711
Phone: 801-530-6747

www.commerce.utah.gov/dre/

VERMONT

Office of Professional
    Regulation
Real Estate Commission
81 River St.
Montpelier, VT 05609-1101
Phone: 802-828-3228

*http://vtprofessionals.org/oprl/
    real_estate/*

VIRGINIA

Department of Professional and
    Occupational Regulation
3600 W. Broad St.
Richmond, VA 23230
Phone: 804-367-8500

www.state.va.us/dpor

WASHINGTON

Department of Licensing
Business and Professions
   Division, Real Estate
P.O. Box 9015
Olympia, WA 98507-9015
Phone: 360-664-6500 or -6488

*www.dol.wa.gov/realestate/refront
   .htm*

WEST VIRGINIA

Real Estate Commission
300 Capitol St., Suite 400
Charleston, WV 25301
Phone: 304-558-3555

www.wvrec.org/

WYOMING

Real Estate Commission
2020 Carey Ave., Suite 702
Cheyenne, WY 82002-0180
Phone: 307-777-7141

http://realestate.state.wy.us/

HUD-1 Statement of Settlement Costs

A. **Settlement Statement**

U.S. Department of Housing
and Urban Development

OMB Approval No. 2502-0265
(expires 9/30/2006)

B. Type of Loan

1. ☐ FHA 2. ☐ FmHA 3. ☐ Conv. Unins.	6. File Number:	7. Loan Number:	8. Mortgage Insurance Case Number:
4. ☐ VA 5. ☐ Conv. Ins.			

C. Note: This form is furnished to give you a statement of actual settlement costs. Amounts paid to and by the settlement agent are shown. Items marked "(p.o.c.)" were paid outside the closing; they are shown here for informational purposes and are not included in the totals.

D. Name & Address of Borrower:	E. Name & Address of Seller:	F. Name & Address of Lender:

G. Property Location:	H. Settlement Agent:	
	Place of Settlement:	I. Settlement Date:

J. Summary of Borrower's Transaction		K. Summary of Seller's Transaction	
100. Gross Amount Due From Borrower		**400. Gross Amount Due To Seller**	
101. Contract sales price		401. Contract sales price	
102. Personal property		402. Personal property	
103. Settlement charges to borrower (line 1400)		403.	
104.		404.	
105.		405.	
Adjustments for items paid by seller in advance		**Adjustments for items paid by seller in advance**	
106. City/town taxes to		406. City/town taxes to	
107. County taxes to		407. County taxes to	
108. Assessments to		408. Assessments to	
109.		409.	
110.		410.	
111.		411.	
112.		412.	

300

120. Gross Amount Due From Borrower			420. Gross Amount Due To Seller		
200. Amounts Paid By Or In Behalf Of Borrower			**500. Reductions In Amount Due To Seller**		
201. Deposit or earnest money			501. Excess deposit (see instructions)		
202. Principal amount of new loan(s)			502. Settlement charges to seller (line 1400)		
203. Existing loan(s) taken subject to			503. Existing loan(s) taken subject to		
204.			504. Payoff of first mortgage loan		
205.			505. Payoff of second mortgage loan		
206.			506.		
207.			507.		
208.			508.		
209.			509.		
Adjustments for items unpaid by seller			**Adjustments for items unpaid by seller**		
210. City/town taxes to			510. City/town taxes to		
211. County taxes to			511. County taxes to		
212. Assessments to			512. Assessments to		
213.			513.		
214.			514.		
215.			515.		
216.			516.		
217.			517.		
218.			518.		
219.			519.		
220. Total Paid By/For Borrower			**520. Total Reduction Amount Due Seller**		
300. Cash At Settlement From/To Borrower			**600. Cash At Settlement To/From Seller**		
301. Gross Amount due from borrower (line 120)			601. Gross amount due to seller (line 420)		
302. Less amounts paid by/for borrower (line 220)	(	)	602. Less reductions in amt. due seller (line 520)	(	)
303. Cash ☐ From ☐ To Borrower			**603. Cash** ☐ To ☐ From Seller		

L. Settlement Charges

			Paid From Borrowers Funds at Settlement	Paid From Seller's Funds at Settlement
700. Total Sales/Broker's Commission based on price $ @ % =				
Division of Commission (line 700) as follows:				
701. $ to				
702. $ to				
703. Commission paid at Settlement				
704.				
800. Items Payable In Connection With Loan				
801. Loan Origination Fee %				
802. Loan Discount %				
803. Appraisal Fee to				
804. Credit Report to				
805. Lender's Inspection Fee				
806. Mortgage Insurance Application Fee to				
807. Assumption Fee				
808.				
809.				
810.				
811.				
900. Items Required By Lender To Be Paid In Advance				
901. Interest from to @ $ /day				
902. Mortgage Insurance Premium for months to				
903. Hazard Insurance Premium for years to				
904. years to				
905.				
1000. Reserves Deposited With Lender				
1001. Hazard insurance months @ $ per month				
1002. Mortgage insurance months @ $ per month				
1003. City property taxes months @ $ per month				
1004. County property taxes months @ $ per month				
1005. Annual assessments months @ $ per month				
1006. months @ $ per month				
1007. months @ $ per month				

1008.	months @ $	per month		

1100. Title Charges

1101. Settlement or closing fee	to		
1102. Abstract or title search	to		
1103. Title examination	to		
1104. Title insurance binder	to		
1105. Document preparation	to		
1106. Notary fees	to		
1107. Attorney's fees	to		
(includes above items numbers:		)	
1108. Title insurance	to		
(includes above items numbers:		)	
1109. Lender's coverage	$		
1110. Owner's coverage	$		
1111.			
1112.			
1113.			

1200. Government Recording and Transfer Charges

1201. Recording fees: Deed $	; Mortgage $	; Releases $	
1202. City/county tax/stamps: Deed $	; Mortgage $		
1203. State tax/stamps: Deed $	; Mortgage $		
1204.			
1205.			

1300. Additional Settlement Charges

1301. Survey to		
1302. Pest inspection to		
1303.		
1304.		
1305.		

1400. Total Settlement Charges (enter on lines 103, Section J and 502, Section K)

Section 5 of the Real Estate Settlement Procedures Act (RESPA) requires the following: • HUD must develop a Special Information Booklet to help persons borrowing money to finance the purchase of residential real estate to better understand the nature and costs of real estate settlement services; • Each lender must provide the booklet to all applicants from whom it receives or for whom it prepares a written application to borrow money to finance the purchase of residential real estate; • Lenders must prepare and distribute with the Booklet a Good Faith Estimate of the settlement costs that the borrower is likely to incur in connection with the settlement. These disclosures are manadatory.

Section 4(a) of RESPA mandates that HUD develop and prescribe this standard form to be used at the time of loan settlement to provide full disclosure of all charges imposed upon the borrower and seller. These are third party disclosures that are designed to provide the borrower with pertinent information during the settlement process in order to be a better shopper.

The Public Reporting Burden for this collection of information is estimated to average one hour per response, including the time for reviewing instructions, searching existing data sources, gathering and maintaining the data needed, and completing and reviewing the collection of information.

This agency may not collect this information, and you are not required to complete this form, unless it displays a currently valid OMB control number.

The information requested does not lend itself to confidentiality.

Examples of Real Estate Contracts

On the following pages you will find the contracts and disclosure forms used during a home sale in California. While each state has its own laws governing the sale of real estate and will require specific forms tailored to those laws, reviewing the California documents can help you get a feel for what you can expect to encounter.

Appendices

Residential ListingAgreement

**CALIFORNIA
ASSOCIATION
OF REALTORS®**

RESIDENTIAL LISTING AGREEMENT
(Exclusive Authorization and Right to Sell)
(C.A.R. Form RLA, Revised 4/06)

1. **EXCLUSIVE RIGHT TO SELL:** _____ ("Seller")
   hereby employs and grants _____ ("Broker")
   beginning (date) _____ and ending at 11:59 P.M. on (date) _____ ("Listing Period")
   the exclusive and irrevocable right to sell or exchange the real property in the City of _____,
   County of_____, Assessor's Parcel No. _____,
   California, described as:_____ ("Property").
2. **ITEMS EXCLUDED AND INCLUDED:** Unless otherwise specified in a real estate purchase agreement, all fixtures and fittings that
   are attached to the Property are included, and personal property items are excluded, from the purchase price.
   ADDITIONAL ITEMS EXCLUDED: _____
   ADDITIONAL ITEMS INCLUDED: _____.
   Seller intends that the above items be excluded or included in offering the Property for sale, but understands that: (I) the purchase
   agreement supersedes any intention expressed above and will ultimately determine which items are excluded and included in the sale;
   and (II) Broker is not responsible for and does not guarantee that the above exclusions and/or inclusions will be in the purchase
   agreement.
3. **LISTING PRICE AND TERMS:**
   A. The listing price shall be: _____
   _____ Dollars ($ _____).
   B. Additional Terms: _____
4. **COMPENSATION TO BROKER:**
   **Notice: The amount or rate of real estate commissions is not fixed by law. They are set by each Broker
   individually and may be negotiable between Seller and Broker (real estate commissions include all
   compensation and fees to Broker).**
   A. Seller agrees to pay to Broker as compensation for services irrespective of agency relationship(s), either □ _____ percent
   of the listing price (or if a purchase agreement is entered into, of the purchase price), or □ $ _____
   AND _____, as follows:
      (1) If during the Listing Period, or any extension, Broker, Seller, cooperating broker, or any other person procures a buyer(s)
   who offers to purchase the Property on the above price and terms, or on any price and terms acceptable to Seller. (Broker
   is entitled to compensation whether any escrow resulting from such offer closes during or after the expiration of the Listing
   Period.)
   OR (2) If within _____ calendar days **(a)** after the end of the Listing Period or any extension, or **(b)** after any cancellation of this
   Agreement, unless otherwise agreed, Seller enters into a contract to sell, convey, lease or otherwise transfer the Property to
   anyone ("Prospective Buyer") or that person's related entity: **(i)** who physically entered and was shown the Property during
   the Listing Period or any extension by Broker or a cooperating broker; or **(ii)** for whom Broker or any cooperating broker
   submitted to Seller a signed, written offer to acquire, lease, exchange or obtain an option on the Property. Seller, however,
   shall have no obligation to Broker under paragraph 4A(2) unless, not later than **3 calendar days** after the end of the Listing
   Period or any extension or cancellation, Broker has given Seller a written notice of the names of such Prospective Buyers.
   OR (3) If, without Broker's prior written consent, the Property is withdrawn from sale, conveyed, leased, rented, otherwise transferred,
   or made unmarketable by a voluntary act of Seller during the Listing Period, or any extension.
   B. If completion of the sale is prevented by a party to the transaction other than Seller, then compensation due under paragraph
   4A shall be payable only if and when Seller collects damages by suit, arbitration, settlement or otherwise, and then in an amount
   equal to the lesser of one-half of the damages recovered or the above compensation, after first deducting title and escrow
   expenses and the expenses of collection, if any.
   C. In addition, Seller agrees to pay Broker: _____
   D. Seller has been advised of Broker's policy regarding cooperation with, and the amount of compensation offered to, other brokers.
      (1) Broker is authorized to cooperate with and compensate brokers participating through the multiple listing service(s)
   ("MLS"): **(i)** by offering MLS brokers: either □ _____ percent of the purchase price, or □ $ _____;
   OR (ii) (if checked) □ as per Broker's policy.
      (2) Broker is authorized to cooperate with and compensate brokers operating outside the MLS as per Broker's policy.
   E. Seller hereby irrevocably assigns to Broker the above compensation from Seller's funds and proceeds in escrow. Broker may
   submit this Agreement, as instructions to compensate Broker pursuant to paragraph 4A, to any escrow regarding the Property
   involving Seller and a buyer, Prospective Buyer or other transferee.
   F. **(1)** Seller represents that Seller has not previously entered into a listing agreement with another broker regarding the Property,
   unless specified as follows: _____
      (2) Seller warrants that Seller has no obligation to pay compensation to any other broker regarding the Property unless the
   Property is transferred to any of the following individuals or entities: _____
   _____.
      (3) If the Property is sold to anyone listed above during the time Seller is obligated to compensate another broker: **(i)** Broker is
   not entitled to compensation under this Agreement; and **(ii)** Broker is not obligated to represent Seller in such transaction.

Seller acknowledges receipt of a copy of this page.
Seller's Initials (_____)(_____)

RLA REVISED 4/06 (PAGE 1 OF 3)   Print Date

Reviewed by _____ Date _____

**EQUAL HOUSING
OPPORTUNITY**

Residential ListingAgreement

Property Address: _____ Date: _____

5. **OWNERSHIP, TITLE AND AUTHORITY:** Seller warrants that: **(i)** Seller is the owner of the Property; **(ii)** no other persons or entities have title to the Property; and **(iii)** Seller has the authority to both execute this Agreement and sell the Property. Exceptions to ownership, title and authority are as follows: _____.

6. **MULTIPLE LISTING SERVICE:** All terms of the transaction, including financing, if applicable, will be provided to the selected MLS for publication, dissemination and use by persons and entities on terms approved by the MLS. Seller authorizes Broker to comply with all applicable MLS rules. MLS rules allow MLS data to be made available by the MLS to additional Internet sites unless Broker gives the MLS instructions to the contrary. MLS rules generally provide that residential real property and vacant lot listings be submitted to the MLS within 48 hours or some other period of time after all necessary signatures have been obtained on the listing agreement. However, Broker will not have to submit this listing to the MLS if, within that time, Broker submits to the MLS a form signed by Seller (C.A.R. Form SEL or the locally required form) instructing Broker to withhold the listing from the MLS. Information about this listing will be provided to the MLS of Broker's selection unless a form instructing Broker to withhold the listing from the MLS is attached to this listing Agreement.

7. **SELLER REPRESENTATIONS:** Seller represents that, unless otherwise specified in writing, Seller is unaware of: **(i)** any Notice of Default recorded against the Property; **(ii)** any delinquent amounts due under any loan secured by, or other obligation affecting, the Property; **(iii)** any bankruptcy, insolvency or similar proceeding affecting the Property; **(iv)** any litigation, arbitration, administrative action, government investigation or other pending or threatened action that affects or may affect the Property or Seller's ability to transfer it; and **(v)** any current, pending or proposed special assessments affecting the Property. Seller shall promptly notify Broker in writing if Seller becomes aware of any of these items during the Listing Period or any extension thereof.

8. **BROKER'S AND SELLER'S DUTIES:** Broker agrees to exercise reasonable effort and due diligence to achieve the purposes of this Agreement. Unless Seller gives Broker written instructions to the contrary, Broker is authorized to order reports and disclosures as appropriate or necessary and advertise and market the Property by any method and in any medium selected by Broker, including MLS and the Internet, and, to the extent permitted by these media, control the dissemination of the information submitted to any medium. Seller agrees to consider offers presented by Broker, and to act in good faith to accomplish the sale of the Property by, among other things, making the Property available for showing at reasonable times and referring to Broker all inquiries of any party interested in the Property. Seller is responsible for determining at what price to list and sell the Property. **Seller further agrees to indemnify, defend and hold Broker harmless from all claims, disputes, litigation, judgments and attorney fees arising from any incorrect information supplied by Seller, or from any material facts that Seller knows but fails to disclose.**

9. **DEPOSIT:** Broker is authorized to accept and hold on Seller's behalf any deposits to be applied toward the purchase price.

10. **AGENCY RELATIONSHIPS:**

   A. Disclosure: If the Property includes residential property with one-to-four dwelling units, Seller shall receive a "Disclosure Regarding Agency Relationships" form prior to entering into this Agreement.

   B. Seller Representation: Broker shall represent Seller in any resulting transaction, except as specified in paragraph 4F.

   C. Possible Dual Agency With Buyer: Depending upon the circumstances, it may be necessary or appropriate for Broker to act as an agent for both Seller and buyer, exchange party, or one or more additional parties ("Buyer"). Broker shall, as soon as practicable, disclose to Seller any election to act as a dual agent representing both Seller and Buyer. If a Buyer is procured directly by Broker or an associate-licensee in Broker's firm, Seller hereby consents to Broker acting as a dual agent for Seller and such Buyer. In the event of an exchange, Seller hereby consents to Broker collecting compensation from additional parties for services rendered, provided there is disclosure to all parties of such agency and compensation. Seller understands and agrees that: **(i)** Broker, without the prior written consent of Seller, will not disclose to Buyer that Seller is willing to sell the Property at a price less than the listing price; **(ii)** Broker, without the prior written consent of Seller, will not disclose to Seller that Buyer is willing to pay a price greater than the offered price; and **(iii)** except for (i) and (ii) above, a dual agent is obligated to disclose known facts materially affecting the value or desirability of the Property to both parties.

   D. Other Sellers: Seller understands that Broker may have or obtain listings on other properties, and that potential buyers may consider, make offers on, or purchase through Broker, property the same as or similar to Seller's Property. Seller consents to Broker's representation of sellers and buyers of other properties before, during and after the end of this Agreement.

   E. Confirmation: If the Property includes residential property with one-to-four dwelling units, Broker shall confirm the agency relationship described above, or as modified, in writing, prior to or concurrent with Seller's execution of a purchase agreement.

11. **SECURITY AND INSURANCE:** Broker is not responsible for loss of or damage to personal or real property, or person, whether attributable to use of a keysafe/lockbox, a showing of the Property, or otherwise. Third parties, including, but not limited to, appraisers, inspectors, brokers and prospective buyers, may have access to, and take videos and photographs of, the interior of the Property. Seller agrees: **(i)** to take reasonable precautions to safeguard and protect valuables that might be accessible during showings of the Property; and **(ii)** to obtain insurance to protect against these risks. Broker does not maintain insurance to protect Seller.

12. **KEYSAFE/LOCKBOX:** A keysafe/lockbox is designed to hold a key to the Property to permit access to the Property by Broker, cooperating brokers, MLS participants, their authorized licensees and representatives, authorized inspectors, and accompanied prospective buyers. Broker, cooperating brokers, MLS and Associations/Boards of REALTORS® are **not** insurers against injury, theft, loss, vandalism or damage attributed to the use of a keysafe/lockbox. Seller does (or if checked ☐ does not) authorize Broker to install a keysafe/lockbox. If Seller does not occupy the Property, Seller shall be responsible for obtaining occupant(s)' written permission for use of a keysafe/lockbox.

13. **SIGN:** Seller does (or if checked ☐ does not) authorize Broker to install a FOR SALE/SOLD sign on the Property.

14. **EQUAL HOUSING OPPORTUNITY:** The Property is offered in compliance with federal, state and local anti-discrimination laws.

15. **ATTORNEY FEES:** In any action, proceeding or arbitration between Seller and Broker regarding the obligation to pay compensation under this Agreement, the prevailing Seller or Broker shall be entitled to reasonable attorney fees and costs from the non-prevailing Seller or Broker, except as provided in paragraph 19A.

16. **ADDITIONAL TERMS:** _____
_____
_____

Seller acknowledges receipt of a copy of this page.
Seller's Initials (_____)(_____)

Reviewed by _____ Date _____

RLA REVISED 4/06 (PAGE 2 OF 3)

EQUAL HOUSING OPPORTUNITY

Reprinted with permission, CALIFORNIA ASSOCIATION OF REALTORS®. Endorsement not implied.

Residential Listing Agreement

Property Address: _____   Date: _____

17. **MANAGEMENT APPROVAL:** If an associate-licensee in Broker's office (salesperson or broker-associate) enters into this Agreement on Broker's behalf, and Broker or Manager does not approve of its terms, Broker or Manager has the right to cancel this Agreement, in writing, within **5 Days** After its execution.

18. **SUCCESSORS AND ASSIGNS:** This Agreement shall be binding upon Seller and Seller's successors and assigns.

19. **DISPUTE RESOLUTION:**

  A. MEDIATION: Seller and Broker agree to mediate any dispute or claim arising between them out of this Agreement, or any resulting transaction, before resorting to arbitration or court action, subject to paragraph 19B(2) below. Paragraph 19B(2) below applies whether or not the arbitration provision is initialed. Mediation fees, if any, shall be divided equally among the parties involved. If, for any dispute or claim to which this paragraph applies, any party commences an action without first attempting to resolve the matter through mediation, or refuses to mediate after a request has been made, then that party shall not be entitled to recover attorney fees, even if they would otherwise be available to that party in any such action. THIS MEDIATION PROVISION APPLIES WHETHER OR NOT THE ARBITRATION PROVISION IS INITIALED.

  B. ARBITRATION OF DISPUTES: (1) Seller and Broker agree that any dispute or claim in law or equity arising between them regarding the obligation to pay compensation under this Agreement, which is not settled through mediation, shall be decided by neutral, binding arbitration, including and subject to paragraph 19B(2) below. The arbitrator shall be a retired judge or justice, or an attorney with at least 5 years of residential real estate law experience, unless the parties mutually agree to a different arbitrator, who shall render an award in accordance with substantive California law. The parties shall have the right to discovery in accordance with Code of Civil Procedure §1283.05. In all other respects, the arbitration shall be conducted in accordance with Title 9 of Part III of the California Code of Civil Procedure. Judgment upon the award of the arbitrator(s) may be entered in any court having jurisdiction. Interpretation of this agreement to arbitrate shall be governed by the Federal Arbitration Act.
  (2) EXCLUSIONS FROM MEDIATION AND ARBITRATION: The following matters are excluded from mediation and arbitration: (i) a judicial or non-judicial foreclosure or other action or proceeding to enforce a deed of trust, mortgage, or installment land sale contract as defined in Civil Code §2985; (ii) an unlawful detainer action; (iii) the filing or enforcement of a mechanic's lien; and (iv) any matter that is within the jurisdiction of a probate, small claims, or bankruptcy court. The filing of a court action to enable the recording of a notice of pending action, for order of attachment, receivership, injunction, or other provisional remedies, shall not constitute a waiver of the mediation and arbitration provisions.

  "NOTICE: BY INITIALING IN THE SPACE BELOW YOU ARE AGREEING TO HAVE ANY DISPUTE ARISING OUT OF THE MATTERS INCLUDED IN THE 'ARBITRATION OF DISPUTES' PROVISION DECIDED BY NEUTRAL ARBITRATION AS PROVIDED BY CALIFORNIA LAW AND YOU ARE GIVING UP ANY RIGHTS YOU MIGHT POSSESS TO HAVE THE DISPUTE LITIGATED IN A COURT OR JURY TRIAL. BY INITIALING IN THE SPACE BELOW YOU ARE GIVING UP YOUR JUDICIAL RIGHTS TO DISCOVERY AND APPEAL, UNLESS THOSE RIGHTS ARE SPECIFICALLY INCLUDED IN THE 'ARBITRATION OF DISPUTES' PROVISION. IF YOU REFUSE TO SUBMIT TO ARBITRATION AFTER AGREEING TO THIS PROVISION, YOU MAY BE COMPELLED TO ARBITRATE UNDER THE AUTHORITY OF THE CALIFORNIA CODE OF CIVIL PROCEDURE. YOUR AGREEMENT TO THIS ARBITRATION PROVISION IS VOLUNTARY."

  "WE HAVE READ AND UNDERSTAND THE FOREGOING AND AGREE TO SUBMIT DISPUTES ARISING OUT OF THE MATTERS INCLUDED IN THE 'ARBITRATION OF DISPUTES' PROVISION TO NEUTRAL ARBITRATION."

Seller's Initials _____ / _____	Broker's Initials _____ / _____

20. **ENTIRE AGREEMENT:** All prior discussions, negotiations and agreements between the parties concerning the subject matter of this Agreement are superseded by this Agreement, which constitutes the entire contract and a complete and exclusive expression of their agreement, and may not be contradicted by evidence of any prior agreement or contemporaneous oral agreement. If any provision of this Agreement is held to be ineffective or invalid, the remaining provisions will nevertheless be given full force and effect. This Agreement and any supplement, addendum or modification, including any photocopy or facsimile, may be executed in counterparts.

By signing below, Seller acknowledges that Seller has read, understands, received a copy of and agrees to the terms of this Agreement.

Seller _____ Date _____

Address _____ City _____ State _____ Zip _____

Telephone _____ Fax _____ E-mail _____

Seller _____ Date _____

Address _____ City _____ State _____ Zip _____

Telephone _____ Fax _____ E-mail _____

Real Estate Broker (Firm) _____ DRE Lic. # _____

By (Agent) _____ DRE Lic. # _____ Date _____

Address _____ City _____ State _____ Zip _____

Telephone _____ Fax _____ E-mail _____

THIS FORM HAS BEEN APPROVED BY THE CALIFORNIA ASSOCIATION OF REALTORS® (C.A.R.). NO REPRESENTATION IS MADE AS TO THE LEGAL VALIDITY OR ADEQUACY OF ANY PROVISION IN ANY SPECIFIC TRANSACTION. A REAL ESTATE BROKER IS THE PERSON QUALIFIED TO ADVISE ON REAL ESTATE TRANSACTIONS. IF YOU DESIRE LEGAL OR TAX ADVICE, CONSULT AN APPROPRIATE PROFESSIONAL.

This form is available for use by the entire real estate industry. It is not intended to identify the user as a REALTOR®. REALTOR® is a registered collective membership mark which may be used only by members of the NATIONAL ASSOCIATION OF REALTORS® who subscribe to its Code of Ethics.

RLA REVISED 4/06 (PAGE 3 OF 3)

Reviewed by _____ Date _____

Real Estate Transfer Disclosure Statement

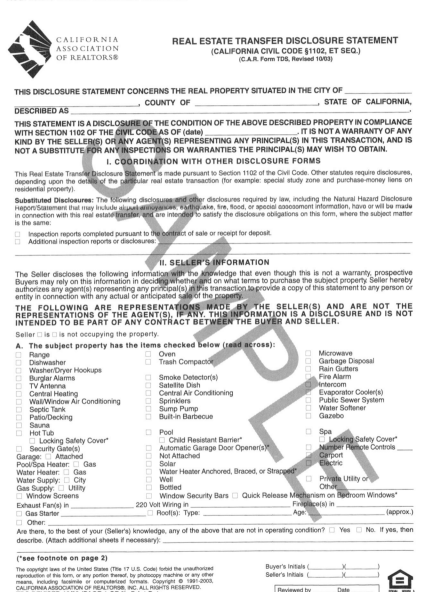

CALIFORNIA
ASSOCIATION
OF REALTORS®

REAL ESTATE TRANSFER DISCLOSURE STATEMENT
(CALIFORNIA CIVIL CODE §1102, ET SEQ.)
(C.A.R. Form TDS, Revised 10/03)

THIS DISCLOSURE STATEMENT CONCERNS THE REAL PROPERTY SITUATED IN THE CITY OF _____
_____, COUNTY OF _____, STATE OF CALIFORNIA,
DESCRIBED AS _____.
THIS STATEMENT IS A DISCLOSURE OF THE CONDITION OF THE ABOVE DESCRIBED PROPERTY IN COMPLIANCE
WITH SECTION 1102 OF THE CIVIL CODE AS OF (date) _____. IT IS NOT A WARRANTY OF ANY
KIND BY THE SELLER(S) OR ANY AGENT(S) REPRESENTING ANY PRINCIPAL(S) IN THIS TRANSACTION, AND IS
NOT A SUBSTITUTE FOR ANY INSPECTIONS OR WARRANTIES THE PRINCIPAL(S) MAY WISH TO OBTAIN.

I. COORDINATION WITH OTHER DISCLOSURE FORMS

This Real Estate Transfer Disclosure Statement is made pursuant to Section 1102 of the Civil Code. Other statutes require disclosures, depending upon the details of the particular real estate transaction (for example: special study zone and purchase-money liens on residential property).

Substituted Disclosures: The following disclosures and other disclosures required by law, including the Natural Hazard Disclosure Report/Statement that may include airport annoyances, earthquake, fire, flood, or special assessment information, have or will be made in connection with this real estate transfer, and are intended to satisfy the disclosure obligations on this form, where the subject matter is the same:

☐ Inspection reports completed pursuant to the contract of sale or receipt for deposit.
☐ Additional inspection reports or disclosures: _____
_____

II. SELLER'S INFORMATION

The Seller discloses the following information with the knowledge that even though this is not a warranty, prospective Buyers may rely on this information in deciding whether and on what terms to purchase the subject property. Seller hereby authorizes any agent(s) representing any principal(s) in this transaction to provide a copy of this statement to any person or entity in connection with any actual or anticipated sale of the property.

THE FOLLOWING ARE REPRESENTATIONS MADE BY THE SELLER(S) AND ARE NOT THE
REPRESENTATIONS OF THE AGENT(S), IF ANY. THIS INFORMATION IS A DISCLOSURE AND IS NOT
INTENDED TO BE PART OF ANY CONTRACT BETWEEN THE BUYER AND SELLER.

Seller ☐ is ☐ is not occupying the property.

A. The subject property has the items checked below (read across):

☐ Range	☐ Oven	☐ Microwave
☐ Dishwasher	☐ Trash Compactor	☐ Garbage Disposal
☐ Washer/Dryer Hookups		☐ Rain Gutters
☐ Burglar Alarms	☐ Smoke Detector(s)	☐ Fire Alarm
☐ TV Antenna	☐ Satellite Dish	☐ Intercom
☐ Central Heating	☐ Central Air Conditioning	☐ Evaporator Cooler(s)
☐ Wall/Window Air Conditioning	☐ Sprinklers	☐ Public Sewer System
☐ Septic Tank	☐ Sump Pump	☐ Water Softener
☐ Patio/Decking	☐ Built-in Barbecue	☐ Gazebo
☐ Sauna		
☐ Hot Tub	☐ Pool	☐ Spa
☐ Locking Safety Cover*	☐ Child Resistant Barrier*	☐ Locking Safety Cover*
☐ Security Gate(s)	☐ Automatic Garage Door Opener(s)*	☐ Number Remote Controls ____
Garage: ☐ Attached	☐ Not Attached	☐ Carport
Pool/Spa Heater: ☐ Gas	☐ Solar	☐ Electric
Water Heater: ☐ Gas	☐ Water Heater Anchored, Braced, or Strapped*	
Water Supply: ☐ City	☐ Well	☐ Private Utility or
Gas Supply: ☐ Utility	☐ Bottled	Other _____
☐ Window Screens	☐ Window Security Bars ☐ Quick Release Mechanism on Bedroom Windows*	

Exhaust Fan(s) in _____ 220 Volt Wiring in _____ Fireplace(s) in _____
☐ Gas Starter _____ ☐ Roof(s): Type: _____ Age: _____ (approx.)
☐ Other: _____
Are there, to the best of your (Seller's) knowledge, any of the above that are not in operating condition? ☐ Yes ☐ No. If yes, then describe. (Attach additional sheets if necessary): _____

(*see footnote on page 2)

TDS REVISED 10/03 (PAGE 1 OF 3) Print Date

Buyer's Initials (_____)(_____)
Seller's Initials (_____)(_____)

Reviewed by _____ Date _____

EQUAL HOUSING
OPPORTUNITY

Appendices

Real Estate Transfer Disclosure Statement

Property Address: _____   Date: _____

B. Are you (Seller) aware of any significant defects/malfunctions in any of the following? ☐ Yes ☐ No. If yes, check appropriate space(s) below.

☐ Interior Walls ☐ Ceilings ☐ Floors ☐ Exterior Walls ☐ Insulation ☐ Roof(s) ☐ Windows ☐ Doors ☐ Foundation ☐ Slab(s) ☐ Driveways ☐ Sidewalks ☐ Walls/Fences ☐ Electrical Systems ☐ Plumbing/Sewers/Septics ☐ Other Structural Components

(Describe: _____
_____
_____
_____)

If any of the above is checked, explain. (Attach additional sheets if necessary.): _____
_____
_____
_____
_____

*This garage door opener or child resistant pool barrier may not be in compliance with the safety standards relating to automatic reversing devices as set forth in Chapter 12.5 (commencing with Section 19890) of Part 3 of Division 13 of, or with the pool safety standards of Article 2.5 (commencing with Section 115920) of Chapter 5 of Part 10 of Division 104 of, the Health and Safety Code. The water heater may not be anchored, braced, or strapped in accordance with Section 19211 of the Health and Safety Code. Window security bars may not have quick release mechanisms in compliance with the 1995 edition of the California Building Standards Code.

C. Are you (Seller) aware of any of the following:

1. Substances, materials, or products which may be an environmental hazard such as, but not limited to, asbestos, formaldehyde, radon gas, lead-based paint, mold, fuel or chemical storage tanks, and contaminated soil or water on the subject property . . . . ☐ Yes ☐ No
2. Features of the property shared in common with adjoining landowners, such as walls, fences, and driveways, whose use or responsibility for maintenance may have an effect on the subject property . . . . ☐ Yes ☐ No
3. Any encroachments, easements or similar matters that may affect your interest in the subject property . . . . ☐ Yes ☐ No
4. Room additions, structural modifications, or other alterations or repairs made without necessary permits . . . . ☐ Yes ☐ No
5. Room additions, structural modifications, or other alterations or repairs not in compliance with building codes . . . . ☐ Yes ☐ No
6. Fill (compacted or otherwise) on the property or any portion thereof . . . . ☐ Yes ☐ No
7. Any settling from any cause, or slippage, sliding, or other soil problems . . . . ☐ Yes ☐ No
8. Flooding, drainage or grading problems . . . . ☐ Yes ☐ No
9. Major damage to the property or any of the structures from fire, earthquake, floods, or landslides . . . . ☐ Yes ☐ No
10. Any zoning violations, nonconforming uses, violations of "setback" requirements . . . . ☐ Yes ☐ No
11. Neighborhood noise problems or other nuisances . . . . ☐ Yes ☐ No
12. CC&R's or other deed restrictions or obligations . . . . ☐ Yes ☐ No
13. Homeowners' Association which has any authority over the subject property . . . . ☐ Yes ☐ No
14. Any "common area" (facilities such as pools, tennis courts, walkways, or other areas co-owned in undivided interest with others) . . . . ☐ Yes ☐ No
15. Any notices of abatement or citations against the property . . . . ☐ Yes ☐ No
16. Any lawsuits by or against the Seller threatening to or affecting this real property, including any lawsuits alleging a defect or deficiency in this real property or "common areas" (facilities such as pools, tennis courts, walkways, or other areas co-owned in undivided interest with others) . . . . ☐ Yes ☐ No

If the answer to any of these is yes, explain. (Attach additional sheets if necessary.): _____
_____
_____
_____
_____

Seller certifies that the information herein is true and correct to the best of the Seller's knowledge as of the date signed by the Seller.

Seller_____   Date _____

Seller_____   Date _____

Buyer's Initials (_____)(_____)
Seller's Initials (_____)(_____)

Copyright © 1991-2003, CALIFORNIA ASSOCIATION OF REALTORS®, INC.
TDS REVISED 10/03 (PAGE 2 OF 3)

Reviewed by _____ Date _____

Real Estate Transfer Disclosure Statement

Property Address: _____ Date: _____

III. AGENT'S INSPECTION DISCLOSURE
(To be completed only if the Seller is represented by an agent in this transaction.)

THE UNDERSIGNED, BASED ON THE ABOVE INQUIRY OF THE SELLER(S) AS TO THE CONDITION OF THE PROPERTY AND BASED ON A REASONABLY COMPETENT AND DILIGENT VISUAL INSPECTION OF THE ACCESSIBLE AREAS OF THE PROPERTY IN CONJUNCTION WITH THAT INQUIRY, STATES THE FOLLOWING:

☐ Agent notes no items for disclosure.

☐ Agent notes the following items: _____

_____

_____

_____

_____

Agent (Broker Representing Seller) _____ By _____ Date _____
(Please Print)   (Associate Licensee or Broker Signature)

IV. AGENT'S INSPECTION DISCLOSURE
(To be completed only if the agent who has obtained the offer is other than the agent above.)

THE UNDERSIGNED, BASED ON A REASONABLY COMPETENT AND DILIGENT VISUAL INSPECTION OF THE ACCESSIBLE AREAS OF THE PROPERTY, STATES THE FOLLOWING:

☐ Agent notes no items for disclosure.

☐ Agent notes the following items: _____

_____

_____

_____

_____

Agent (Broker Obtaining the Offer) _____ By _____ Date _____
(Please Print)   (Associate Licensee or Broker Signature)

V. BUYER(S) AND SELLER(S) MAY WISH TO OBTAIN PROFESSIONAL ADVICE AND/OR INSPECTIONS OF THE PROPERTY AND TO PROVIDE FOR APPROPRIATE PROVISIONS IN A CONTRACT BETWEEN BUYER AND SELLER(S) WITH RESPECT TO ANY ADVICE/INSPECTIONS/DEFECTS.

I/WE ACKNOWLEDGE RECEIPT OF A COPY OF THIS STATEMENT.

Seller _____ Date _____ Buyer _____ Date _____

Seller _____ Date _____ Buyer _____ Date _____

Agent (Broker Representing Seller) _____ By _____ Date _____
(Please Print)   (Associate Licensee or Broker Signature)

Agent (Broker Obtaining the Offer) _____ By _____ Date _____
(Please Print)   (Associate Licensee or Broker Signature)

SECTION 1102.3 OF THE CIVIL CODE PROVIDES A BUYER WITH THE RIGHT TO RESCIND A PURCHASE CONTRACT FOR AT LEAST THREE DAYS AFTER THE DELIVERY OF THIS DISCLOSURE IF DELIVERY OCCURS AFTER THE SIGNING OF AN OFFER TO PURCHASE. IF YOU WISH TO RESCIND THE CONTRACT, YOU MUST ACT WITHIN THE PRESCRIBED PERIOD.

A REAL ESTATE BROKER IS QUALIFIED TO ADVISE ON REAL ESTATE. IF YOU DESIRE LEGAL ADVICE, CONSULT YOUR ATTORNEY.

SURE TRAC Published and Distributed by:
REAL ESTATE BUSINESS SERVICES, INC.
a subsidiary of the California Association of REALTORS®
The System for Success® 525 South Virgil Avenue, Los Angeles, California 90020

TDS REVISED 10/03 (PAGE 3 OF 3)

Reviewed by _____ Date _____

EQUAL HOUSING OPPORTUNITY

Reprinted with permission, CALIFORNIA ASSOCIATION OF REALTORS®. Endorsement not implied.

Appendices

Buyer's Inspection Advisory

CALIFORNIA
ASSOCIATION
OF REALTORS®

BUYER'S INSPECTION ADVISORY
(C.A.R. Form BIA, Revised 10/02)

Property Address: _____ ("Property").

A. IMPORTANCE OF PROPERTY INVESTIGATION: The physical condition of the land and improvements being purchased is not guaranteed by either Seller or Brokers. For this reason, you should conduct thorough investigations of the Property personally and with professionals who should provide written reports of their investigations. A general physical inspection typically does not cover all aspects of the Property nor items affecting the Property that are not physically located on the Property. If the professionals recommend further investigations, including a recommendation by a pest control operator to inspect inaccessible areas of the Property, you should contact qualified experts to conduct such additional investigations.

B. BUYER RIGHTS AND DUTIES: You have an affirmative duty to exercise reasonable care to protect yourself, including discovery of the legal, practical and technical implications of disclosed facts, and the investigation and verification of information and facts that you know or that are within your diligent attention and observation. The purchase agreement gives you the right to investigate the Property. If you exercise this right, and you should, you must do so in accordance with the terms of that agreement. This is the best way for you to protect yourself. It is extremely important for you to read all written reports provided by professionals and to discuss the results of inspections with the professional who conducted the inspection. You have the right to request that Seller make repairs, corrections or take other action based upon items discovered in your investigations or disclosed by Seller. If Seller is unwilling or unable to satisfy your requests, or you do not want to purchase the Property in its disclosed and discovered condition, you have the right to cancel the agreement if you act within specific time periods. If you do not cancel the agreement in a timely and proper manner, you may be in breach of contract.

C. SELLER RIGHTS AND DUTIES: Seller is required to disclose to you material facts known to him/her that affect the value or desirability of the Property. However, Seller may not be aware of some Property defects or conditions. Seller does not have an obligation to inspect the Property for your benefit nor is Seller obligated to repair, correct or otherwise cure known defects that are disclosed to you or previously unknown defects that are discovered by you or your inspectors during escrow. The purchase agreement obligates Seller to make the Property available to you for investigations.

D. BROKER OBLIGATIONS: Brokers do not have expertise in all areas and therefore cannot advise you on many items, such as soil stability, geologic or environmental conditions, hazardous or illegal controlled substances, structural conditions of the foundation or other improvements, or the condition of the roof, plumbing, heating, air conditioning, electrical, sewer, septic, waste disposal, or other system. The only way to accurately determine the condition of the Property is through an inspection by an appropriate professional selected by you. If Broker gives you referrals to such professionals, Broker does not guarantee their performance. You may select any professional of your choosing. In sales involving residential dwellings with no more than four units, Brokers have a duty to make a diligent visual inspection of the accessible areas of the Property and to disclose the results of that inspection. However, as some Property defects or conditions may not be discoverable from a visual inspection, it is possible Brokers are not aware of them. If you have entered into a written agreement with a Broker, the specific terms of that agreement will determine the nature and extent of that Broker's duty to you. **YOU ARE STRONGLY ADVISED TO INVESTIGATE THE CONDITION AND SUITABILITY OF ALL ASPECTS OF THE PROPERTY. IF YOU DO NOT DO SO, YOU ARE ACTING AGAINST THE ADVICE OF BROKERS.**

E. YOU ARE ADVISED TO CONDUCT INVESTIGATIONS OF THE ENTIRE PROPERTY, INCLUDING, BUT NOT LIMITED TO THE FOLLOWING:
   1. **GENERAL CONDITION OF THE PROPERTY, ITS SYSTEMS AND COMPONENTS:** Foundation, roof, plumbing, heating, air conditioning, electrical, mechanical, security, pool/spa, other structural and non-structural systems and components, fixtures, built-in appliances, any personal property included in the sale, and energy efficiency of the Property. (Structural engineers are best suited to determine possible design or construction defects, and whether improvements are structurally sound.)
   2. **SQUARE FOOTAGE, AGE, BOUNDARIES:** Square footage, room dimensions, lot size, age of improvements and boundaries. Any numerical statements regarding these items are APPROXIMATIONS ONLY and have not been verified by Seller and cannot be verified by Brokers. Fences, hedges, walls, retaining walls and other natural or constructed barriers or markers do not necessarily identify true Property boundaries. (Professionals such as appraisers, architects, surveyors and civil engineers are best suited to determine square footage, dimensions and boundaries of the Property.)
   3. **WOOD DESTROYING PESTS:** Presence of, or conditions likely to lead to the presence of wood destroying pests and organisms and other infestation or infection. Inspection reports covering these items can be separated into two sections: Section 1 identifies areas where infestation or infection is evident. Section 2 identifies areas where there are conditions likely to lead to infestation or infection. A registered structural pest control company is best suited to perform these inspections.
   4. **SOIL STABILITY:** Existence of fill or compacted soil, expansive or contracting soil, susceptibility to slippage, settling or movement, and the adequacy of drainage. (Geotechnical engineers are best suited to determine such conditions, causes and remedies.)

Buyer's Initials (_____)(_____)
Seller's Initials (_____)(_____)

Reviewed by _____ Date _____

EQUAL HOUSING
OPPORTUNITY

Buyer's Inspection Advisory

Property Address: _____ Date: _____

5. **ROOF:** Present condition, age, leaks, and remaining useful life. (Roofing contractors are best suited to determine these conditions.)

6. **POOL/SPA:** Cracks, leaks or operational problems. (Pool contractors are best suited to determine these conditions.)

7. **WASTE DISPOSAL:** Type, size, adequacy, capacity and condition of sewer and septic systems and components, connection to sewer, and applicable fees.

8. **WATER AND UTILITIES; WELL SYSTEMS AND COMPONENTS:** Water and utility availability, use restrictions and costs. Water quality, adequacy, condition, and performance of well systems and components.

9. **ENVIRONMENTAL HAZARDS:** Potential environmental hazards, including, but not limited to, asbestos, lead-based paint and other lead contamination, radon, methane, other gases, fuel oil or chemical storage tanks, contaminated soil or water, hazardous waste, waste disposal sites, electromagnetic fields, nuclear sources, and other substances, materials, products, or conditions (including mold (airborne, toxic or otherwise), fungus or similar contaminants). (For more in formation on these items, you may consult an appropriate professional or read the booklets "Environmental Hazards: A Guide for Homeowners, Buyers, Landlords and Tenants," "Protect Your Family From Lead in Your Home" or both.)

10. **EARTHQUAKES AND FLOODING:** Susceptibility of the Property to earthquake/seismic hazards and propensity of the Property to flood. (A Geologist or Geotechnical Engineer is best suited to provide information on these conditions.)

11. **FIRE, HAZARD AND OTHER INSURANCE:** The availability and cost of necessary or desired insurance may vary. The location of the Property in a seismic, flood or fire hazard zone, and other conditions, such as the age of the Property and the claims history of the Property and Buyer, may affect the availability and need for certain types of insurance. Buyer should explore insurance options early as this information may affect other decisions, including the removal of loan and inspection contingencies. (An insurance agent is best suited to provide information on these conditions.)

12. **BUILDING PERMITS, ZONING AND GOVERNMENTAL REQUIREMENTS:** Permits, inspections, certificates, zoning, other governmental limitations, restrictions, and requirements affecting the current or future use of the Property, its development or size. (Such information is available from appropriate governmental agencies and private information providers. Brokers are not qualified to review or interpret any such information.)

13. **RENTAL PROPERTY RESTRICTIONS:** Some cities and counties impose restrictions that limit the amount of rent that can be charged, the maximum number of occupants, and the right of a landlord to terminate a tenancy. Deadbolt or other locks and security systems for doors and windows, including window bars, should be examined to determine whether they satisfy legal requirements. (Government agencies can provide information about these restrictions and other requirements.)

14. **SECURITY AND SAFETY:** State and local Law may require the installation of barriers, access alarms, self-latching mechanisms and/or other measures to decrease the risk to children and other persons of existing swimming pools and hot tubs, as well as various fire safety and other measures concerning other features of the Property. Compliance requirements differ from city to city and county to county. Unless specifically agreed, the Property may not be in compliance with these requirements. (Local government agencies can provide information about these restrictions and other requirements.)

15. **NEIGHBORHOOD, AREA, SUBDIVISION CONDITIONS; PERSONAL FACTORS:** Neighborhood or area conditions, including schools, proximity and adequacy of law enforcement, crime statistics, the proximity of registered felons or offenders, fire protection, other government services, availability, adequacy and cost of any speed-wired, wireless internet connections or other telecommunications or other technology services and installations, proximity to commercial, industrial or agricultural activities, existing and proposed transportation, construction and development that may affect noise, view, or traffic, airport noise, noise or odor from any source, wild and domestic animals, other nuisances, hazards, or circumstances, protected species, wetland properties, botanical diseases, historic or other governmentally protected sites or improvements, cemeteries, facilities and condition of common areas of common interest subdivisions, and possible lack of compliance with any governing documents or Homeowners' Association requirements, conditions and influences of significance to certain cultures and/or religions, and personal needs, requirements and preferences of Buyer.

Buyer and Seller acknowledge and agree that Broker: **(i)** Does not decide what price Buyer should pay or Seller should accept; **(ii)** Does not guarantee the condition of the Property; **(iii)** Does not guarantee the performance, adequacy or completeness of inspections, services, products or repairs provided or made by Seller or others; **(iv)** Does not have an obligation to conduct an inspection of common areas or areas off the site of the Property; **(v)** Shall not be responsible for identifying defects on the Property, in common areas, or offsite unless such defects are visually observable by an inspection of reasonably accessible areas of the Property or are known to Broker; **(vi)** Shall not be responsible for inspecting public records or permits concerning the title or use of Property; **(vii)** Shall not be responsible for identifying the location of boundary lines or other items affecting title; **(viii)** Shall not be responsible for verifying square footage, representations of others or information contained in Investigation reports, Multiple Listing Service, advertisements, flyers or other promotional material; **(ix)** Shall not be responsible for providing legal or tax advice regarding any aspect of a transaction entered into by Buyer or Seller; and **(x)** Shall not be responsible for providing other advice or information that exceeds the knowledge, education and experience required to perform real estate licensed activity. Buyer and Seller agree to seek legal, tax, insurance, title and other desired assistance from appropriate professionals.

By signing below, Buyer and Seller each acknowledge that they have read, understand, accept and have received a Copy of this Advisory. Buyer is encouraged to read it carefully.

_____   _____   _____   _____
Buyer Signature   Date   Buyer Signature   Date

_____   _____   _____   _____
Seller Signature   Date   Seller Signature   Date

Published and Distributed by:
REAL ESTATE BUSINESS SERVICES, INC.
a subsidiary of the California Association of REALTORS®
525 South Virgil Avenue, Los Angeles, California 90020

The System for Success®

Reviewed by _____ Date _____

EQUAL HOUSING OPPORTUNITY

BIA REVISED 10/02 (PAGE 2 OF 2)

Reprinted with permission, CALIFORNIA ASSOCIATION OF REALTORS®. Endorsement not implied.

California Residential Purchase Agreement

CALIFORNIA ASSOCIATION OF REALTORS®

CALIFORNIA RESIDENTIAL PURCHASE AGREEMENT AND JOINT ESCROW INSTRUCTIONS
For Use With Single Family Residential Property — Attached or Detached
(C.A.R. Form RPA-CA, Revised 1/06)

Date _____, at _____, California.
1. **OFFER:**
   A. **THIS IS AN OFFER FROM** _____ ("Buyer").
   B. **THE REAL PROPERTY TO BE ACQUIRED** is described as _____
   _____, Assessor's Parcel No. _____, situated in
   _____, County of _____, California, ("Property").
   C. **THE PURCHASE PRICE** offered is _____
   _____ Dollars $ _____
   D. **CLOSE OF ESCROW** shall occur on _____ (date)(or □ _____ **Days** After Acceptance).
2. **FINANCE TERMS:** Obtaining the loans below **is a contingency** of this Agreement unless: (I) either 2K or 2L is checked below; or
   (ii) otherwise agreed in writing. Buyer shall act diligently and in good faith to obtain the designated loans. Obtaining deposit, down
   payment and closing costs **is not a contingency.** Buyer represents that funds will be good when deposited with Escrow Holder.
   A. **INITIAL DEPOSIT:** Buyer has given a deposit in the amount of ....$ _____
   to the agent submitting the offer (or to □ _____), by personal check
   (or □ _____), made payable to _____,
   which shall be held uncashed until Acceptance and then deposited within **3** business days after
   Acceptance (or □ _____), with
   Escrow Holder, (or □ into Broker's trust account).
   B. **INCREASED DEPOSIT:** Buyer shall deposit with Escrow Holder an increased deposit in the amount of ....$ _____
   within _____ **Days** After Acceptance, or □ _____.
   C. **FIRST LOAN IN THE AMOUNT OF** ....$ _____
   (1) NEW First Deed of Trust in favor of lender, encumbering the Property, securing a note payable at
   maximum interest of _____% fixed rate, or _____% initial adjustable rate with a maximum
   interest rate of _____%, balance due in _____ years, amortized over _____ years. Buyer
   shall pay loan fees/points not to exceed _____. (These terms apply whether the designated loan
   is conventional, FHA or VA.)
   (2) □ FHA □ VA: (The following terms only apply to the FHA or VA loan that is checked.)
   Seller shall pay _____% discount points. Seller shall pay other fees not allowed to be paid by
   Buyer, □ not to exceed $_____ Seller shall pay the cost of lender required Repairs
   (including those for wood destroying pest) not otherwise provided for in this Agreement, □ not to
   exceed $ _____. (Actual loan amount may increase if mortgage insurance premiums,
   funding fees or closing costs are financed.)
   D. **ADDITIONAL FINANCING TERMS:** □ Seller financing, (C.A.R. Form SFA); □ secondary financing, ...$ _____
   (C.A.R. Form PAA, paragraph 4A); □ assumed financing (C.A.R. Form PAA, paragraph 4B) _____
   _____
   E. **BALANCE OF PURCHASE PRICE** (not including costs of obtaining loans and other closing costs) in the amount of ...$ _____
   to be deposited with Escrow Holder in sufficient time to close escrow.
   F. **PURCHASE PRICE (TOTAL):** ....$ _____
   G. **LOAN APPLICATIONS:** Within 7 (or □ _____) **Days** After Acceptance, Buyer shall provide Seller a letter from lender or
   mortgage loan broker stating that, based on a review of Buyer's written application and credit report, Buyer is prequalified or
   preapproved for the NEW loan specified in 2C above.
   H. **VERIFICATION OF DOWN PAYMENT AND CLOSING COSTS:** Buyer (or Buyer's lender or loan broker pursuant to 2G) shall, within
   7 (or □ _____) **Days** After Acceptance, provide Seller written verification of Buyer's down payment and closing costs.
   I. **LOAN CONTINGENCY REMOVAL:** (I) Within 17 (or □ _____) **Days** After Acceptance, Buyer shall, as specified in paragraph
   14, remove the loan contingency or cancel this Agreement; **OR** (ii) (if checked) □ the loan contingency shall remain in effect
   until the designated loans are funded.
   J. **APPRAISAL CONTINGENCY AND REMOVAL:** This Agreement is (**OR**, if checked, □ is NOT) contingent upon the Property
   appraising at no less than the specified purchase price. If there is a loan contingency, at the time the loan contingency is
   removed (or, if checked, □ within 17 (or _____) **Days** After Acceptance) Buyer shall, as specified in paragraph 14B(3), remove
   the appraisal contingency or cancel this Agreement. If there is no loan contingency, Buyer shall, as specified in paragraph
   14B(3), remove the appraisal contingency within 17 (or _____) **Days** After Acceptance.
   K. □ **NO LOAN CONTINGENCY** (if checked): Obtaining any loan in paragraphs 2O, 2D or elsewhere in this Agreement is NOT
   a contingency of this Agreement. If Buyer does not obtain the loan and as a result Buyer does not purchase the Property, Seller
   may be entitled to Buyer's deposit or other legal remedies.
   L. □ **ALL CASH OFFER** (if checked): No loan is needed to purchase the Property. Buyer shall, within 7 (or □ _____) **Days** After Acceptance,
   provide Seller written verification of sufficient funds to close this transaction.
3. **CLOSING AND OCCUPANCY:**
   A. Buyer intends (or □ does not intend) to occupy the Property as Buyer's primary residence.
   B. **Seller-occupied or vacant property:** Occupancy shall be delivered to Buyer at _____ AM/PM, □ on the date of Close Of
   Escrow; □ on _____; or □ no later than _____ **Days** After Close Of Escrow. (C.A.R. Form PAA, paragraph 2.) If
   transfer of title and occupancy do not occur at the same time, Buyer and Seller are advised to: (i) enter into a written occupancy
   agreement; and (ii) consult with their insurance and legal advisors.

RPA-CA REVISED 1/06 (PAGE 1 OF 8) Print Date

Buyer's Initials (_____)(_____)
Seller's Initials (_____)(_____)

Reviewed by _____ Date _____

EQUAL HOUSING OPPORTUNITY

California Residential Purchase Agreement

Property Address: _____   Date: _____

    C. **Tenant-occupied property: (i) Property shall be vacant** at least 5 (or ☐ _____) **Days** Prior to Close Of Escrow, unless otherwise agreed in writing. **Note to Seller: If you are unable to deliver Property vacant in accordance with rent control and other applicable Law, you may be in breach of this Agreement.**

    OR (ii) (if checked) ☐ **Tenant to remain in possession.** The attached addendum is incorporated into this Agreement (C.A.R. Form PAA, paragraph 3.);

    OR (iii) (if checked) ☐ **This Agreement is contingent** upon Buyer and Seller entering into a written agreement regarding occupancy of the Property within the time specified in paragraph 14B(1). If no written agreement is reached within this time, either Buyer or Seller may cancel this Agreement in writing.

    D. At Close Of Escrow, Seller assigns to Buyer any assignable warranty rights for items included in the sale and shall provide any available Copies of such warranties. Brokers cannot and will not determine the assignability of any warranties.

    E. At Close Of Escrow, unless otherwise agreed in writing, Seller shall provide keys and/or means to operate all locks, mailboxes, security systems, alarms and garage door openers. If Property is a condominium or located in a common interest subdivision, Buyer may be required to pay a deposit to the Homeowners' Association ("HOA") to obtain keys to accessible HOA facilities.

4. **ALLOCATION OF COSTS** (If checked): Unless otherwise specified here, this paragraph only determines who is to pay for the report, inspection, test or service mentioned. If not specified here or elsewhere in this Agreement, the determination of who is to pay for any work recommended or identified by any such report, inspection, test or service shall be by the method specified in paragraph 14B(2).

    A. **WOOD DESTROYING PEST INSPECTION:**

        (1) ☐ Buyer ☐ Seller shall pay for an inspection and report for wood destroying pests and organisms ("Report") which shall be prepared by _____, a registered structural pest control company. The Report shall cover the accessible areas of the main building and attached structures and, if checked: ☐ detached garages and carports, ☐ detached decks, ☐ the following other structures or areas _____. The Report shall not include roof coverings. If Property is a condominium or located in a common interest subdivision, the Report shall include only the separate interest and any exclusive-use areas being transferred and shall not include common areas, unless otherwise agreed. Water tests of shower pans on upper level units may not be performed without consent of the owners of property below the shower.

        OR (2) ☐ **(If checked)** The attached addendum (C.A.R. Form WPA) regarding wood destroying pest inspection and allocation of cost is incorporated into this Agreement.

    B. **OTHER INSPECTIONS AND REPORTS:**

        (1) ☐ Buyer ☐ Seller shall pay to have septic or private sewage disposal systems inspected _____.

        (2) ☐ Buyer ☐ Seller shall pay to have domestic wells tested for water potability and productivity _____.

        (3) ☐ Buyer ☐ Seller shall pay for a natural hazard zone disclosure report prepared by _____.

        (4) ☐ Buyer ☐ Seller shall pay for the following inspection or report _____.

        (5) ☐ Buyer ☐ Seller shall pay for the following inspection or report _____.

    C. **GOVERNMENT REQUIREMENTS AND RETROFIT:**

        (1) ☐ Buyer ☐ Seller shall pay for smoke detector installation and/or water heater bracing, if required by Law. Prior to Close Of Escrow, Seller shall provide Buyer a written statement of compliance in accordance with state and local Law, unless exempt.

        (2) ☐ Buyer ☐ Seller shall pay the cost of compliance with any other minimum mandatory government retrofit standards, inspections and reports if required as a condition of closing escrow under any Law. _____.

    D. **ESCROW AND TITLE:**

        (1) ☐ Buyer ☐ Seller shall pay escrow fee _____.
        Escrow Holder shall be _____.

        (2) ☐ Buyer ☐ Seller shall pay for **owner's** title insurance policy specified in paragraph 12E _____.
        Owner's title policy to be issued by _____.
        (Buyer shall pay for any title insurance policy insuring Buyer's **lender**, unless otherwise agreed in writing.)

    E. **OTHER COSTS:**

        (1) ☐ Buyer ☐ Seller shall pay County transfer tax or transfer fee _____.

        (2) ☐ Buyer ☐ Seller shall pay City transfer tax or transfer fee _____.

        (3) ☐ Buyer ☐ Seller shall pay HOA transfer fee _____.

        (4) ☐ Buyer ☐ Seller shall pay HOA document preparation fees _____.

        (5) ☐ Buyer ☐ Seller shall pay the cost, not to exceed $ _____, of a one-year home warranty plan, issued by _____,
        with the following optional coverage: _____.

        (6) ☐ Buyer ☐ Seller shall pay for _____.

        (7) ☐ Buyer ☐ Seller shall pay for _____.

5. **STATUTORY DISCLOSURES (INCLUDING LEAD-BASED PAINT HAZARD DISCLOSURES) AND CANCELLATION RIGHTS:**

    A. **(1)** Seller shall, within the time specified in paragraph 14A, deliver to Buyer, if required by Law: **(i)** Federal Lead-Based Paint Disclosures and pamphlet ("Lead Disclosures"); and **(ii)** disclosures or notices required by sections 1102 et. seq. and 1103 et. seq. of the California Civil Code ("Statutory Disclosures"). Statutory Disclosures include, but are not limited to, a Real Estate Transfer Disclosure Statement ("TDS"), Natural Hazard Disclosure Statement ("NHD"), notice or actual knowledge of release of illegal controlled substance, notice of special tax and/or assessments (or, if allowed, substantially equivalent notice regarding the Mello-Roos Community Facilities Act and Improvement Bond Act of 1915) and, if Seller has actual knowledge, an industrial use and military ordnance location disclosure (C.A.R. Form SSD).

        (2) Buyer shall, within the time specified in paragraph 14B(1), return Signed Copies of the Statutory and Lead Disclosures to Seller.

        (3) In the event Seller, prior to Close Of Escrow, becomes aware of adverse conditions materially affecting the Property, or any material inaccuracy in disclosures, information or representations previously provided to Buyer of which Buyer is otherwise unaware, Seller shall promptly provide a subsequent or amended disclosure or notice, in writing, covering those items. **However, a subsequent or amended disclosure shall not be required for conditions and material inaccuracies disclosed in reports ordered and paid for by Buyer.**

Buyer's Initials (_____)(_____)
Seller's Initials (_____)(_____)

RPA-CA REVISED 1/06 (PAGE 2 OF 8)

Reviewed by _____ Date _____

☖ EQUAL HOUSING OPPORTUNITY

Reprinted with permission, CALIFORNIA ASSOCIATION OF REALTORS®. Endorsement not implied.

Appendices

California Residential Purchase Agreement

Property Address: _____   Date: _____

   (4) If any disclosure or notice specified in 5A(1), or subsequent or amended disclosure or notice is delivered to Buyer after the offer
       is Signed, Buyer shall have the right to cancel this Agreement within **3 Days** After delivery in person, or **5 Days** After delivery
       by deposit in the mail, by giving written notice of cancellation to Seller or Seller's agent. (Lead Disclosures sent by mail must
       be sent certified mail or better.)
   (5) Note to Buyer and Seller: Waiver of Statutory and Lead Disclosures is prohibited by Law.
   B. **NATURAL AND ENVIRONMENTAL HAZARDS:** Within the time specified in paragraph 14A, Seller shall, if required by Law:
       (i) deliver to Buyer earthquake guides (and questionnaire) and environmental hazards booklet; **(ii)** even if exempt from the
       obligation to provide a NHD, disclose if the Property is located in a Special Flood Hazard Area; Potential Flooding (Inundation)
       Area; Very High Fire Hazard Zone; State Fire Responsibility Area; Earthquake Fault Zone; Seismic Hazard Zone; and **(iii)**
       disclose any other zone as required by Law and provide any other information required for those zones.
   C. **DATA BASE DISCLOSURE:** Notice: Pursuant to Section 290.46 of the Penal Code, information about specified registered sex
       offenders is made available to the public via an Internet Web site maintained by the Department of Justice at
       www.meganslaw.ca.gov. Depending on an offender's criminal history, this information will include either the address at which
       the offender resides or the community of residence and ZIP Code in which he or she resides. (Neither Seller nor Brokers are
       required to check this website. If Buyer wants further information, Broker recommends that Buyer obtain information from this
       website during Buyer's inspection contingency period. Brokers do not have expertise in this area.)
6. **CONDOMINIUM/PLANNED UNIT DEVELOPMENT DISCLOSURES:**
   A. **SELLER HAS: 7 (or ☐ _____) Days** After Acceptance to disclose to Buyer whether the Property is a condominium, or is
       located in a planned unit development or other common interest subdivision (C.A.R. Form SSD).
   B. If the Property is a condominium or is located in a planned unit development or other common interest subdivision, Seller
       has **3 (or ☐ _____) Days** After Acceptance to request from the HOA (C.A.R. Form HOA): **(i)** Copies of any documents
       required by Law; **(ii)** disclosure of any pending or anticipated claim or litigation by or against the HOA; **(iii)** a statement
       containing the location and number of designated parking and storage spaces; **(iv)** Copies of the most recent 12 months of
       HOA minutes for regular and special meetings; and **(v)** the names and contact information of all HOAs governing the Property
       (collectively, "CI Disclosures"). Seller shall itemize and deliver to Buyer all CI Disclosures received from the HOA and any CI
       Disclosures in Seller's possession. Buyer's approval of CI Disclosures is a contingency of this Agreement as specified in
       paragraph 14B(3).
7. **CONDITIONS AFFECTING PROPERTY:**
   A. Unless otherwise agreed: **(i) the Property is sold (a) in its PRESENT physical condition as of the date of Acceptance and
       (b) subject to Buyer's Investigation rights; (ii)** the Property, including pool, spa, landscaping and grounds, is to be
       maintained in substantially the same condition as on the date of Acceptance; and **(iii)** all debris and personal property not
       included in the sale shall be removed by Close Of Escrow.
   B. **SELLER SHALL, within the time specified in paragraph 14A, DISCLOSE KNOWN MATERIAL FACTS AND DEFECTS
       affecting the Property, including known insurance claims within the past five years, AND MAKE OTHER DISCLOSURES
       REQUIRED BY LAW (C.A.R. Form SSD).**
   C. **NOTE TO BUYER:** You are strongly advised to conduct investigations of the entire Property in order to determine its
       present condition since Seller may not be aware of all defects affecting the Property or other factors that you consider
       important. Property improvements may not be built according to code, in compliance with current Law, or have had
       permits issued.
   D. **NOTE TO SELLER:** Buyer has the right to inspect the Property and, as specified in paragraph 14B, based upon
       information discovered in those inspections: **(i)** cancel this Agreement; or **(ii)** request that you make Repairs or take
       other action.
8. **ITEMS INCLUDED AND EXCLUDED:**
   A. **NOTE TO BUYER AND SELLER:** Items listed as included or excluded in the MLS, flyers or marketing materials are **not**
       included in the purchase price or excluded from the sale unless specified in 8B or C.
   B. **ITEMS INCLUDED IN SALE:**
       (1) All EXISTING fixtures and fittings that are attached to the Property;
       (2) Existing electrical, mechanical, lighting, plumbing and heating fixtures, ceiling fans, fireplace inserts, gas logs and grates,
           solar systems, built-in appliances, window and door screens, awnings, shutters, window coverings, attached floor coverings,
           television antennas, satellite dishes, private integrated telephone systems, air coolers/conditioners, pool/spa equipment,
           garage door openers/remote controls, mailbox, in-ground landscaping, trees/shrubs, water softeners, water purifiers,
           security systems/alarms; and
       (3) The following items: _____
       _____.
       (4) Seller represents that all items included in the purchase price, unless otherwise specified, are owned by Seller.
       (5) All items included shall be transferred free of liens and without Seller warranty.
   C. **ITEMS EXCLUDED FROM SALE:** _____

9. **BUYER'S INVESTIGATION OF PROPERTY AND MATTERS AFFECTING PROPERTY:**
   A. Buyer's acceptance of the condition of, and any other matter affecting the Property, is a contingency of this Agreement as
       specified in this paragraph and paragraph 14B. Within the time specified in paragraph 14B(1), Buyer shall have the right, at
       Buyer's expense unless otherwise agreed, to conduct inspections, investigations, tests, surveys and other studies ("Buyer
       Investigations"), including, but not limited to, the right to: **(i)** inspect for lead-based paint and other lead-based paint hazards;
       (ii) inspect for wood destroying pests and organisms; **(iii)** review the registered sex offender database; **(iv)** confirm the
       insurability of Buyer and the Property; and **(v)** satisfy Buyer as to any matter specified in the attached Buyer's Inspection
       Advisory (C.A.R. Form BIA). Without Seller's prior written consent, Buyer shall neither make nor cause to be made: **(i)** invasive
       or destructive Buyer Investigations; or **(ii)** inspections by any governmental building or zoning inspector or government
       employee, unless required by Law.
   B. Buyer shall complete Buyer Investigations and, as specified in paragraph 14B, remove the contingency or cancel this
       Agreement. Buyer shall give Seller, at no cost, complete Copies of all Buyer Investigation reports obtained by Buyer. Seller
       shall make the Property available for all Buyer Investigations. Seller shall have water, gas, electricity and all operable pilot lights
       on for Buyer's Investigations and through the date possession is made available to Buyer.

Buyer's Initials (_____)(_____)
Seller's Initials (_____)(_____)

Reviewed by _____ Date _____

☰ EQUAL HOUSING OPPORTUNITY

California Residential Purchase Agreement

Property Address: _____   Date: _____

10. **REPAIRS:** Repairs shall be completed prior to final verification of condition unless otherwise agreed in writing. Repairs to be performed at Seller's expense may be performed by Seller or through others, provided that the work complies with applicable Law, including governmental permit, inspection and approval requirements. Repairs shall be performed in a good, skillful manner with materials of quality and appearance comparable to existing materials. It is understood that exact restoration of appearance or cosmetic items following all Repairs may not be possible. Seller shall: **(i)** obtain receipts for Repairs performed by others; **(ii)** prepare a written statement indicating the Repairs performed by Seller and the date of such Repairs; and **(iii)** provide Copies of receipts and statements to Buyer prior to final verification of condition.

11. **BUYER INDEMNITY AND SELLER PROTECTION FOR ENTRY UPON PROPERTY:** Buyer shall: **(i)** keep the Property free and clear of liens; **(ii)** Repair all damage arising from Buyer Investigations; and **(iii)** indemnify and hold Seller harmless from all resulting liability, claims, demands, damages and costs. Buyer shall carry, or Buyer shall require anyone acting on Buyer's behalf to carry, policies of liability, workers' compensation and other applicable insurance, defending and protecting Seller from liability for any injuries to persons or property occurring during any Buyer Investigations or work done on the Property at Buyer's direction prior to Close Of Escrow. Seller is advised that certain protections may be afforded Seller by recording a "Notice of Non-responsibility" (C.A.R. Form NNR) for Buyer Investigations and work done on the Property at Buyer's direction. Buyer's obligations under this paragraph shall survive the termination of this Agreement.

12. **TITLE AND VESTING:**
    A. Within the time specified in paragraph 14, Buyer shall be provided a current preliminary (title) report, which is only an offer by the title insurer to issue a policy of title insurance and may not contain every item affecting title. Buyer's review of the preliminary report and any other matters which may affect title are a contingency of this Agreement as specified in paragraph 14B.
    B. Title is taken in its present condition subject to all encumbrances, easements, covenants, conditions, restrictions, rights and other matters, whether of record or not, as of the date of Acceptance except: **(i)** monetary liens of record unless Buyer is assuming those obligations or taking the Property subject to those obligations; and **(ii)** those matters which Seller has agreed to remove in writing.
    C. Within the time specified in paragraph 14A, Seller has a duty to disclose to Buyer all matters known to Seller affecting title, whether of record or not.
    D. At Close Of Escrow, Buyer shall receive a grant deed conveying title (or, for stock cooperative or long-term lease, an assignment of stock certificate or of Seller's leasehold interest), including oil, mineral and water rights if currently owned by Seller. Title shall vest as designated in Buyer's supplemental escrow instructions. THE MANNER OF TAKING TITLE MAY HAVE SIGNIFICANT LEGAL AND TAX CONSEQUENCES. CONSULT AN APPROPRIATE PROFESSIONAL.
    E. Buyer shall receive a CLTA/ALTA Homeowner's Policy of Title Insurance. A title company, at Buyer's request, can provide information about the availability, desirability, coverage, and cost of various title insurance coverages and endorsements. If Buyer desires title coverage other than that required by this paragraph, Buyer shall instruct Escrow Holder in writing and pay any increase in cost.

13. **SALE OF BUYER'S PROPERTY:**
    A. This Agreement is NOT contingent upon the sale of any property owned by Buyer.
    OR B. ☐ (If checked): The attached addendum (C.A.R. Form COP) regarding the contingency for the sale of property owned by Buyer is incorporated into this Agreement.

14. **TIME PERIODS; REMOVAL OF CONTINGENCIES; CANCELLATION RIGHTS: The following time periods may only be extended, altered, modified or changed by mutual written agreement. Any removal of contingencies or cancellation under this paragraph must be in writing (C.A.R. Form CR).**
    A. SELLER HAS: 7 (or ☐ _____) Days After Acceptance to deliver to Buyer all reports, disclosures and information for which Seller is responsible under paragraphs 4, 5A and B, 6A, 7B and 12.
    B. (1) BUYER HAS: 17 (or ☐ _____) Days After Acceptance, unless otherwise agreed in writing, to:
        (i) complete all Buyer Investigations; approve all disclosures, reports and other applicable information, which Buyer receives from Seller; and approve all matters affecting the Property (including lead-based paint and lead-based paint hazards as well as other information specified in paragraph 5 and insurability of Buyer and the Property); and
        (ii) return to Seller Signed Copies of Statutory and Lead Disclosures delivered by Seller in accordance with paragraph 5A.
        (2) Within the time specified in 14B(1), Buyer may request that Seller make repairs or take any other action regarding the Property (C.A.R. Form RR). Seller has no obligation to agree to or respond to Buyer's requests.
        (3) By the end of the time specified in 14B(1) (or 2I for loan contingency or 2J for appraisal contingency), Buyer shall, in writing, remove the applicable contingency (C.A.R. Form CR) or cancel this Agreement. However, if **(i)** government-mandated inspections/ reports required as a condition of closing; or **(ii)** Common Interest Disclosures pursuant to paragraph 6B are not made within the time specified in 14A, then Buyer has **5 (or ☐ _____) Days** After receipt of any such items, or the time specified in 14B(1), whichever is later, to remove the applicable contingency or cancel this Agreement in writing.
    C. CONTINUATION OF CONTINGENCY OR CONTRACTUAL OBLIGATION; SELLER RIGHT TO CANCEL:
        (1) Seller right to Cancel; Buyer Contingencies: Seller, after first giving Buyer a Notice to Buyer to Perform (as specified below), may cancel this Agreement in writing and authorize return of Buyer's deposit if, by the time specified in this Agreement, Buyer does not remove in writing the applicable contingency or cancel this Agreement. Once all contingencies have been removed, failure of Buyer or Seller to close escrow on time may be a breach of this Agreement.
        (2) Continuation of Contingency: Even after the expiration of the time specified in 14B, Buyer retains the right to make requests to Seller, remove in writing the applicable contingency or cancel this Agreement until Seller cancels pursuant to 14C(1). Once Seller receives Buyer's written removal of all contingencies, Seller may not cancel this Agreement pursuant to 14C(1).
        (3) Seller right to Cancel; Buyer Contract Obligations: Seller, after first giving Buyer a Notice to Buyer to Perform (as specified below), may cancel this Agreement in writing and authorize return of Buyer's deposit for any of the following reasons: **(i)** if Buyer fails to deposit funds as required by 2A or 2B; **(ii)** if the funds deposited pursuant to 2A or 2B are not good when deposited; **(iii)** if Buyer fails to provide a letter as required by 2G; **(iv)** if Buyer fails to provide verification as required by 2H or 2L; **(v)** if Seller reasonably disapproves of the verification provided by 2H or 2L; **(vi)** if Buyer fails to return Statutory and Lead Disclosures as required by paragraph 5A(2); or **(vii)** if Buyer fails to sign or initial a separate liquidated damage form for an increased deposit as required by paragraph 16. **Seller is not required to give Buyer a Notice to Perform regarding Close of Escrow.**
        (4) Notice To Buyer To Perform: The Notice to Buyer to Perform (C.A.R. Form NBP) shall: **(i)** be in writing; **(ii)** be signed by Seller; and **(iii)** give Buyer at least **24 (or _____)** hours (or until the time specified in the applicable paragraph, whichever occurs last) to take the applicable action. A Notice to Buyer to Perform may not be given any earlier than **2 Days** Prior to the expiration of the applicable time for Buyer to remove a contingency or cancel this Agreement or meet a 14C(3) obligation.

Buyer's Initials (_____)(_____)
Seller's Initials (_____)(_____)

RPA-CA REVISED 1/06 (PAGE 4 OF 8)

Reviewed by _____ Date _____

EQUAL HOUSING
OPPORTUNITY

California Residential Purchase Agreement

Property Address: _____   Date: _____

D. **EFFECT OF BUYER'S REMOVAL OF CONTINGENCIES :** If Buyer removes, in writing, any contingency or cancellation rights, unless otherwise specified in a separate written agreement between Buyer and Seller, Buyer shall conclusively be deemed to have: **(i)** completed all Buyer Investigations, and review of reports and other applicable information and disclosures pertaining to that contingency or cancellation right; **(ii)** elected to proceed with the transaction; and **(iii)** assumed all liability, responsibility and expense for Repairs or corrections pertaining to that contingency or cancellation right, or for inability to obtain financing.

E. **EFFECT OF CANCELLATION ON DEPOSITS:** If Buyer or Seller gives written notice of cancellation pursuant to rights duly exercised under the terms of this Agreement, Buyer and Seller agree to Sign mutual instructions to cancel the sale and escrow and release deposits to the party entitled to the funds, less fees and costs incurred by that party. Fees and costs may be payable to service providers and vendors for services and products provided during escrow. **Release of funds will require mutual Signed release instructions from Buyer and Seller, judicial decision or arbitration award. A party may be subject to a civil penalty of up to $1,000 for refusal to sign such instructions if no good faith dispute exists as to who is entitled to the deposited funds (Civil Code §1057.3).**

15. **FINAL VERIFICATION OF CONDITION:** Buyer shall have the right to make a final inspection of the Property within **5 (or _____) Days** Prior to Close Of Escrow, NOT AS A CONTINGENCY OF THE SALE, but solely to confirm: **(i)** the Property is maintained pursuant to paragraph 7A; **(ii)** Repairs have been completed as agreed; and **(iii)** Seller has complied with Seller's other obligations under this Agreement.

16. **LIQUIDATED DAMAGES: If Buyer fails to complete this purchase because of Buyer's default, Seller shall retain, as liquidated damages, the deposit actually paid. If the Property is a dwelling with no more than four units, one of which Buyer intends to occupy, then the amount retained shall be no more than 3% of the purchase price. Any excess shall be returned to Buyer. Release of funds will require mutual, Signed release instructions from both Buyer and Seller, judicial decision or arbitration award.**
BUYER AND SELLER SHALL SIGN A SEPARATE LIQUIDATED DAMAGES PROVISION FOR ANY INCREASED DEPOSIT. (C.A.R. FORM RID)

Buyer's Initials _____/_____	Seller's Initials _____/_____

17. **DISPUTE RESOLUTION:**

A. **MEDIATION:** Buyer and Seller agree to mediate any dispute or claim arising between them out of this Agreement, or any resulting transaction, before resorting to arbitration or court action. Paragraphs 17B(2) and (3) below apply to mediation whether or not the Arbitration provision is initialed. Mediation fees, if any, shall be divided equally among the parties involved. If, for any dispute or claim to which this paragraph applies, any party commences an action without first attempting to resolve the matter through mediation, or refuses to mediate after a request has been made, then that party shall not be entitled to recover attorney fees, even if they would otherwise be available to that party in any such action. THIS MEDIATION PROVISION APPLIES WHETHER OR NOT THE ARBITRATION PROVISION IS INITIALED.

B. **ARBITRATION OF DISPUTES: (1) Buyer and Seller agree that any dispute or claim in Law or equity arising between them out of this Agreement or any resulting transaction, which is not settled through mediation, shall be decided by neutral, binding arbitration, including and subject to paragraphs 17B(2) and (3) below. The arbitrator shall be a retired judge or justice, or an attorney with at least 5 years of residential real estate Law experience, unless the parties mutually agree to a different arbitrator, who shall render an award in accordance with substantive California Law. The parties shall have the right to discovery in accordance with California Code of Civil Procedure §1283.05. In all other respects, the arbitration shall be conducted in accordance with Title 9 of Part III of the California Code of Civil Procedure. Judgment upon the award of the arbitrator(s) may be entered into any court having jurisdiction. Interpretation of this agreement to arbitrate shall be governed by the Federal Arbitration Act.**
(2) EXCLUSIONS FROM MEDIATION AND ARBITRATION: The following matters are excluded from mediation and arbitration: **(i)** a judicial or non-judicial foreclosure or other action or proceeding to enforce a deed of trust, mortgage or installment land sale contract as defined in California Civil Code §2985; **(ii)** an unlawful detainer action; **(iii)** the filing or enforcement of a mechanic's lien; and **(iv)** any matter that is within the jurisdiction of a probate, small claims or bankruptcy court. The filing of a court action to enable the recording of a notice of pending action, for order of attachment, receivership, injunction, or other provisional remedies, shall not constitute a waiver of the mediation and arbitration provisions.
(3) BROKERS: Buyer and Seller agree to mediate and arbitrate disputes or claims involving either or both Brokers, consistent with 17A and B, provided either or both Brokers shall have agreed to such mediation or arbitration prior to, or within a reasonable time after, the dispute or claim is presented to Brokers. Any election by either or both Brokers to participate in mediation or arbitration shall not result in Brokers being deemed parties to the Agreement.
"**NOTICE: BY INITIALING IN THE SPACE BELOW YOU ARE AGREEING TO HAVE ANY DISPUTE ARISING OUT OF THE MATTERS INCLUDED IN THE 'ARBITRATION OF DISPUTES' PROVISION DECIDED BY NEUTRAL ARBITRATION AS PROVIDED BY CALIFORNIA LAW AND YOU ARE GIVING UP ANY RIGHTS YOU MIGHT POSSESS TO HAVE THE DISPUTE LITIGATED IN A COURT OR JURY TRIAL. BY INITIALING IN THE SPACE BELOW YOU ARE GIVING UP YOUR JUDICIAL RIGHTS TO DISCOVERY AND APPEAL, UNLESS THOSE RIGHTS ARE SPECIFICALLY INCLUDED IN THE 'ARBITRATION OF DISPUTES' PROVISION. IF YOU REFUSE TO SUBMIT TO ARBITRATION AFTER AGREEING TO THIS PROVISION, YOU MAY BE COMPELLED TO ARBITRATE UNDER THE AUTHORITY OF THE CALIFORNIA CODE OF CIVIL PROCEDURE. YOUR AGREEMENT TO THIS ARBITRATION PROVISION IS VOLUNTARY.**"
"**WE HAVE READ AND UNDERSTAND THE FOREGOING AND AGREE TO SUBMIT DISPUTES ARISING OUT OF THE MATTERS INCLUDED IN THE 'ARBITRATION OF DISPUTES' PROVISION TO NEUTRAL ARBITRATION.**"

Buyer's Initials _____/_____	Seller's Initials _____/_____

Buyer's Initials (_____)(_____)
Seller's Initials (_____)(_____)

Reviewed by _____ Date _____

California Residential Purchase Agreement

Property Address: _____   Date: _____

18. **PRORATIONS OF PROPERTY TAXES AND OTHER ITEMS:** Unless otherwise agreed in writing, the following items shall be PAID CURRENT and prorated between Buyer and Seller as of Close Of Escrow: real property taxes and assessments, interest, rents, HOA regular, special, and emergency dues and assessments imposed prior to Close Of Escrow, premiums on insurance assumed by Buyer, payments on bonds and assessments assumed by Buyer, and payments on Mello-Roos and other Special Assessment District bonds and assessments that are now a lien. The following items shall be assumed by Buyer WITHOUT CREDIT toward the purchase price: prorated payments on Mello-Roos and other Special Assessment District bonds and assessments and HOA special assessments that are now a lien but not yet due. Property will be reassessed upon change of ownership. Any supplemental tax bills shall be paid as follows: **(i)** for periods after Close Of Escrow, by Buyer; and **(ii)** for periods prior to Close Of Escrow, by Seller. TAX BILLS ISSUED AFTER CLOSE OF ESCROW SHALL BE HANDLED DIRECTLY BETWEEN BUYER AND SELLER. Prorations shall be made based on a 30-day month.
19. **WITHHOLDING TAXES:** Seller and Buyer agree to execute any instrument, affidavit, statement or instruction reasonably necessary to comply with federal (FIRPTA) and California withholding Law, if required (C.A.R. Forms AS and AB).
20. **MULTIPLE LISTING SERVICE ("MLS"):** Brokers are authorized to report to the MLS a pending sale and, upon Close Of Escrow, the terms of this transaction to be published and disseminated to persons and entities authorized to use the information on terms approved by the MLS.
21. **EQUAL HOUSING OPPORTUNITY:** The Property is sold in compliance with federal, state and local anti-discrimination Laws.
22. **ATTORNEY FEES:** In any action, proceeding, or arbitration between Buyer and Seller arising out of this Agreement, the prevailing Buyer or Seller shall be entitled to reasonable attorney fees and costs from the non-prevailing Buyer or Seller, except as provided in paragraph 17A.
23. **SELECTION OF SERVICE PROVIDERS:** If Brokers refer Buyer or Seller to persons, vendors, or service or product providers ("Providers"), Brokers do not guarantee the performance of any Providers. Buyer and Seller may select ANY Providers of their own choosing.
24. **TIME OF ESSENCE; ENTIRE CONTRACT; CHANGES:** Time is of the essence. All understandings between the parties are incorporated in this Agreement. Its terms are intended by the parties as a final, complete and exclusive expression of their Agreement with respect to its subject matter, and may not be contradicted by evidence of any prior agreement or contemporaneous oral agreement. If any provision of this Agreement is held to be ineffective or invalid, the remaining provisions will nevertheless be given full force and effect. **Neither this Agreement nor any provision in it may be extended, amended, modified, altered or changed, except in writing Signed by Buyer and Seller.**
25. **OTHER TERMS AND CONDITIONS,** including attached supplements:
    A. ☑ Buyer's Inspection Advisory (C.A.R. Form BIA)
    B. ☐ Purchase Agreement Addendum (C.A.R. Form PAA paragraph numbers: _____)
    C. ☐ Statewide Buyer and Seller Advisory (C.A.R. Form SBSA)
    D. _____
26. **DEFINITIONS:** As used in this Agreement:
    A. **"Acceptance"** means the time the offer or final counter offer is accepted in writing by a party and is delivered to and personally received by the other party or that party's authorized agent in accordance with the terms of this offer or a final counter offer.
    B. **"Agreement"** means the terms and conditions of this accepted California Residential Purchase Agreement and any accepted counter offers and addenda.
    C. **"C.A.R. Form"** means the specific form referenced or another comparable form agreed to by the parties.
    D. **"Close Of Escrow"** means the date the grant deed, or other evidence of transfer of title, is recorded. If the scheduled close of escrow falls on a Saturday, Sunday or legal holiday, then close of escrow shall be the next business day after the scheduled close of escrow date.
    E. **"Copy"** means copy by any means including photocopy, NCR, facsimile and electronic.
    F. **"Days"** means calendar days, unless otherwise required by Law.
    G. **"Days After"** means the specified number of calendar days after the occurrence of the event specified, not counting the calendar date on which the specified event occurs, and ending at 11:59PM on the final day.
    H. **"Days Prior"** means the specified number of calendar days before the occurrence of the event specified, not counting the calendar date on which the specified event is scheduled to occur.
    I. **"Electronic Copy" or "Electronic Signature"** means, as applicable, an electronic copy or signature complying with California Law. Buyer and Seller agree that electronic means will not be used by either party to modify or alter the content or integrity of this Agreement without the knowledge and consent of the other.
    J. **"Law"** means any law, code, statute, ordinance, regulation, rule or order, which is adopted by a controlling city, county, state or federal legislative, judicial or executive body or agency.
    K. **"Notice to Buyer to Perform"** means a document (C.A.R. Form NBP), which shall be in writing and Signed by Seller and shall give Buyer at least 24 hours **(or as otherwise specified in paragraph 14C(4))** to remove a contingency or perform as applicable.
    L. **"Repairs"** means any repairs (including pest control), alterations, replacements, modifications or retrofitting of the Property provided for under this Agreement.
    M. **"Signed"** means either a handwritten or electronic signature on an original document, Copy or any counterpart.
    N. **Singular and Plural** terms each include the other, when appropriate.

Buyer's Initials (_____)(_____)
Seller's Initials (_____)(_____)

Reviewed by _____ Date _____

Appendices

California Residential Purchase Agreement

Property Address: _____ Date: _____

27. AGENCY:

    A. DISCLOSURE: Buyer and Seller each acknowledge prior receipt of C.A.R. Form AD "Disclosure Regarding Real Estate Agency Relationships."

    B. POTENTIALLY COMPETING BUYERS AND SELLERS: Buyer and Seller each acknowledge receipt of a disclosure of the possibility of multiple representation by the Broker representing that principal. This disclosure may be part of a listing agreement, buyer-broker agreement or separate document (C.A.R. Form DA). Buyer understands that Broker representing Buyer may also represent other potential buyers, who may consider, make offers on or ultimately acquire the Property. Seller understands that Broker representing Seller may also represent other sellers with competing properties of interest to this Buyer.

    C. CONFIRMATION: The following agency relationships are hereby confirmed for this transaction:
Listing Agent _____ (Print Firm Name) is the agent of (check one): ☐ the Seller exclusively; or ☐ both the Buyer and Seller.
Selling Agent _____ (Print Firm Name) (if not same as Listing Agent) is the agent of (check one): ☐ the Buyer exclusively; or ☐ the Seller exclusively; or ☐ both the Buyer and Seller. Real Estate Brokers are not parties to the Agreement between Buyer and Seller.

28. JOINT ESCROW INSTRUCTIONS TO ESCROW HOLDER:

    A. The following paragraphs, or applicable portions thereof, of this Agreement constitute the joint escrow instructions of Buyer and Seller to Escrow Holder, which Escrow Holder is to use along with any related counter offers and addenda, and any additional mutual instructions to close the escrow: 1, 2, 4, 12, 13B, 14E, 18, 19, 24, 25B and 25D, 26, 28, 29, 32A, 33 and paragraph D of the section titled Real Estate Brokers on page 8. If a Copy of the separate compensation agreement(s) provided for in paragraph 29 or 32A, or paragraph D of the section titled Real Estate Brokers on page 8 is deposited with Escrow Holder by Broker, Escrow Holder shall accept such agreement(s) and pay out from Buyer's or Seller's funds, or both, as applicable, the Broker's compensation provided for in such agreement(s). The terms and conditions of this Agreement not set forth in the specified paragraphs are additional matters for the information of Escrow Holder, but about which Escrow Holder need not be concerned. Buyer and Seller will receive Escrow Holder's general provisions directly from Escrow Holder and will execute such provisions upon Escrow Holder's request. To the extent the general provisions are inconsistent or conflict with this Agreement, the general provisions will control as to the duties and obligations of Escrow Holder only. Buyer and Seller will execute additional instructions, documents and forms provided by Escrow Holder that are reasonably necessary to close the escrow.

    B. A Copy of this Agreement shall be delivered to Escrow Holder within **3** business days after Acceptance (or ☐ _____). Buyer and Seller authorize Escrow Holder to accept and rely on Copies and Signatures as defined in this Agreement as originals, to open escrow and for other purposes of escrow. The validity of this Agreement as between Buyer and Seller is not affected by whether or when Escrow Holder Signs this Agreement.

    C. Brokers are a party to the escrow for the sole purpose of compensation pursuant to paragraphs 29, 32A and paragraph D of the section titled Real Estate Brokers on page 8. Buyer and Seller irrevocably assign to Brokers compensation specified in paragraphs 29 and 32A, respectively, and irrevocably instruct Escrow Holder to disburse those funds to Brokers at Close Of Escrow or pursuant to any other mutually executed cancellation agreement. Compensation instructions can be amended or revoked only with the written consent of Brokers. Escrow Holder shall immediately notify Brokers: **(i)** if Buyer's initial or any additional deposit is not made pursuant to this Agreement, or is not good at time of deposit with Escrow Holder; or **(ii)** if Buyer and Seller instruct Escrow Holder to cancel escrow.

    D. A Copy of any amendment that affects any paragraph of this Agreement for which Escrow Holder is responsible shall be delivered to Escrow Holder within **2** business days after mutual execution of the amendment.

29. BROKER COMPENSATION FROM BUYER: If applicable, upon Close Of Escrow, **Buyer** agrees to pay compensation to Broker as specified in a separate written agreement between Buyer and Broker.

30. TERMS AND CONDITIONS OF OFFER:
This is an offer to purchase the Property on the above terms and conditions. All paragraphs with spaces for initials by Buyer and Seller are incorporated in this Agreement only if initialed by all parties. If at least one but not all parties initial, a counter offer is required until agreement is reached. Seller has the right to continue to offer the Property for sale and to accept any other offer at any time prior to notification of Acceptance. Buyer has read and acknowledges receipt of a Copy of the offer and agrees to the above confirmation of agency relationships. If this offer is accepted and Buyer subsequently defaults, Buyer may be responsible for payment of Brokers' compensation. This Agreement and any supplement, addendum or modification, including any Copy, may be Signed in two or more counterparts, all of which shall constitute one and the same writing.

Buyer's Initials (_____)(_____)
Seller's Initials (_____)(_____)

Reviewed by _____ Date _____

California Residential Purchase Agreement

Property Address: _____ Date: _____

31. EXPIRATION OF OFFER: This offer shall be deemed revoked and the deposit shall be returned unless the offer is Signed by Seller and a Copy of the Signed offer is personally received by Buyer, or by _____, who is authorized to receive it by 5:00 PM on the third Day after this offer is signed by Buyer (or, if checked, ☐ by _____ (date), at _____ AM/PM).

Date _____ Date _____

BUYER _____ BUYER _____

(Print name) _____ **(Print name)** _____

(Address) _____

32. BROKER COMPENSATION FROM SELLER:
  A. Upon Close Of Escrow, Seller agrees to pay compensation to Broker as specified in a separate written agreement between Seller and Broker.
  B. If escrow does not close, compensation is payable as specified in that separate written agreement.

33. ACCEPTANCE OF OFFER: Seller warrants that Seller is the owner of the Property, or has the authority to execute this Agreement. Seller accepts the above offer, agrees to sell the Property on the above terms and conditions, and agrees to the above confirmation of agency relationships. Seller has read and acknowledges receipt of a Copy of this Agreement, and authorizes Broker to deliver a Signed Copy to Buyer.
  ☐ (If checked) **SUBJECT TO ATTACHED COUNTER OFFER, DATED** _____.

Date _____ Date _____

SELLER _____ SELLER _____

(Print name) _____ **(Print name)** _____

(Address) _____

(___ / ___) **CONFIRMATION OF ACCEPTANCE:** A Copy of Signed Acceptance was personally received by Buyer or Buyer's authorized
(Initials) agent on (date) _____ at _____ AM/PM. **A binding Agreement is created when a Copy of Signed Acceptance is personally received by Buyer or Buyer's authorized agent whether or not confirmed in this document. Completion of this confirmation is not legally required in order to create a binding Agreement; it is solely intended to evidence the date that Confirmation of Acceptance has occurred.**

REAL ESTATE BROKERS:
A. Real Estate Brokers are not parties to the Agreement between Buyer and Seller.
B. Agency relationships are confirmed as stated in paragraph 27.
C. If specified in paragraph 2A, Agent who submitted the offer for Buyer acknowledges receipt of deposit.
D. **COOPERATING BROKER COMPENSATION:** Listing Broker agrees to pay Cooperating Broker (**Selling Firm**) and Cooperating Broker agrees to accept, out of Listing Broker's proceeds in escrow: **(i)** the amount specified in the MLS, provided Cooperating Broker is a Participant of the MLS in which the Property is offered for sale or a reciprocal MLS; or **(ii)** ☐ (if checked) the amount specified in a separate written agreement (C.A.R. Form CBC) between Listing Broker and Cooperating Broker.

Real Estate Broker (Selling Firm) _____ License # _____ Date _____
By _____ License # _____
Address _____ City _____ State _____ Zip _____
Telephone _____ Fax _____ E-mail _____

Real Estate Broker (Listing Firm) _____ License # _____
By _____ License # _____ Date _____
Address _____ City _____ State _____ Zip _____
Telephone _____ Fax _____ E-mail _____

ESCROW HOLDER ACKNOWLEDGMENT:
Escrow Holder acknowledges receipt of a Copy of this Agreement, (if checked, ☐ a deposit in the amount of $ _____), counter offer numbers _____ and _____, and agrees to act as Escrow Holder subject to paragraph 28 of this Agreement, any supplemental escrow instructions and the terms of Escrow Holder's general provisions.

Escrow Holder is advised that the date of Confirmation of Acceptance of the Agreement as between Buyer and Seller is _____

Escrow Holder _____ Escrow # _____
By _____ Date _____
Address _____
Phone/Fax/E-mail_____
Escrow Holder is licensed by the California Department of ☐ Corporations, ☐ Insurance, ☐ Real Estate. License # _____

(___ / ___) **REJECTION OF OFFER:** No counter offer is being made. This offer was reviewed and rejected by Seller on
(Seller's Initials) _____ (Date)

THIS FORM HAS BEEN APPROVED BY THE CALIFORNIA ASSOCIATION OF REALTORS® (C.A.R.). NO REPRESENTATION IS MADE AS TO THE LEGAL VALIDITY OR ADEQUACY OF ANY PROVISION IN ANY SPECIFIC TRANSACTION. A REAL ESTATE BROKER IS THE PERSON QUALIFIED TO ADVISE ON REAL ESTATE TRANSACTIONS. IF YOU DESIRE LEGAL OR TAX ADVICE, CONSULT AN APPROPRIATE PROFESSIONAL.
This form is available for use by the entire real estate industry. It is not intended to identify the user as a REALTOR®. REALTOR® is a registered collective membership mark which may be used only by members of the NATIONAL ASSOCIATION OF REALTORS® who subscribe to its Code of Ethics.

Published and Distributed by:
REAL ESTATE BUSINESS SERVICES, INC.
a subsidiary of the California Association of REALTORS®
525 South Virgil Avenue, Los Angeles, California 90020
The System for Success®

Reviewed by _____ Date _____

RPA-CA REVISED 1/06 (PAGE 8 OF 8)

Reprinted with permission, CALIFORNIA ASSOCIATION OF REALTORS®. Endorsement not implied.

Glossary

This glossary includes many terms that are primarily of interest to buyers as well as terms that typically concern sellers.

ABR: Accredited Buyer Representative. A designation available to Realtors who have documented their experience representing home buyers, completed coursework, and passed a test.

Abstract: Short for *abstract of title*, this is a history of all deeds or other legal documents (such as *lien*) affecting ownership of the property.

Accessorial services: The moving industry's term for extras such as packing or unpacking boxes.

Adjusted basis: The amount of money you paid for a home, adjusted for sales expenses, home improvements, and old capital gains rolled over from pre-1997 home sales.

Adjustment period: The frequency with which the interest rate changes on an adjustable-rate loan. A one-year ARM, for example, has an annual adjustment period.

Agent: Someone who acts on behalf of someone else. A real estate agent is working on behalf of a *broker*, who, in turn, is an agent of the buyer or seller who hired that broker. A buyer cannot assume a real estate agent is representing the buyer's interests unless the buyer has signed an agreement with a broker who agrees to act as the buyer's agent.

Amortization: The process of paying off a debt through a series of regularly scheduled payments of *principal* and *interest*.

Appraisal: A licensed appraiser's estimate of market value based on recent completed sales of comparable properties and taking into account a home's special features and flaws.

APR: Annual Percentage Rate. This single number, stated as a percentage (0 to 10 percent, for example) combines prepaid interest and the monthly rate to indicate the real cost of a loan. Federal law requires that lenders disclose the APR on all loans.

ARM: Adjustable rate mortgage. These loans carry interest rates that will rise and fall with market rates from year to year, or perhaps at shorter intervals, depending on the specifics of the loan.

ASHI: The American Society of Home Inspectors and its members.

Assessment: An estimate of a property's market value conducted by an assessor (either a government employee or private contractor). Local governments use these assessments in calculating property taxes. The assessment will assign a dollar value to the land and a dollar value to the home or other structures built upon it.

Balloon: A single, lump-sum payment required at the end of a loan's term if the schedule of monthly payments has not been great enough to pay off the loan's *principal*. See *negative amortization*.

Bill of lading: The main document governing the move of your household goods. It serves as a contract for services and your receipt.

Binding estimate: A moving company's firm price based on a specific quantity of goods to be shipped. Extra goods and services can increase the final bill, and you could be expected to pay up to 15 percent more than the binding estimate upon delivery. Any amount owed beyond that is payable within thirty days.

Bridge loan: A loan (often a home-equity loan on your old residence) designed to provide money to make the down payment on a new home before the old one has been sold.

Broker: Someone who is licensed by the state to represent buyers and/or sellers in the purchase or sale of real estate. Some states require that all people who offer real estate sales services hold a broker's license; others issue different licenses to brokers and to salespeople (agents). Typically, a licensed real estate agent works under the umbrella of a licensed broker, and it is the broker with whom buyers and sellers have contracts for representation in the sale or purchase of real estate. Often, if an experienced agent has qualified for a broker's license but is still performing the duties of an agent, he or she will be called a broker-associate and still will work under the umbrella of another broker.

Brokers' open: Also called a caravan, this is an open house restricted to local real estate brokers and agents who use them to get familiar with new listings.

Broom clean: The standard condition expected when a home changes hands. All the old occupant's belongings have been removed, trash has been taken out, and floors and carpets have been swept.

Buy down: To lower the interest rate by paying upfront interest, or *points*, at closing. A seller may offer to buy down the interest rate for a buyer by paying for those points, typically 1 to 3 percent of the loan amount. See *points*.

Buyer's broker, buyer's agent: A real estate salesperson who has agreed (preferably in writing) to represent the buyer in a transaction.

Buyer's market: A market in which there are more sellers than buyers, and therefore buyers have an easier time winning negotiations over price and other terms of the sale.

Buyer's remorse: The nearly inevitable period of doubt that hits after signing a contract to buy a home marked by worry that the price is too high, the property is in disrepair, and that a better deal lies elsewhere.

Cap: The maximum interest rate that can be charged on an adjustable-rate mortgage (ARM). ARMs typically have two caps, one limiting how much your interest rate can change at each adjustment period and the other setting a maximum rate over the life of the loan. *Interest-rate caps* limit how much interest the lender may charge. They are preferable to *payment caps*, which limit how much the borrower can be required to pay each month but do not limit the interest rate that is being charged. If there is only an interest-rate cap in place, a lender may boost the interest rate, but hold the monthly payments to the capped amount. When this happens, unpaid interest charges will build up, slowly increasing the borrower's indebtedness and possibly setting up the need for a *balloon payment* at the end of the loan.

Capital gain: Profit from a home sale, from the tax collector's point of view. The amount the seller receives from the sale of the home, minus the original cash down payment and the monthly payments toward mortgage principal and the money spent on renovations and remodeling over the years results in the capital gain amount.

Cash reserve: The amount of money left in savings or investments after a borrower has closed on a home.

CCRs: Codes, Covenants and Restrictions. These are the rules that legally bind the owners of condominiums, co-ops, and homeowners associations. They govern things including finances, dues, architectural standards, and lifestyle rules such as prohibitions on decorative banners or parking trucks or boats within the community.

Closing costs: Fees payable at closing for expenses associated with a home purchase, including taxes, termite inspection fees, title insurance, loan origination fees, and other expenses.

Closing or close of escrow: The transfer of property ownership from one party to another. It involves the seller's signing over of the deed to the buyer; the buyer's signing of the loan promissory note and the mortgage document, plus signing assorted disclosure forms, providing proof of a valid homeowners insurance policy and paying for assorted last-minute closing fees, either through the mortgage loan or in cash at the closing table.

Cloud on title: An outstanding claim on the title that calls ownership into question.

CLUE report: A report from the insurance industry's database, called the Comprehensive Loss Underwriting Exchange. It tracks both the history of insurance claims filed for a specific property and the history of claims submitted by home owners. A significant claims history raises the cost of insurance premiums.

COFI: The Cost of Funds Index, based on interest rates prevailing in the Federal Home Loan Bank's 11th District, which encompasses Arizona, California, and Nevada. Some adjustable-rate mortgages, particularly those with an interest rate that adjusts monthly, are pegged to the COFI index, which tends to rise and fall more slowly than other commonly used indexes. However, more-frequent adjustments mean the overall interest rates remain close to those on ARMs pegged to other indexes.

Commission: A fee for real estate brokerage services that is calculated as a percentage of the sales price.

Comparable: Recently sold homes that are similar in size, location, and amenities. When estimating sales prices or performing official appraisals, real estate agents and appraisers will research the selling prices of comparable properties to back up their price estimates, adjusting those prices for the special features and flaws that are present in one home but not the other.

Comparative Market Analysis: CMA. An analysis performed by a real estate agent to help determine a likely selling price for a property based on the prices of other properties currently on the market, the prices of those sold within the past year and the prices on any listings that failed to sell. It is not as rigorous an examination as an appraisal.

Condo or co-op fee: Also called "maintenance," this is the monthly payment owed by owners of condo and co-op homes to cover the expenses of maintaining and improving the property and its amenities, such as the services of a doorman or a fitness center.

Condo: A condo, short for condominium, is a form of ownership. Most frequently, apartments are owned this way, but the term can refer to townhomes and detached houses. Owners own the inside of their unit and a share of the common grounds, including the exterior of the building, parking lots, fitness facilities or other features. Condo owners vote among themselves to appoint a condo board, which oversees the business of running the property, including the assessment of mandatory condo fees on owners and, usually, the hiring of a management company to handle day-to-day affairs.

Conforming loan: Mortgage loans that conform to the guidelines established by secondary mortgage market companies Fannie Mae and Freddie Mac. In particular, conforming loans must meet their limits on the size of the loan, which were $417,000 in 2006. The limit is adjusted at the beginning of each year. See *jumbo loan.*

Contingencies: Clauses added to a purchase contract that must be satisfied and removed before the deal can be closed. Common contingencies include those requiring a satisfactory home-inspection and an appraisal.

Conventional loan: Any mortgage except those that are FHA-insured or VA-guaranteed.

Convey: Items that are included with the home sale *convey* to the new owners. This especially refers to items that are not considered real estate, such as window coverings and furniture.

Co-op: Short for co-operative, this is a form of ownership in which several people own shares in a corporation that owns, typically, an apartment building. Ownership of shares entitles the owner to reside in one specific unit in that building and to vote on how the co-op will be run. A monthly maintenance fee will be charged to all owners to cover upkeep of common facilities and services.

Counteroffer: A seller's response to a buyer's purchase offer that rejects the seller's proposal and proposes, instead, price and/or terms that are more favorable to the seller. The buyer may, in turn, make his own *counteroffer* in response.

Covenants: See *CCRs*.

CRS: Certified Residential Specialist. A designation available to Realtors who have met specific standards for experience and have completed coursework on listing and selling homes.

Curb appeal: The attractiveness of a home and garden as viewed from the curb. A lack of curb appeal can limit the number of buyers who ask for a showing.

Deed of trust: See *mortgage*.

Deed: A legal document that conveys title to a property. See *title*.

Default: A buyer's failure to abide by the terms of a loan agreement, mainly by not making the payments due. If the borrower does not soon catch up with the payment schedule, default can go into *foreclosure*.

Delinquent: A loan in which the payments are three or more months past-due.

Deposit: See *earnest money*.

Disclosure: A seller is usually expected (or required) to fill out *disclosure* forms that alert prospective buyers to conditions that would affect the price and their decision to buy the property. There are disclosures about overall property condition and the presence of hazardous substances such as lead-based paint and radon gas.

Discount broker: A real estate broker or agent who offers services for a flat fee or who charges commissions significantly lower than local competitors. Sellers should find out whether the discounted fee or commission will include the full range of services usually expected with a listing contract.

Due-on-sale clause: A provision present in many mortgage contracts that allows the lender to require that the loan be paid off when the original borrower sells the home. It means the new buyer cannot assume the terms of the old loan without the lender's permission.

Earnest money: Also called a *deposit,* this is an amount of cash that a buyer offers the seller when presenting an offer to buy a property. Because this cash can be forfeited to the seller if the buyer backs out of the deal for reasons that are not already spelled out as contingencies in the contract (such as the buyer's dissatisfaction with a home-inspection report), it is considered a sign of the buyer's good-faith intent to buy the property. Earnest money checks should be held by a third party (such as in a broker's special escrow account) until the transaction is complete.

Easement: A legal right, recorded with the deed, for one party to use part of someone else's real estate. A neighbor may have an *easement* to use a neighbor's driveway because that is the only way for them to access the street, or the local utility may have an *easement* to a swath of a homeowner's land which gives it the right to bury and maintain a gas line through the area. An easement may diminish a property's value.

Equity: Home equity is the amount of ownership someone has in a property after any loans against it have been paid off. If a home sells for $300,000 and there is a mortgage against it for $100,000, the owner's equity is $200,000.

Escalation clause: This addition to a purchase contract says the buyer will increase his or her offer by certain increments (say $5,000 each) over the offers of any legitimate, competing buyer. These are used in *seller's markets* in which there are likely to be many buyers competing for a single property. An escalation clause should have a top dollar amount to limit the buyer's eventual bid.

Escrow: The holding of money or documents (such as the deed to a property) by a neutral third party while waiting for the buyer and seller to satisfy all the conditions of a contract. In California, when a purchase offer has been placed on a property and accepted by the seller, the transaction is considered to have gone into escrow while the details of title searches, termite inspections, and document preparations are handled. When all terms of the contract have been complied with and title changes hands, escrow is closed.

Another common use of the term is when a mortgage company collects property taxes and homeowners' insurance payments and holds them *in escrow* until the payment is due. Earnest-money deposits also should be held in an *escrow* account by a real estate broker or lawyer.

Estimated proceeds of sale: At the listing presentation, a real estate agent or broker usually gives the homeowner this document outlining how much they might reasonably expect to net from a sale at the recommended listing price minus brokerage commissions and the amount needed to pay off old mortgages.

Exclusive right-to-sell: The most common form of listing, which entitles a listing broker/agent to a commission during the listing period regardless of who actually finds the buyer.

FHA mortgage: A low-down payment mortgage program in which mortgage insurance is provided by the federal government. FHA loans are targeted toward purchasers of moderately priced homes.

Fixed-rate mortgage: A mortgage loan that carries the same interest rate through the life of the loan.

Flat-fee broker: A broker or agent who charges a fixed fee for real estate services. Some limit their services to posting a listing on the MLS for a flat fee of several hundred dollars.

Flight charge: The amount that moving companies will charge for hauling goods up or down steps.

Foreclosure: The legal process a lien holder (such as the mortgage lender or tax authority) undertakes when a borrower or owner fails to make required payments. The lender or tax authority will take possession of the property and sell it to provide cash to pay off the loan.

FSBO: For Sale By Owner. It refers both to the property and to the owner who is selling without the help of a broker/agent.

Full value protection: Liability coverage offered by movers for an additional fee, which requires them to repair, replace, or pay for lost or damaged items.

Full service broker: A broker/agent who offers the traditional, full range of services under a listing contract, including MLS posting, advertising, providing contracts, showing the property, and assisting with negotiations. Full-service brokers may or may not charge discounted commissions or fees.

Good faith estimate: Federal law requires that lenders give borrowers a written good-faith estimate of closing costs associated with taking out the loan and purchasing a property.

GRI: Graduate, Realtor Institute. A designation available to Realtors who work primarily in residential real estate and who complete coursework on technical aspects and fundamentals of real estate.

High value article: A term used by movers to describe an item worth more than one hundred dollars per pound.

HOA: Homeowners Association. While this term can apply to condo and co-op associations, it more commonly refers to communities of individually owned townhomes and freestanding houses. Owners of these homes are mandatory members of the association, which takes care of community property, which may include road maintenance, streetlights, community swimming pools, tennis courts and parks, landscaping, and other amenities. The HOA charges members monthly or annual dues and can place a lien against a member's home for unpaid dues and fees.

Holdback: Money held back from settlement until certain requirements have been met. For example, buyer and seller may agree to a holdback of some of the sales proceeds due the seller if the property was not in acceptable condition at the time of the pre-closing walk-through.

Home-equity loan: See *second mortgage*.

Homeowners insurance: An insurance policy that covers the home and its contents for damage or destruction due to fire, lightning, hail, wind storms, and burglary. In some high-risk areas, there are limits on coverage for wind storms and hail. Flood insurance and earthquake insurance must be purchased separately.

Homestead laws: Laws in some states that protect a person's home against claims by creditors.

HUD-1: The "U.S. Department of Housing and Urban Development Settlement Statement," which the government requires to be used at each closing. It details all amounts paid to and from the seller and the buyer.

Hybrid loan: A mortgage loan that combines features of fixed-rate loans and adjustable-rate loans. With a 30-year hybrid loan, for example, the interest rate will be fixed for the first five, seven or 10 years, after which it converts to an interest rate that adjusts every year for the remaining term of the loan.

Impracticable operations: A moving-industry term describing conditions such as bad roads or dangerous environment that make it impossible for a truck to be positioned for pickup or delivery. Consumers may be charged extra fees for use of a smaller truck that can transport goods between their large truck and the building.

Index: A specific, regularly published list of interest rates that is used as a basis for setting the new interest rate on adjustable-rate mortgages at each adjustment period. Common indexes are the one-year *Treasury index*; the *COFI*, or Eleventh District Cost of Funds Index; and the *LIBOR*, or London Interbank Offered Rate. See *margin*.

Interest rate: Expressed as a percentage, this is the "rent" paid on money borrowed from someone else. It always should be evaluated along with any upfront interest (points) paid at closing. See *points*.

Interest-only mortgage: A mortgage loan that gives the home buyer the option of making only interest payments during the early years of the loan, typically the first 10 to 15. While they make only interest payments, the loan balance will not decrease. After that 10- or

15-year period, the loan switches to a new payment schedule that pays off the remaining principal and interest over the remaining 15 to 20 years.

Joint tenancy with right of survivorship: A form of holding title used by two or more owners. Each person must have an equal share of ownership.

Jumbo loan: Mortgage loans for more than Fannie Mae and Freddie Mac's limit, which was $417,000 in 2006. (It's adjusted at the beginning of each year.) They typically carry higher interest rates than loans under the jumbo threshold, which are called *conforming loans.*

Junk fees: Closing costs that are suspected of being superfluous add-ons or that inflate the cost of legitimate closing services. Some fees to question as being junk: "processing fee," "shipping fee," "appraisal review fee," or high fees for photocopying or courier services.

Kick-out: A clause added to a contingency in a purchase contract that allows the seller to demand that the buyer remove the contingency (say within 24 or 48 hours) and buy the home if another buyer were to come forward with a competing offer.

Lead-based paint: Paint containing lead was outlawed in 1978, and sellers of homes built before that year need to provide a disclosure to buyers revealing any information they have about its presence in the home.

Lease with option to buy: A rental agreement that credits part of each month's rent toward the eventual down payment on the home.

Leverage: The ability to use borrowed money to help turn a small investment into a larger amount of wealth.

LIBOR: London Interbank Offered Rate. An index based on the interest rates charged on large loans in Europe. The index is sometimes used as a basis for pegging adjustable-rate mortgages in the U.S.

Lien: A creditor's financial claim against the value of a property. Mortgage lenders; homeowners associations and condo/co-op boards; local, state, and federal governments; and contractors are among those who can place a lien against your property for unpaid debts, taxes, or fees.

Lifetime cap: See *Caps.*

Listing: A legal agreement by which a homeowner hires a real estate broker to market his or her property. Brokers consider listings, or the information on homes that they are marketing, to be their property and their inventory.

Listing price: The asking price for a home as detailed in the listing agreement.

Loan-to-value ratio: LTV. A ratio that lenders use to determine how much equity the borrower has at stake in a mortgage deal. A high LTV is risky for the lender because the odds are higher that a troubled borrower will walk away from his or her obligation to pay off the loan. A $300,000 home bought with a $30,000 (or 10 percent) down payment has an LTV of 90 percent.

Lock: When a borrower applies for a mortgage loan, he or she can choose to *lock* in the loan's interest rate at the price that's being charged that day or to allow the rate to *float* with the day-to-day changes in rates until the borrower chooses to lock, or until the loan closes.

Lockbox: A box securely affixed near a home's entry that holds a key to that home. Qualified local agents and brokers have a code or other way to open the box and access the key so they can conduct showings without having to make an appointment with the seller or the listing agent.

Maintenance fee: The monthly fee paid by owners of condominiums, co-operatives, or homeowners association to pay for upkeep of commonly owned property, taxes, insurance, and special services, such as a doorman or security service. Also called a condo or co-op fee.

Margin: The markup added to the published interest-rate index to determine the new interest rate to be charged on an adjustable-rate loan at each adjustment period. For example, an ARM's rate might be set at the one-year Treasury index plus a *margin* of 1.5 percentage points. See *index*.

MLS: Multiple Listing Service. A system used by participating real estate brokers that allows them to post listings of homes available for sale and promising a split of the sales commission with another broker who comes up with a buyer for that property.

Mortgage banker: A business that originates, sells, and services mortgage loans.

Mortgage broker: A person who deals with a number of different loan originators and can shop a borrower's loan application around for the best combination of interest rate and terms. The broker will earn a fee for each mortgage he or she originates. While good mortgage brokers will shop hard on behalf of borrowers, there is nothing to require a mortgage broker to represent the interests of the borrower. Some steer borrowers into loans that earn the most profit for the broker.

Mortgage life insurance: Life insurance policies payable to the mortgage lender if one or both of the homeowners dies during the term of the policy. Usually you're better off buying an ordinary term life insurance policy that pays the survivor—and not the lender— which allows the survivor to decide whether it's prudent to pay off the loan, or to use the insurance proceeds for other purposes.

Mortgage: A document the borrower signs placing a lien against the property giving the lender the right to foreclose, or seize the property, if the borrower fails to pay back the loan. In some places a "deed of trust" is used instead, which allows an easier foreclosure process for the lender.

Mortgagee, mortgagor: The *mortgagee* is the lender. The *mortgagor* is the borrower, who agrees to offer his or her property as security for the loan.

Mortgage-interest deduction: The deduction from taxable income for interest paid on a mortgage of up to $1 million used to buy, build, or significantly rehabilitate a primary residence and one vacation home. Also deductible is interest on an additional $100,000 in home-equity debt (such as a home equity line of credit) used for any purpose. The deduction applies to both state and federal income tax returns.

NAR: An acronym for the National Association of Realtors, the main trade association representing real estate brokers, agents, and rental property managers. See *Realtor*.

Negative amortization: A loan repayment plan in which the monthly payments are not enough to pay off the borrowed amount by the end of the loan term. If your loan has negative amortization, the amount of money you owe gradually increases and you will have to pay it off in a lump sum, usually by refinancing to a new loan. See *balloon*.

Net listing: Illegal in many states, a net listing allows brokers and agents to set whatever price they choose on a property. If it sells, the owner is guaranteed a set dollar amount; any remainder goes to the broker/agent as commission.

Nonbinding estimate: A moving company's written estimate which will be revised based on the shipment's actual weight. Movers can demand cash payment of up to 110 percent of the nonbinding estimate (plus other fees) before unloading at the new address. Any remainder is payable within 30 days.

Open listing: An owner may sign such a contract for brokerage services with more than one broker at a time, and only owes a commission to the broker who actually produces a buyer. Also known as a *nonexclusive* or *general listing*.

Origination fee: A fee charged by lenders for a mortgage, perhaps 1 percent of the loan amount.

Ownership in severalty: A form of holding title to a property used when there is a single owner.

Perc test: Short for *percolation test*. A test by a qualified contractor to determine if the land has the proper drainage to support the operation of a septic tank and drain field. If the land does not pass the perc test, you may not build a home there.

Personal property: Property that is not considered *real estate*, such as furniture, appliances that are not permanently attached to the home, and mobile homes that do not have permanent foundations.

PITI: Principal, Interest, Taxes, and Insurance. These are the four components of a monthly mortgage payment. Principal pays off part of the original loan balance; Interest is, essentially, the rent paid on the borrowed money; Taxes cover local property taxes, and Insurance covers the homeowner's policy.

Pledged-asset mortgages: These loan programs allow buyers to pledge assets such as stocks, bonds, mutual funds, or certificates of deposit as collateral for the mortgage loan, instead of making a down payment.

Pocket listing: Slang describing a situation where a real estate agent keeps word of his new listing closely held within his own office or brokerage for a few days in hopes of securing a buyer who is represented by that same office, thereby keeping both the seller's and buyer's sides of the commission in-house. Such behavior does not benefit the seller who is paying for representation.

Points: Pre-paid interest, due at closing, designed to reduce the interest rate charged on the loan. One point equals 1 percent of the loan amount. Each point of prepaid interest typically reduces the interest rate by 1/8 percentage point.

Pre-approval, pre-qualification: Pre-approval for a mortgage loan requires that the borrower submit a full loan application, supplying information on employment, income, debts, bank accounts, and other assets and liabilities and allowing the lender to pull credit scores. Based on this, the lender will pre-approve the borrower for a loan of a certain size, subject only to a property appraisal once the borrower has found a home. "Pre-qualification" means someone has simply looked at the applicant's income and debts to estimate the size of a mortgage the applicant *probably* could obtain. It's not enough to persuade a seller that this is a viable buyer.

Prepaid interest: See *points.*

Prepayment of principal: Most mortgage loans allow borrowers to make additional payments toward principal at any time, either as a recurring addition to their monthly payment or as an occasional lump-sum. These prepayments help the borrower pay off the loan early and can result in significant savings on the amount of interest paid over the life of the loan.

Prepayment penalty: A provision in the mortgage loan contract that requires the borrower to pay a significant penalty if he or she pays off the loan early. While some borrowers may choose to accept a prepayment penalty in exchange for a discount on the interest rate, these penalties are common among the loans offered to borrowers with poor credit scores—and without any break on the interest rate.

Principal: The amount of money borrowed.

Purchase agreement: Also known as a *contract of sale.* This offer, submitted by the buyers, becomes a binding contract once the sellers sign and accept it.

Radon: A tasteless, odorless, colorless radioactive gas that can cause lung cancer. Special tests can reveal its presence in a home.

Ratified contract: The purchase agreement, or contract of sale, once all the contingencies (home inspection, loan qualification, appraisal, etc.) have been satisfied and removed.

Real property: Also called *real estate.* Land and the buildings put upon it. See *personal property.*

Realtor: A member of the National Association of Realtors, a trade association for real estate brokers, salespeople, and rental property managers. Members agree to abide by a Code of Ethics.

Released value protection: The liability coverage provided at no extra cost by interstate movers. Compensation for lost or damaged goods is calculated at sixty cents per pound.

RESPA: The Real Estate Settlement Procedures Act. This federal law prohibits unearned kickbacks (such as a free cruise to the real estate agent who refers the most business to a title insurance company each year) among professionals who provide settlement services. It also requires that all fees related to the real estate transaction be detailed on the HUD-1 settlement statement.

Second mortgage: A loan, usually a home equity loan or a home equity line of credit, that is secured by your home. It's called a "second" mortgage, because, if you were to quit paying off the loan, the holder of this loan is second in line, behind the holder of your "first" mortgage (usually the one used to buy the home) in sharing the proceeds from a foreclosure sale.

Seller financing: Mortgage credit provided by the sellers in lieu of having the buyers take out a loan from a bank or other institution. Sellers receive payment for their home in monthly installments, plus interest, and they hold a lien against the property.

Seller's market: A market in which there are more buyers than homes available for sale. This gives the sellers the advantage in negotiations, resulting in sales at the asking price, or higher.

Seller's remorse: The nearly inevitable period of doubt that hits after signing a contract to sell a home, marked by worry that the price was too low and possibly including regret over the decision to sell.

Special assessment: A mandatory collection of extra fees by a condo or cooperative board or a homeowners' association to pay a large, unbudgeted bill. Well-managed boards and associations try to avoid the need for special assessments by maintaining a contingency fund and by routinely budgeting for periodic maintenance and rehabilitation.

Staging: The practice of dressing up and decorating a home to maximize its appeal to buyers. It may include re-arranging existing furniture, removing belongings and even borrowing props.

Tenancy by the entirety: A form of holding title available only to married couples. It gives each spouse 100 percent ownership.

Tenancy in common: A form of holding title available to two or more co-owners who may have unequal shares in the property.

Time is of the essence: A phrase commonly used in real estate contracts to indicate that dates specified in the contract are binding, and failure to meet deadlines could void the contract.

Title company: A company that researches title histories and issues title insurance.

Title insurance: An insurance policy issued by title companies after they have searched the history of ownership of a property. Lenders require a policy to cover their financial risk if someone were to come forward claiming ownership; borrowers are wise to pay extra to have the coverage apply to them as well.

Title search: An examination of land ownership records on file with the local government to determine the history of how ownership of that property has changed hands over the years.

Title: Evidence of ownership of a property. There are specific, legal formats for holding title, including *tenancy in common* and *tenancy by the entirety.*

Townhouse, townhome: A home that is attached to others on one or two sides, formerly known as a *row house.* It may be owned as a condominium or individually.

Treasury rates: Indexes of interest rates paid on U.S. government securities. Many adjustable-rate loans are pegged to Treasury indexes that match their adjustment periods. The one-year ARM, for example, would be tied to one-year Treasuries.

Unrepresented seller: A new term being promoted by the real estate industry to refer to homeowners who sell without hiring a broker. It is intended to replace FSBO, or For Sale By Owner.

VA mortgage: A zero down-payment mortgage loan available to active-duty military and veterans. The federal government guarantees that, if the borrower doesn't repay the loan, the lender will recover part of the money they lent, replacing the need for a down payment or mortgage insurance.

Home-repair warranty: A policy that covers repairs to heating, cooling, electrical and plumbing systems, plus some appliances. Sellers may offer warranties on an older home to reassure buyers and possibly gain a marketing edge.

Zillow: The name of a free database of home value estimates, maps and aerial photographs accessible at www.Zillow.com. It is rapidly becoming a verb as well as a proper noun.

Index